New England Soups *from the* Sea

New England Soups *from the* Sea

Recipes for

CHOWDERS, BISQUES, BOILS, STEWS,
AND CLASSIC SEAFOOD MEDLEYS

CRAIG FEAR

The Countryman Press

An Imprint of W. W. Norton & Company
Independent Publishers Since 1923

For information about permission to reproduce selections from this book, write to Permissions, The Countryman Press, 500 Fifth Avenue, New York, NY 10110

For information about special discounts for bulk purchases, please contact W. W. Norton Special Sales at specialsales@wwnorton.com or 800-233-4830

Manufacturing by Versa Press
Book design by Allison Chi
Production manager: Devon Zahn

The Countryman Press
www.countrymanpress.com

Library of Congress Cataloging-in-Publication Data

Names: Fear, Craig, author.
Title: New England soups from the sea : recipes for chowders, bisques, boils, stews, and classic seafood medleys / Craig Fear.
Description: New York, NY : The Countryman Press, a division of W. W. Norton & Company, Independent Publishers Since 1923, [2022] | Includes bibliographical references and index.
Identifiers: LCCN 2021047630 | ISBN 9781682687130 (paperback) | ISBN 9781682687147 (epub)
Subjects: LCSH: Cooking (Seafood) | Cooking, American—New England style. | LCGFT: Cookbooks.
Classification: LCC TX747 .F376 2022 | DDC 641.6/9–dc23/eng/20211021
LC record available at https://lccn.loc .gov/2021047630

A division of W. W. Norton & Company, Inc.
500 Fifth Avenue, New York, NY 10110
www.wwnorton.com

10 9 8 7 6 5 4 3 2 1

For my uncle Bill Papp (1948–2019), whose delicious homemade clam chowder simmered in my subconscious for years, and was part of my inspiration to write this book.

Contents

11 Introduction:
Beyond Clam Chowder and
Lobster Bisque

Section 1. Understanding New England Soups from the Sea

17 Chapter 1. Know Your Fisherman/Fisherwoman

29 Chapter 2. The Native Fish of New England

43 Chapter 3. The Native Shellfish of New England

57 Chapter 4. The Portuguese Influence

Section 2. The Key Foundation of All New England Soups from the Sea

65 Chapter 5. Stocks and Broths

73 Basic Fish Stock

74 Robust Fish Stock

78 Basic Lobster Stock

79 Robust Lobster Stock

82 Basic Crab Stock

86 Hard-Shell Clam Broth

87 Soft-Shell Clam Broth

88 Mussel Broth

Section 3. New England Soups and Stews

94 Chapter 6. Chowders

105 Classic Creamy New England Clam Chowder

107 Rhode Island Clam Chowder

110 Milky Maine Steamer Clam Chowder

112 Manhattan Clam Chowder

115 Portuguese Clam Chowder

117 Connecticut Clam Chowder

120 Classic New England Whitefish Chowder

123 Wild Salmon Chowder

126 Portuguese Fish Chowder

128 Bluefish Chowder with Cherry Tomatoes, Basil, and Tarragon

130 Smoked Haddock Chowder with a Poached Egg

132 Hake and Skate Chowder

134 Lobster Corn Chowder

137 Mussel Chowder with Fennel

140 Crab, Bacon, and Cheddar Corn Chowder

142 Scallop and Wild Mushroom Chowder with Chives

144 Oyster Spinach Chowder

146 Curried Butternut Squash Squid Chowder

148 **Chapter 7. Brothy Soups**

151 Monkfish (or Dogfish) Soup with Ginger, Lemongrass, and Lime

154 Lemony Haddock (or Black Sea Bass) Soup

156 Portuguese Two Fish Soup

159 Pesto Noodle Soup with Striped Bass (or Halibut)

162 Tomato Swordfish (or Mackerel) Soup with Fresh Italian Herbs

164 Wild Salmon (or Bluefish) and Dill Soup

166 Traditional Clam Stew

167 Spinach-Tarragon Clam Soup

170 Clams Newburg Soup

173 Steamer Clam Soup in a Tomato-Basil-Lemon Broth

174 Steamer Clam Soup in a Ginger-Garlic-Tarragon-Lime Broth

178 Mussel Dijonnaise Soup

180 Atlantic Blue Mussel Mediterranean Soup

182 Aromatic Mussel Soup

186 Malty Mussel Soup

188 PBR Mussel Soup

193 Traditional Oyster Stew

194 Oysters Rockefeller Soup

196 Oysters Mariniere Soup

198 Oysters Bienville Soup

200 Maine Lobster Stew

203 New England Jonah Crab Stew

204 New England Summer Crab Soup

207 Portuguese Kale Soup with Scallops

210 New England-Style Hot and Sour Soup with Scallops

212 Portuguese Squid Soup

215 Caldo Verde with Squid

217 Traditional Scallop Stew

218 **Chapter 8. Bisques**

221 Lobster Bisque

224 New England Jonah Crab Bisque

228 Traditional New England Clam Bisque

231 Tomato-Clam Bisque

233 Mussel and Fennel Bisque

235 Scallop Bisque with Sage

237 Oyster Bisque with Fried Shallots and Garlic

239 Salmon Bisque with Dill

241 Whitefish Bisque

243 Chapter 9. Classic Medleys and Stews

246 Bouillabaisse

251 Bourride

253 Cioppino

256 Zarzuela

258 Zuppa di Pesce with Black Sea Bass

259 Simple Portuguese Clam Stew

262 Elegant Portuguese Clam Stew

264 Portuguese Squid Stew

266 Portuguese Mussel Stew

268 Portuguese Shrimp Mozambique

271 Chapter 10. Boils

276 Traditional New England Clam Boil

279 New England Blue Mussel Boil

280 Portuguese Clam Boil

282 New England Fish Boil

284 A Seasonal New England Fish and Clam Boil—Four Ways

287 Thanks

289 Notes

290 Index

Introduction: Beyond Clam Chowder and Lobster Bisque

Clam chowder and lobster bisque. I've eaten at countless New England area restaurants in my 45 years on this earth, and I don't recall a time when these two were not the predominant choices of seafood soups. Even native New Englanders might be unable to name another type of seafood soup.

Not that there's anything wrong with clam chowder and lobster bisque! When made with fresh, real ingredients, they are two of the most delicious soups on the planet. Who doesn't love New England's most iconic meal: clam chowder, made from juicy local New England hard-shell clams, smoky bacon, onions, and cream? Who doesn't love a rich, sweet, and succulent bowl of lobster bisque? I know no one.

However, there was a time you could find a much greater diversity of seafood soups. You could also find these soups not just in restaurants but on the stovetops in New England home kitchens.

Prior to the middle of the 20th century, cookbooks showcase a time when Americans living on the East Coast embraced the bounty of the sea in all its forms and everything was fair game for the soup pot. *The Soup Book* by Chef Louis De Gouy,

published in 1949, contains one hundred different chowder recipes, using dozens of different fish and shellfish species. Only six of the recipes use clams. *The Soup Book*'s bisque chapter contains 34 different recipes. Only three of those use lobster. The *Long Island Seafood Cookbook*, published in 1939 by J. George Frederick, has numerous recipes for soups, chowders, and stews, very few of which are seen anymore. Some of those recipes include mussel chowder, oyster bisque, watercress clam soup, flounder stew, and many varieties of simple broth-based soups.

For generations, those living near the sea, those who depended on it, knew how to prepare seafood in myriad ways, especially in the form of simple, thrifty soups. Before World War II, fish chowder was as common as clam chowder. Oyster stew, a super simple soup made of oysters, onions, and milk, was widely popular up and down the East Coast. You might also have found brothy soups made without any milk or cream. The highly concentrated liquors (the briny liquid held inside the shells) of shellfish, especially clams, make incredible broths when steamed in water. Similarly, the rich juices of crustaceans (like lobsters) and the wonderful ocean-fresh flavors of fish make beautiful stocks when simmered with vegetables, wine, and herbs. They can be used as a base in countless economical soup recipes. You *rarely* see broth-based seafood soups anymore, and yet they are some of the most delicious soups I've ever tasted.

Sadly, in the decades after World War II, many societal changes removed fresh seafood from our kitchens. The increasingly powerful food industry replaced our culinary traditions with chemically laden processed foods. Quick and convenient became America's new food culture. Fish was packaged into frozen fish sticks, fast-food sandwiches, and, of course, the staple of both kids' lunch boxes and the 9 to 5 workforce—canned tuna fish. Seafood soups were now more likely to be consumed from a can than as a home-cooked meal. Not surprisingly, the wonderful flavors, aromas, and textures of fresh seafood were quickly lost. Even worse, they took on a rancid, overly fishy character. This is because, in canning, fish is cooked to very high temperatures, which causes it to lose all its color and flavor. It's why you need gobs of mayonnaise to make canned tuna fish palatable, why canned clams are tough and rubbery, and why canned seafood stocks and broths have lost their fresh ocean essence. These are just a few examples.

As a result, in the decades following World War II, many Americans grew up with a distaste for seafood that they carried into adulthood. Millions more, including even those who lived near the sea, lost the passed-down, traditional knowledge within families for how to cook and prepare seafood, including, of course, soups. Canned soup companies, diners, and fast-food and chain restaurants responded with highly processed seafood soups that had less pronounced seafood flavors. The creamy richness of clam chowder and lobster bisque fit the bill perfectly and were easy sellers for food establishments both in and beyond New England. The heretofore diversity of New England area seafood soups, like many regional traditional foods, slowly ebbed away and became a thing of the past.

But there's good news.

Around the turn of the 21st century, Americans, on a large scale, started demanding better-quality food. Decades of consuming processed foods left us with a long list of increasingly common and easily preventable diet-related illnesses such as heart disease and type 2 diabetes. The locavore movement, that is, the emphasis on fresh, high-quality, organic, locally grown food, which has a lower environmental impact and greater benefit to local economies than processed food, has created a resurgence in farmers' markets and regional culinary traditions.

Soups have been a huge part of this! In particular, there's been a revival of interest in homemade bone broths and stocks the way our grandmothers and great grandmothers used to make them, which was from pasture-fed and humanely raised animals. Leftover chicken carcasses, which might include the collagen-rich feet, head, wings, and backs would go in the stockpot along with onions, carrots, and celery, and the ingredients would all simmer for hours to both develop flavor and allow the beneficial nutrients to leach out. Similar stocks and broths were made using beef, pork, and wild game. We also learned in recent years that these infusions have powerful health benefits. And of course, stocks and broths serve as a foundation for innumerable soup recipes.

The rebirth in making traditional stocks, broths, and soups has mostly remained in the realm of agricultural-based foods. Interest in seafood still lags way behind because, let's face it, American's comfort level with cooking and preparing it is tepid at best. Seafood stocks and broths are rarely, if ever, made at home anymore. And yet, they are just as nutrient-dense, just as healthy, and contrary to popular belief, can be a lot cheaper and simpler to make than chicken and beef stock. Who knew?! And when made in time-honored ways, they acquire an exquisite, delicate essence of the sea that elevates and enhances countless seafood soup recipes. New England, with its rich seafaring history and culinary traditions, can teach us much in this arena. There is *so much to rediscover* beyond clam chowder and lobster bisque. There's also unlimited potential to create new recipes too!

That said, there's more to this book than just soup recipes. As you probably know, our oceans are in crisis, and our seafood-buying choices have a powerful impact on the health of our oceans. Fishermen and fisherwomen who fish the right way—ethically, legally, sustainably, and with concern for their impact on our oceans—are desperately asking us as consumers to do more to support them. And that's what Chapter 1 is all about.

Section 1

Understanding New England Soups from the Sea

Chapter 1

Know Your Fisherman/ Fisherwoman

In *American Seafood,* Barton Seaver writes: "Within the US exclusive economic zone (our sovereign territory that extends 200 miles offshore), more of America is underwater than above it."[1] Crazy as it sounds, we have more acreage available for seafood than we do land for farming. And contrary to popular belief, we have extremely well-managed fisheries in the United States that ensure both healthy fish stocks and clean waters. And yet, approximately 90 percent of the seafood we consume in America is imported. To understand how ludicrous this is, consider the following:

As the crow flies, we have approximately 12,000 miles of coastline in America. But if you include the actual shoreline, which is not a straight line, and which includes harbors, bays, inlets, estuaries, and islands, it's estimated we have about 95,000 miles of coastline. Keep in mind, some countries have *zero* miles of coastline. We're fortunate to have an incredible scope and diversity of underwater ecosystems right off our shores. And we're even more fortunate that these coastlines harbor some of the most sustainable fisheries in the world.

Of course, it wasn't always this way. Innovations in fishing technology in the late 19th and early 20th centuries, namely, steam and then gas-powered engines, large nets (called otter trawls), and bigger and faster fishing vessels allowed for exponential increases in the volume of fish caught. In one day, modern fishing vessels could now catch as much fish as pre-20th-century sail-powered boats could catch in several weeks. Despite reports of plummeting catches, the first half of the 20th century was an era when a collective belief in "progress" could not be stopped, no matter the consequences. In the decades after World War II many fishing stocks became threatened by overfishing.

In response to the crisis, the United States passed historic legislation in 1976 under the Magnuson-Stevens Act to prevent overfishing, rebuild stocks, and ensure a sustainable seafood supply. It extended US jurisdiction from 12 miles from shore to 200 nautical miles. This covers an area of 4.4 million square miles of ocean more than any country on earth.[2] Two other historic pieces of legislation, the Marine Mammal Protection Act (1972) and the Endangered Species Act (1973), were created to protect dozens of marine species that play vital roles in our ocean ecosystems including whales, seals, dolphins, and sea lions, as well as critical marine habitat that they depend upon.

This does not mean everything is perfect. Managing fish stocks is an imperfect science. Sometimes, stocks are overfished and need to recover. Two revisions to the original Magnuson-Stevens Act, the Sustainable Fisheries Act (1996) and the Magnuson-Stevens Fishery Conservation and Management Reauthorization Act (2006), put further restrictions on fisheries and mandated better scientific monitoring of stocks. In 2016 the National Oceanic and Atmospheric Administration (NOAA), the federal agency responsible for managing our national fisheries, celebrated its 40th rebuilt fish stock since the year 2000.

Of course, threats still exist for our marine systems. Pollution, habitat loss from the overdevelopment of our shorelines, and the rise in ocean temperatures from global warming continue to endanger marine habitats and fish species. Most people are now aware of these to some extent, but another less spoken of threat persists: globalization.

While the United States has made progress to ensure a sustainable seafood system, we still import a tremendous amount of seafood from overseas sources that do not follow the same stringent standards that our national fisheries do.

This means, as consumers, we frequently buy seafood that was caught on the opposite side of the world. We consume massive quantities of farmed shrimp, farmed fish, and canned seafood products like tuna, to name a few, all sourced from beyond our coastlines. The reality is, seafood sourced from overseas provides a cheap alternative to locally caught seafood.

All the while, healthy, plentiful, sustainably caught fish and shellfish, harvested right from our own shores, are being ignored. Our local fishermen, fisherwomen, and local fishing economies are struggling mightily in the face of this globalized seafood trade. Furthermore, seafood that is transported over long distances leaves a heavy carbon footprint.

Meanwhile, our oceans are struggling in the face of overfishing and mindless consumption. By shopping for your seafood locally, you can help contribute to

the success of small businesses, shrink your carbon footprint, and help support the fishermen and fisherwmen who work within strict regional and federal standards to keep fish and shellfish stocks sustainable.

What does this have to do with soups, you might ask? Everything! Supporting sustainably raised or wild-caught seafood from local New England waters is an inherent part of making good-quality stocks, broths, and New England seafood soups. They go hand in hand. Sure, you can make decent tasting soups with boxed and canned foods from your "local" mega-supermarket. But you really can't make epic *soul-stirring* ones. Ones that awaken that ancient connection we all feel to the sea. Ones that reacquaint our taste buds to what seafood should taste like, not overly fishy, weird, or icky, but rather like a familiar, refreshing dip in the ocean after years away. This is, in my opinion, a key to reconnecting us to our culinary seafood traditions. And this is my mission in this book.

Five Ways to Support US Fisheries

Certainly there are barriers today to cooking with seafood the way people did before World War II, when families and communities were smaller and more close knit. Modern life is vastly different and things such as cost, time, and accessibility are real challenges, especially if you have a full-time job and are raising kids. Furthermore, you might not live in New England. I'll address some of those challenges in the coming pages. But regardless of where you live, when it comes to supporting our national fisheries, there are things you can do, perhaps more than you realize.

1. Join a Community Supported Fishery

Community supported fishery (CSF) programs are the seafood version of the increasingly popular community supported agriculture (CSA) programs. In a CSA, members of a community pay a one-time upfront fee for a weekly share in a local farm's seasonal output of fruits and vegetables. CSA members then either go directly to the farm for their weekly share or to a designated pickup location. Similarly, in a CSF, community members pay upfront for a weekly or biweekly share in the catch of one or several local fishermen and fisherwomen. The benefits of joining a CSF are immense.

Paying local fishermen and fisherwomen directly allows them to bypass the global demand-based market system with a more sustainable supply-based market system. In a demand-based market, the consumer dictates what the fisherman supplies. In the United States, because our taste in seafood has become overly simplified since World War II, that means only a handful of species are available in stores, in particular, these are tuna, cod, shrimp, and salmon. In the case of tuna and cod, it has led to overfishing to meet the demand. In the case of shrimp and salmon, it has led to environmentally destructive fish and shrimp farms to meet the demand.

But in a supply-based system, fishermen and fisherwomen supply fish based on what's *in season, abundant, and available locally*. This direct and simple chain encourages more transparency and trust between consumers and fishermen. It gives consumers increased access to locally caught seafood. It pays fishermen and fisherwomen a fairer price for their work. It benefits the health of our seas. And it strengthens the economies of our community-based fisheries. Bottom line: everybody benefits.

CSFs are still in their infancy and there are not nearly as many options as CSAs. Most are concentrated in the Northeast and California, but they are slowly catching on in other places. If you live near the coast, there's a good chance you can find one via the Local Catch Network, a fantastic online resource. Simply go to their website (www.localcatch.org) to search for CSFs in your area.

CSFs are one of several direct buying options. Your local farmers' market may include a local fishery. If you live close to the sea, you may be able to buy direct from a boat or a fisherwoman's market located on the dock. But not everyone has access to CSFs or buying direct. In that case, your next best option would be #2.

2. Know Your Fishmonger

Fishmongers are the folks who select and purchase seafood for sale to the public. Generally speaking, there are two basic types of fishmongers—those who work in the seafood department of supermarkets and those who own their own independent specialty shops and/or seafood markets. However, the latter is more in the spirit of a true fishmonger. They are typically more connected to local seafood options, have more knowledge and experience working with seafood, and have a lot more freedom to choose what fisheries they support. They're also more likely to make special preparations such as fish stock, smoked fish, or pâté. Many independent fishmongers struggle to compete with supermarket seafood departments that operate within the global demand-based market. That said, many supermarkets are improving their options and offering more choices from US fisheries.

the Marine Stewardship Council (MSC). Check out each seafood department and notice who's doing more to support US-based fisheries. Ask them the same questions as previously mentioned and notice which of the seafood department fishmongers have more knowledge and expertise. Support the best options possible!

That said, there's an even better option than supermarkets. And that brings me to option #3.

3. Buy Direct Online

Thanks to the power of modern technology, more and more fishermen, fisherwomen, and seafood suppliers are circumventing the global seafood supply chain by shipping to consumers through direct purchases via the internet. In the process they're also circumventing another problem with the global seafood industry: seafood fraud.

Because many types of fish have similar tastes and texture, some sellers intentionally mislabel cheaper varietes for more expensive ones. An example would be pollock that's passed off as cod. In the global supply chain, seafood passes through a complex chain of middlemen that include distributors, packagers, processing facilities, importers, and transporters. Accurately tracking everything along the way can be almost impossible, especially when so much of those transactions happen overseas. Only a very small percentage of imported seafood is inspected by the FDA. According to Oceana, a marine conserva-

If you have a choice, always try to support your local independent fishmonger! They are a valuable resource in our communities. Ask them questions such as what's local and what's in season. Ask for cooking tips. Ask them to scale, gut, or fillet a whole fish, if necessary. Ask for a specific species if they don't carry it. Ask for a bulk order for a special event. Most can place special orders with advance notice. My favorite thing to ask for? Whole fish carcasses for soup stocks! Most independent fishmongers do what they do because of their enthusiasm and love of seafood. Some are even former fishermen or fisherwomen themselves. They'll be more than happy to help you.

If there are no independent fishmongers in your area, you'll probably have a choice of supermarket chains. All seafood sold in supermarkets is required to have a country of origin label, so it's easy to determine if the supermarket carries seafood from US sources. Also, look for labels that certify sustainable practices, such as from

tion nonprofit organization that has studied seafood fraud, some fish, like Atlantic cod and wild salmon, may be purposefully mislabeled from 25 percent to as much as 70 percent of the time.[3] Large-scale suppliers that buy wholesale from the global supply chain, such as supermarkets and chain restaurants, are the most vulnerable to seafood fraud.

The most direct transfer of seafood from fisherman to your dinner plate (or soup bowl), the better for all involved: Fishermen and fisherwomen get paid more, you consume fresher seafood, and the environment benefits from the much smaller carbon footprint.

HOW TO BUY DIRECT ONLINE

There are a growing number of New England area CSFs and seafood businesses that are expanding their market via direct sales online. One of my personal favorites is Red's Best (www.redsbest.com), headquartered on the historic Boston Fish Pier.

Red's Best processes, packages, and transports the catches of hundreds of small-scale New England fishing boats. Not only do they do it quickly and efficiently, they've also developed innovative software that tracks everything from the moment the catch is unloaded to when it reaches the buyer. By taking care of most of the supply chain operations—tracking each transaction and labeling each package with who caught it, where, and how—Red's Best ensures ultimate consumer trust and confidence. Furthermore, by aggregating catches from hundreds of small boats, Red's Best is helping form a larger market presence for small-scale fishermen, thereby leveling the global playing field. And best of all, they can ship directly to your doorstep.

There are many other online sources for purchasing native US seafood. The New England–based nonprofit, Eating with the Ecosystem (www.eatingwiththeecosystem .org), whose mission is to promote a place-based approach to sustaining New England's wild seafood, has an excellent "Local Seafood Resources" page that includes a link for New England seafood businesses that offer online sales.

If you live outside New England, companies like Vital Choice (www.vitalchoice .com) and Sea to Table (www.sea2table .com) source sustainable seafood from small-scale domestic suppliers and ship it all over the United States. A quick online search may reveal a fishery that is closer to where you live. In the coming years, I'm confident there will be many more options.

Finally, it's interesting to note that the only item Red's Best sells via their website that's not local to New England is wild-caught shrimp. That's because shrimp can no longer be caught in New England waters. And that brings me to #4.

4. Please Stop Eating Shrimp from Abroad

Judging from the popularity of shrimp on menus and its year-round availability in supermarkets, you might think that we've always eaten a lot of shrimp in America. But, prior to the 1960s, most Americans were not regularly consuming shrimp. Shrimp was more of a regional delicacy, especially in the Cajun country of Louisiana. As our consumer taste in seafood narrowed, ironically, our taste for shrimp expanded dramatically. Shrimp's meaty texture and sweet taste runs contrary to many types of seafood with negative connotations of "slimy" or "fishy." Most people I know who say they don't like seafood make an exception with shrimp. Today, the average American consumes over 4 pounds of it per year, more than any other seafood by a long shot.

Another reason for this trend is that shrimp is an ideal fit for the global demand-based market system. Shrimp freezes well and can be efficiently stored, packaged, and shipped all over the world. It is available year round, has a short life cycle, and reproduces quickly—a combination that ensures a constant supply. Finally, it can be caught in the wild in prodigious quantities, but it can also be farmed in prodigious quantities too. And that last reason is perhaps the biggest reason of all for its widespread availability.

In the 1970s and 1980s, seafood franchises like Red Lobster and Long John Silver's rose to prominence and expanded our national appetite for shrimp. Initially, most of the shrimp came from our Gulf Coast states. But as demand grew, cheaper, more consistent supplies were sought and corporations found oppor-

tunity with Asian countries known for their historically rich and fertile shrimp grounds. To fulfill the American demand for shrimp, millions of acres of native mangrove forests were converted to farmed shrimp operations. And with it, thousands of historically small, subsistence-based shrimping operations, using sustainable methods meant to feed small communities, were transformed into highly intensive unsustainable operations designed to maximize yields to feed wealthy nations. Not surprisingly, there's been a heavy price to pay.

For starters, mangrove forests are vital tropical coastline ecosystems. They are an essential habitat for countless types of marine life. They act as a buffer against typhoons and hurricanes and help prevent erosion. Their dense network of roots and vegetation helps improve water quality by filtering pollutants. They also sequester carbon from the atmosphere and are thus a buffer against climate change. And they provide livelihoods to countless native populations that have historically lived along the coasts as subsistence fishing communities.

Shrimp farms pose many other problems. Shrimp grown in contained areas, known as shrimp ponds, are highly susceptible to disease. A heavy use of antibiotics has been employed for decades on Asian shrimp farms much the same way they've been used in the factory farming of livestock.

Shrimp ponds can also cause a buildup

of waste. For decades, shrimp farms became so toxic that they were abandoned so that new ones could be built. The vicious cycle continued for years until the problems became so widespread that eventually producers and governments started to recognize the ecological damage and the need for better, more sustainable means of production.

Today, improvements are being made, and that's a good thing, but problems persist and only a very small percentage of imported shrimp is inspected. You really don't know when you buy shrimp from Asia what standards or lack of standards were followed.

Even with more sustainable methods of production, the bottom line is that shrimp aquaculture still operates within the economic model of global demand. And that model means the very countries producing this shrimp, such as China, Thailand, Vietnam, India, and Indonesia, export the overwhelming majority of it to wealthier nations. Countless native subsistence fisheries that once produced food for their own communities have been displaced by multinational shrimp operations. Meanwhile, our national shrimp fisheries have struggled to compete with the low prices of mass-produced farmed shrimp from overseas. Today, 90 percent of shrimp consumed in the United States comes from foreign shrimp farms.

The madness of this system is perhaps even more insane when you consider that our abundant coastlines are rich in many different types of shrimp, both cold and warm water varieties. Furthermore, US shrimp fisheries are sustainably managed and responsibly harvested. They're also mostly wild and are not farmed operations. We have great shrimp right here in the United States! You may know that the most prolific shrimping region is the Gulf of Mexico, which is where the overwhelming majority of US wild shrimp comes from. But there are other smaller shrimp fisheries all along our coasts. That is, with the exception of one—New England.

Since 2014, the fishery for New England's native shrimp, the northern shrimp (also called salad or bay shrimp), has been shut down due to declining populations. Though little-known outside New England, it provided a small but valuable fishery to the region. Warming seas have pushed the habitat for northern shrimp outside the Gulf of Maine and a future return is considered unlikely.

To honor the true spirit of this book, a place-based approach to New England seafood, you therefore won't find many recipes that include shrimp. I do make an exception in Chapter 9, Classic Medleys and Stews. Recipes such as cioppino originated outside of New England, and historically contained shrimp. I frequently encourage substituting different types of seafood in many of the recipes in this book, and shrimp certainly fits the bill as a quick and easy replacement. In those cases, it's fine to use wild shrimp from US-based fisheries.

Of course, some say that the demand for shrimp is so high in America that US shrimp fisheries can't meet it, and therefore we need to buy shrimp from other areas of the world. These arguments almost always come from those who benefit from this circumstance, which in this case is the shrimp aquaculture industry.

So here's an argument that the multinational shrimp companies don't want you to hear: Why not just *not* eat shrimp from abroad and instead look to more local options? Clams, mussels, scallops, crabs, crayfish, and even fish can all be used in place of shrimp in many recipes. It's really not that radical when you think about it. It just takes some awareness and a change in buying habits.

As consumers, we have more power than we think. Our collective choices can make a bold impact. Our oceans and national fisheries desperately need us to encourage a more transparent, just system by supporting a more localized and sustainable supply-based economic model.

An important part of this transition is to reacquaint ourselves with the wonderful diversity of seafood that exists right here on our coasts. And that's what #5 is all about.

5. Embrace Diversity

You might think that along the coast of New England there would be a deep connection to local seafood. Eating with the Ecosystem, the nonprofit mentioned in the How to Buy Direct Online section (page 22), decided to find out. In 2019 they published the results of a unique one-of-a-kind citizen science research project called Eat Like a Fish.[4] They recruited 86 citizens from across New England and for six months asked them to regularly visit almost four hundred different fish markets to assess the availability of 52 types of seafood native to New England. The purpose was to gauge how well the diversity of New England's wild seafood is reflected in the New England marketplace.

The answer shouldn't be very surprising: Not very well at all.

The report revealed that 30 of the 52 species were found in less than 10 percent of the fish markets And 47 of the 52 were found in less than 50 percent of the markets. Only lobster, sea scallops, clams, cod, and haddock were found in over 50 percent of the markets.

And yet, all of the 52 species are abundant in New England waters. Even in New England, a region with a storied connection to the sea, our modern-day global seafood economy has broken that connection.

Clearly the same dynamic occurs on a national level. Over the past one hundred years, consumer taste in seafood has narrowed dramatically. Despite there being hundreds of edible seafood species on our coasts, 90 percent of all seafood consumed in America comes from just 10 species. Canned tuna, salmon, and, of course, farmed shrimp make up over 50 percent of those 10 species. Two others, cod and

Alaskan pollock, are a huge part of the processed food industry, and they are used in things like fast-food fish sandwiches and frozen fish sticks.

This is creating havoc in our oceans. Large-scale industrial fishing is leaving a trail of destruction in a greedy race to fulfill the demand for just a few species. Overfishing, bottom trawling that damages the ocean floor, wasteful bycatch, and lost or abandoned plastic fishing gear that kills sea life are all part of the problem. Throw in ecologically damaging aquaculture operations and it's no wonder our oceans are in crisis. Images of entangled sea life and tales of damaged ocean ecosystems regularly appear on the news and in our social media feeds. It's easy to feel overwhelmed and helpless in the face of it. But, as consumers, we can help shift things by embracing more diversity.

Benefits of Diversity

When we eat a wider variety of local seafood we participate in a more supply-based economic model that, as we've covered, is a more balanced, economically fair, and ecologically sustainable system.

Fishermen and fisherwomen who fish for one or only a few species put themselves at risk. Some years certain fish are plentiful and some years they're not. Diversifying what they can catch reduces that risk, just like farmers reduce their risk by planting a wide variety of crops.

On the consumer side, embracing the diversity of our oceans and buying those undervalued species can be very economical. Times change and so do our cultural perceptions around seafood. It's strange to think that at one time lobsters were considered food for the poor. Oysters, once plentiful, sold for a penny a piece at the turn of the 20th century. Right now, lesser-known species with little market demand can often be purchased at an extremely low price. I've seen fish like mackerel, monkfish, and porgy all priced at under half the cost of more common fish like cod and tuna. Squid is also a great value, as so few people buy it fresh at fish markets anymore. Jonah crab, a native New England crab, is slowly starting to catch on and is an incredible bargain compared to other types of non-native crabs. Blue mussels are often very affordable. Seek all these out while the prices remain low! You never know when demand, hence prices, might go up.

Diversifying our seafood choices also reduces wasteful bycatch. This bycatch, sometimes referred to as "trash fish," are the unwanted fish caught while fishing more commercially popular species. These fish are sometimes sold as bait, to pet food companies, or to specialty markets in ethnic communities that recognize their value. And that's the thing. They have *immense value*. They have their own unique tastes and textures, nutritional benefits, and most are plentiful and highly sustainable. Instead of trash fish, which has a negative connotation, they should really be called undervalued fish. Because there's little domestic demand, some are often quite affordable. Examples of undervalued fish in New England include porgy, skate, sea robin, dogfish, and squid.

Finally, diversifying our seafood choices helps us adapt to the coming shifts in underwater ecosystems. As a result of warming oceans, new species will enter into our local waters and familiar ones will leave, like the New England northern shrimp. Our local fishermen would love to catch and sell us a wider diversity of seafood, and they will if we demand it.

Overcoming Cultural (Mis)Perceptions

But before we demand a new species of fish, we need to refamiliarize ourselves with it. No one's going to demand anything they've never tasted before.

Negative perceptions of seafood are entrenched in our culture. This is due to both unfamiliarity but also negative experiences.

I'll give you one example in my own life. As a kid I loved catching bluefish. But I hated eating it. Why? Nobody knew how to cook it. I brought home fresh fillets, and we put them in the freezer. When we thawed them and cooked them they were utterly awful. Little did we know that unlike other fish, one should never freeze bluefish. Fast forward 30 years to researching this book.

I decided to revisit bluefish. I learned that because of their highly active feeding habits they have a high level of oxygen in their bloodstream, which gives their meat a high oil content (and thus high omega-3 content). This means it can spoil quickly and does not freeze well. As a result, bluefish have earned a cultural reputation as being overly fishy. However, if you cook them fresh, they have an absolutely fantastic rich, full flavor. They are now one of my favorite fish to eat. But what I experienced as a kid was fairly common. Many species have similarly entrenched negative perceptions.

Similarly, the Eat Like a Fish citizen science research project recognized that one of the key challenges facing most people is not just the accessibility to diversity, it's also learning how to cook the diversity! In that study, all 86 citizen scientists were asked to prepare and cook unfamiliar seafood in new ways. Most discovered that previously held prejudices dissolved when they learned how to bring out the unique and varied flavors of unfamiliar seafood. They enjoyed learning new recipes and even discovered new favorites!

When we realize what we've been missing all these years—abundant, cost-effective, healthful seafood right on our shores—and we acquire the cooking skills needed to prepare it in delicious ways, the demand will naturally follow.

Might I suggest seafood soups?

Chapter 2

The Native Fish of New England

If we could see clearly into the dark, murky waters of New England, we'd be amazed at the volume and diversity of fish life. According to the Rhode Island Fishermen's Alliance, a nonprofit dedicated to supporting sustainable fisheries in Rhode Island, the fishery biomass in New England has grown by over 500 percent in recent decades as a result of the strict regulations of our national fisheries.[5] And yet, despite being plentiful and sustainable, very few of these fish make it to our seafood markets or dinner plates.

This chapter is intended to help change that by providing a short overview of the different fish species that are native to New England waters and conducive to the soup recipes in this book. Generally speaking, larger fish yield larger, meatier fillets, which are easier to work with in soups. For that reason, small fish like herring, butterfish, and anchovies, though abundant in New England, are not included here.

This overview is organized into two sections with broad categories: Lean Mild Whitefish and Oily Full-Flavored Fish. Each category is further divided into a few subcategories. Brief descriptions of each fish are followed by a summary of five characteristics: flavor, texture, sustainability, seasonality, and best soup use.

Keep in mind that the sustainability status of each fish pertains to its sustainability in New England waters. Some of these fish are not well-managed in other areas of the world, and you may find generalized labels of them being unsustainable in some seafood guides or websites that don't look at them at a local level. Also, my sustainability designations are meant as a quick and current snapshot. As such, they are not in-depth profiles of their sustainability status. Moreover, the sustainability status of a fish species is not necessarily permanent. Sustainability statuses can change quickly from year to year. For more in-depth and current updates, please check FishWatch (www.fishwatch .gov) or NOAA Fisheries (www.fisheries .noaa.gov/species).

Also, factors such as seasonality and market demand means that not all the fish listed in this chapter will be easily found in seafood markets. At times, you'll need to choose alternatives in recipes. With that in mind, it's important to remember two key things when selecting a fish for a soup:

1. Different species of fish are inter-changeable in soup recipes

You can choose any lean, mild whitefish and substitute it for any other one. Their differences are subtle. Some have a slightly different texture and flavor than others, but they share more in common than not. The same could be said for the oily, full-flavored fish, though their differences can be a little more pronounced. For example, bluefish tastes quite different from salmon or swordfish. But we're not talking apples and oranges. They're close enough so that they won't dramatically change the overall flavor of the soup.

Fish species from regions outside New England are interchangeable in the recipes too. If you don't live in New England and would like to support fisheries closer to where you live, you can use locally available fish. For a helpful guide on suitable substituions, see the chart in New England Fish Substitutes (page 41). The compatibility of different types of fish in soups is a wonderful thing! It allows for more experimentation and, most important, it allows you to try something new.

2. When possible, choose fish that are less familiar to you

Many of these unfamiliar fish will likely be in the Undervalued Whitefish section of the Lean Mild Whitefish category (see page 34). These are the species that need more exposure and more consumer demand. Be curious, and look and/or ask for them at local fish markets. The best way to discover their differences is plain and simple: through experience. You'll find your own likes and dislikes.

Personally speaking, I love more full-flavored tasting fish. I adore their rich, tender, meaty fillets. In fact, I'd choose bluefish, mackerel, or striped bass any day of the week in most soup recipes that call for whitefish such as cod or haddock. This is just my personal preference. Many people I know prefer the opposite. This is to say, you can certainly substitute a lean, mild whitefish for an oily full-flavored fish if that is your preference (or vice versa) in many soup recipes, including the recipes in this cookbook. Cookbook recipes may seem to be set in stone, but they can be changed, adapted, and interpreted in unlimited ways.

Lean Mild Whitefish

Though similar in taste and texture, I've chosen three subcategories of lean, mild whitefish to help distinguish them from each other. The cod family is the most commercially fished, the most familiar, and the most widely available. It is typically in markets year round. The flatfish family are literally flat, bottom-dwelling fish. They are commonly seen in New England markets, though they can have more seasonal fluctuations. And finally, the undervalued whitefish are those that will probably be the hardest to find in markets. They're often the bycatch of more popular whitefish species but have lots of culinary potential. Due to their low demand, many will be very reasonably priced.

The Cod Family

ATLANTIC COD

Historically the most economically important fishery in New England, Atlantic cod has suffered dramatic and tragic population declines due to industrial fishing practices that date back over a hundred years. Unfortunately, cod continues to be a huge portion of the global whitefish trade. This does not mean to never choose cod, but it does mean you should do so sparingly. Fisheries in the United States have strict quotas to allow for a long-term rebuilding of the stock. Most cod in supermarkets comes from Iceland or Norway. Seek out wild-caught US sources from small-scale fisheries. Cod is the default whitefish choice of most people in a variety of soups and stews. Its thick, flaky fillets are a staple in fish chowders, and its unassuming, clean flavor seamlessly blends into many stews and medleys.

Flavor – mild and clean
Texture – delicate and flaky
Sustainability – choose sparingly
Seasonality – year round
Best soup use – chowder, stews, boils

HADDOCK

Very similar in both appearance and flavor to cod, haddock has a firmer texture and slightly stronger flavor. For this reason,

I prefer haddock over cod in soups. Previously overfished, haddock stocks have rebounded well in recent decades. It is a good, sustainable choice; however, its popularity (along with cod) can overshadow other equally delicious and abundant New England fish. Therefore, choose haddock in moderation.

Flavor – mild, slightly sweet

Texture – flaky yet firmer than cod

Sustainability – choose moderately

Seasonality – year round

Best soup use – chowder, brothy soups, stews

ATLANTIC POLLOCK

A great alternative to cod and haddock, Atlantic pollock has been historically neglected but makes for a very sustainable choice. Bluish-gray-colored fillets tend to keep consumers away, but don't let that deter you. It's simply their natural color. They also have a slightly higher fat content and stronger flavor than cod and haddock. Don't confuse Atlantic pollock with Alaskan pollock. The latter is the largest fishery in the world, but almost all of it goes to processed frozen fish products and fast food.

Flavor – mild and sweet, but stronger than cod and haddock

Texture – firm

Sustainability – choose liberally

Seasonality – year round

Best soup use – chowder, brothy soups, stews

SILVER HAKE (WHITING)

The smallest members of the cod family, silver hake, also called whiting, have a softer flesh. They are a good choice in chowders, especially in combination with other fish or shellfish. Red hake and white hake are two other types of hake, though they are less common in markets. Silver hake is a very sustainable option, and it is typically a lot cheaper than other types of whitefish. Avoid frozen hake; it easily becomes waterlogged and turns rubbery when cooked.

Flavor – mild

Texture – soft and less flaky than others in the cod family

Sustainability – choose liberally

Seasonality – year round

Best soup use – chowder

The Flatfish

FLOUNDERS

There are several types of flounders that live in New England waters. The commercial varieties are summer flounder (also called fluke), winter flounder (also called blackback or lemon sole), yellowtail flounder, American dab (also called American plaice), and grey sole (also called witch flounder). They all share similar characteristics, notably a very thin fillet (though some summer flounders grow quite large and have thick fillets) and fairly mild flavors. Their thinness doesn't make them an ideal choice for soups, but that doesn't mean they should never be considered. I find their best use is in stews and medleys. They're also a good choice for the rare but surprisingly delicious Whitefish Bisque (page 241).

Flavor – mild, slightly sweet, hints of shellfish and minerals

Texture – flaky, delicate to moderately firm

Sustainability – choose liberally

Seasonality – year round

Best soup use – stews

HALIBUT

Having lived in the "halibut fishing capital of the world," Homer, Alaska, I have an affinity toward these giant flatfish, the largest in the world, which can reach upward of 500 pounds. Unlike the stock of Pacific halibut, which is healthy and thriving, the stock of Atlantic halibut is severely depleted. For this reason there is no commercial fishery for Atlantic halibut, though some limited harvest is allowed under a long-term rebuilding plan. If you find Atlantic halibut in stores, make sure it's from a US wild-caught fishery and choose it very sparingly. Better yet, seek out Pacific halibut instead to help the once mighty Atlantics recover. Halibut is a good fit for soups because of its thick yet tender and firm fillets. However, it can easily turn mushy if overcooked.

Flavor – mild and sweet

Texture – lean and tender, but dense and firm

Sustainability – choose Atlantic halibut very sparingly; Pacific halibut is a sustainable alternative

Seasonality – year round

Best soup use – chowder, stews

SKATE

Though technically not a flatfish, skates are nevertheless a flat-shaped, cartilaginous, bottom-dwelling fish with many species throughout the world. In New England, the winter skate species is used for food. Skate wing, the part most commonly consumed, is considered a delicacy in France where much of it is exported. With a flavor similar to scallops, we are only beginning to recognize its culinary potential in the United States. Though pricey in restaurants, skate sold at fish markets can be a great bargain because they are in such low demand. Ask your fishmonger to source some for you, if possible. There is some concern over the health of skates because they are often a bycatch of other fish, but the winter skate stocks are relatively healthy and well-managed in New England waters.

Flavor – mild, similar to scallops

Texture – firm and stringy

Sustainability – choose moderately

Seasonality – year round

Best soup use – brothy soups, stews

Flavor – mild and sweet
Texture – dense and firm, similar to lobster meat
Sustainability – choose liberally
Seasonality – year round
Best soup use – stews

The Undervalued Whitefish

MONKFISH

Perhaps the most hideous looking thing in the sea, monkfish are basically a massive head with sharp teeth and a tail. But what the monkfish lacks in appearance it makes up for in fantastic flavor. The dense, firm meat, which comes only from the tail, is often compared to the texture of lobster meat. It's very versatile in all types of soups and is a staple ingredient in bouillabaisse and other Mediterranean-style stews. Monkfish fillets are often covered with a natural gray membrane. It needs to be removed, otherwise the fillets will shrink and toughen when cooked. Whole monkfish with their big gelatinous heads make excellent, rich fish stocks! Though overfished in the 1980s and 1990s, stocks in New England have recovered and are considered healthy and sustainable.

BLACK SEA BASS

An exquisite looking fish, when mature the black sea bass have black spotted skin with a purplish sheen and a large banded and spiny dorsal fin. As beautiful as they look, they taste even better. Many consider them to be among the best tasting whitefish, and I completely concur. Their flesh is delicate but firm and stands up well in soups. I love to use them in brothy concoctions as well as stews and medleys. Their heads and carcasses make fantastic fish stocks. They are a migratory fish and take up residence on the southern New England coast from late spring through early fall. Overfished in past decades, strict quotas have returned black sea bass to sustainable levels in the North Atlantic.

Flavor – mild, slightly sweet and nuanced
Texture – tender but firm
Sustainability – choose moderately
Seasonality – May to October
Best soup use – brothy soups, stews

TAUTOG (BLACKFISH)

A favorite of recreational fishermen and fisherwomen in southern New England, tautog live along the coast and inhabit rocky areas, wrecks, jetties, and breakwaters. They are also called blackfish because of their strikingly dark skin. They have a reputation as a fine eating fish with a flavor and texture similar to black sea bass. However, they are hard to find in markets as they are mostly relegated to sport fishing. Because they grow slowly and don't swim in large schools there are strict limitations on catches. In some locations and at some times of the year fishermen are only permitted to keep one fish. This is a good thing to ensure healthy populations. You're most likely to find them in markets in the fall, when they're at their most abundant. They are a real treat and make a fantastic bowl of chowder. Their carcasses make excellent stocks as well.

Flavor – mild and sweet
Texture – lean but tender and firm
Sustainability – choose sparingly
Seasonality – April to November
Best soup use – chowder, stews

DOGFISH

Named after their tendency to hunt in packs, dogfish are actually small sharks and have enormous commercial and culinary potential. Their firm, meaty flesh has a similar taste to halibut but with more complexity. Often considered a nuisance bycatch, many New England fishermen and fisherwomen have turned to the abundant supply of dogfish in the wake of the dramatic decline in cod. Though overfished in Europe, current dogfish populations are much healthier in the eastern United States where there is a lack of consumer demand. The Cape Cod Commercial Fishermen's Alliance has been collaborating with restaurants, markets, and schools to expand the domestic market for sustainably caught dogfish. Their versatile fillets are adaptable to any soup recipe, but I think a brothy soup is the best way to appreciate their full, rich flavor.

Flavor – rich, mildly sweet, and savory
Texture – firm, meaty, and tender
Sustainability – choose moderately
Seasonality – year round
Best soup use – brothy soups, stews

SEA ROBIN

Beauty is in the eye of the beholder, as they say, and no fish fits that better than the sea robin. They are at once striking, albeit strange looking, with dark orange and red colors and large, winglike fins (thus, their name) that propels them along the sea bottom. There is no commercial fishery for sea robins, and that is a shame because they are abundant and delicious. Their flesh is fairly firm and meaty, which means they work great in soups and stews. The French know this well. A close cousin to the sea robin, the red gurnard is a staple in regional French bouillabaisse recipes. There is a small but growing awareness of their culinary potential in the United States, which means you might find them in markets on occasion. Consider yourself lucky if you do!

Flavor – mild and delicate, similar to flounder
Texture – meaty and moderately firm
Sustainability – choose liberally
Seasonality – April to October
Best soup use – stews

SCUP (PORGY)

Once a popular fish to eat in early America, scup, also called porgy, has fallen out of favor despite its abundance in southern New England waters. Scup is a small fish, typically around 1 pound, and like all small fish, doesn't make a great choice for soups. It's more often prepared whole for grilling and baking. However, larger scup can be filleted, in which case you can certainly use its meat in soups. Scup has a much more pronounced flavor than other mild whitefish and has a firm texture. This combination makes them a good choice in stews. Scup are sustainable, and if you can find them in markets, they are very affordable.

Flavor – moderate and sweet
Texture – lean, flaky, and firm
Sustainability – choose liberally
Seasonality – May to October
Best soup use – stews

ACADIAN REDFISH (OCEAN PERCH)

A slow-growing deep water fish with a long lifespan, Acadian redfish were overfished for many decades, but they have made a nice comeback thanks to conservation efforts. Their unique feature is their bright red color, which is not commonly seen in local fish sold at New England markets. They are small fish, but similar to scup, the larger ones can be filleted. They have a very clean, mild, unassuming flavor and would therefore make a good choice in recipes with bolder flavors such as stews. I have begun to see Acadian redfish in fish markets on more than rare occasions, a good sign that they are making a comeback with consumers.

Flavor – mild, slightly sweet
Texture – moderately firm
Sustainability – choose liberally
Seasonality – year round
Best soup use – stews

Oily Full-Flavored Fish

Oily fish are more active fish compared to lean whitefish. Because they migrate longer distances and attack prey more aggressively, their muscles contain more fat and oxygen-rich blood. This results in both more flavor (and omega-3s) and color. It also means that fatty fish, whose primary fats are delicate polyunsaturated fats, go rancid much quicker than whitefish. Fatty fish need to be consumed and/or preserved quickly when removed from the water. They're also more seasonal than many types of whitefish, often migrating into New England waters during the spring and summer, where some are popular recreational fish. When fresh and in season they make wonderfully luscious and nourishing additions to any soup recipes.

Two broad categories are included to differentiate Atlantic Wild Fish and Farmed Atlantic Salmon. The latter is so widely consumed and so controversial that it requires its own category.

Atlantic Wild Fish

BLUEFISH

This is the fish that tugs at my heartstrings more than any other. It is the fish I grew up catching and dreaming of catching. Sleek and bullet-shaped, bluefish have a luminous white underside with shades of iridescent gray, blue, and green on the backside. They are voracious predators. A "bluefish blitz," when a school of feeding blues thrash the water surface like a violent rainstorm, is an awe-inspiring thing to witness. Bluefish should be very fresh and never frozen. Their flavor is full, buttery, and rich. They make transcendent fish chowders and bold additions to stews and medleys. Bluefish have mysterious migration cycles. They are at times abundant for long periods and then disappear for long periods. These patterns make it hard to discern how fishing impacts their stocks. Though well-managed, their stocks are currently below target population levels. Choose bluefish moderately when they're at their peak in late summer and early fall.

Flavor – rich, full flavor

Texture – coarse and moist

Sustainability – choose moderately

Seasonality – May to October

Best soup use – chowder, stews

STRIPED BASS

Named for the striking black stripes that run along the tops and sides of their sleek silver bodies, striped bass were a profoundly important food for Native Americans and early Anglo settlers. Tales of their past abundance, schools so dense you could walk across them, and massive size, some over 100 pounds, are the stuff of legend. Because they spawn in fresh water, they suffered precipitous declines throughout the 20th century due to coastal habitat loss and overfishing. Aggressive decades-long conservation measures saw them make a remarkable recovery in the mid-2000s. However, recent reports suggest overfishing has reoccurred. Choose striped bass sparingly for now. Though recreational fishermen and fisherwomen can catch striped bass all year long (with strict catch limitations), the commercial fishery is limited mostly to a few summer months, meaning these are the only times you'll find fresh wild-caught striped bass in markets. Not as oily as other fish in this category, their flavor sits right in the middle between stronger tasting fish, like salmon and bluefish, and mild, lean whitefish. This makes them incredibly versatile fish that adapt well to almost any soup recipe.

Flavor – slightly sweet, rich, and full, but not as strong as bluefish
Texture – dense, moderately firm, moderately oily
Sustainability – choose sparingly
Seasonality – June to August
Best soup use – all

ATLANTIC MACKEREL

With wavy vertical bands of black and blue on their top half, the Atlantic mackerel is a fish of unparalleled beauty. Once a mainstay in the diet of seafaring Atlantic communities, most Atlantic mackerel is now shipped overseas where it is still held in high esteem in many countries. Its rich, oily, sweet meat, high in omega-3s, is unlike any other. It is so universally pleasing in taste that it's hard to understand why it's disappeared from our plates. Perhaps it's because this fish is sold whole instead of as fillets. Most small, plentiful fish, like herring and butterfish, have shared similar fates. Mackerel is among the easiest fish to fillet and yields a good amount of meat in relation to the body, especially in late summer and fall when they're at their peak flavor. Pick out the largest ones you can find at your local fish market. You can ask your fishmonger to fillet them for you. You may not get enough meat for a large serving of soup, but what you do get will make smaller-sized preparations totally worth it.

Flavor – sweet, rich, full flavor
Texture – flaky, soft, moist
Sustainability – choose liberally
Seasonality – year round but best in late summer and fall
Best soup use – chowder, brothy soups, stews

NORTH ATLANTIC SWORDFISH

Once fished close to extinction, the North Atlantic swordfish is once again thriving. It's also one of the few fish that thrive on our dinner plates. Its thick, juicy, tender, easy-to-cook fillets are a favorite in both restaurants and home kitchens. The familiarity of swordfish can often supersede lesser-known oily New England fish like bluefish and mackerel. Choose it in moderation but not at the exclusion of others. Swordfish's thick fillets make excellent meaty additions to brothy soups and are a common ingredient in seafood stews around the world.

Flavor – sweet, rich, full flavor
Texture – tender but dense and firm
Sustainability – choose moderately
Seasonality – June to November
Best soup use – brothy soups, stews

TUNA

Although tuna is the most renowned of all the oily wild Atlantic fish, it unfortunately makes a poor choice in soups. Its rich, tender red meat quickly loses its flavor and becomes dry and tough when cooked for too long. It's much better suited to light and quick searing on a hot grill or served completely raw as sushi. I'll never in a million years understand how canned tuna fish, which lacks its natural flavor, color, and freshness, became a staple food in America. Needless to say, do *not* use tuna in any soup recipes.

Farmed Atlantic Salmon

It's almost hard to fathom that at one time the great wild salmon runs on the West Coast also took place on the East Coast. Few people alive today have ever seen or tasted a wild Atlantic salmon. The last fishery in the Gulf of Maine was shut down in 1948. The majority of wild salmon fisheries in New England closed long before that. Dams and industrial pollution in the 19th century destroyed the native freshwater spawning grounds of Atlantic salmon and sent most to extinction.

Today, there are a few remaining wild Atlantic salmon with access to their spawning grounds in Maine rivers. But they are listed as endangered species and all fishing is strictly forbidden. You will never find wild Atlantic salmon for sale anywhere. Know that *all* Atlantic salmon sold in stores is farmed Atlantic salmon. Wild Pacific salmon is also available in stores. There are five different species of wild Pacific salmon: chinook (also called king), coho, pink, sockeye, and chum. About 90 percent of wild Pacific salmon comes from Alaska.

Our demand for salmon has steadily increased since research revealed the many health benefits of omega-3s in the 1980s and 1990s. As a result, salmon has become the most consumed fish in America, surpassing even canned tuna. But instead of wild Pacific salmon, most of what we now consume is farmed Atlantic salmon and most of that is imported from Canada, Norway, Scotland, and Chile. Nor are we the only country that imports it. Farmed Atlantic salmon is now a major global commodity.

However, salmon farms, just like shrimp farms, are not good for the marine environment or the salmon themselves. They are kept in large pens along coastal areas, which can build up a lot of waste and negatively impact the health of local waters. Disease and parasites such as sea lice are widespread amongst farmed salmon. As a result, antibiotic use is prevalent and causes further problems. There's also the problem of fish that escape the pens, putting pressure on wild, native local fish species for increased competition of food and habitat. Escapees can also easily transmit parasitic infections to healthy wild salmon. In 2018, Washington State banned salmon farming after a quarter million Atlantic salmon escaped from their pens into Puget Sound.

Furthermore, the flesh of farmed Atlantic salmon is actually white. Indeed, Atlantic salmon lose their vibrant orange and red colors when they're taken off their natural diet of shrimp and krill. Farmed salmon are given feeds with synthetic colorings that color their flesh a much lighter pinkish color as compared to wild salmon. It's easy to see this in fish markets that display both wild and farmed fillets side by side.

To combat the rampant problems with salmon farming, many companies are now starting huge indoor salmon farms with high-tech water circulation systems. These are very new endeavors, and it remains to be seen whether they will be profitable in the long run. But they are not without controversies either. They are high-tech, high-cost, energy-intensive operations.

The argument you'll often hear in support of fish farms, be it indoor or outdoor, is that we need them to feed the world. Every fish aquaculture industry executive wants you to believe that. But I don't believe it and you shouldn't either. We have enough wild fish and shellfish in America to feed the entire country many times over! Except we ignore it or ship it overseas. We don't need more fish farms with complicated supply chains. I may sound like a broken record, but what we need is an awareness of the abundance of healthy sustainable seafood in our very own waters, and a change in our buying habits to support a more localized sup-ply chain that pays local fishermen and fisherwomen a fair price. Our native wild Alaskan salmon fisheries have struggled to compete with the lower cost of farmed Atlantic salmon that's flooding the market.

Though it's not native to New England, wild Pacific salmon is a much better choice, and purchasing this fish supports our native wild salmon fisheries on the West Coast. Yes, it's a lot more expensive, but it's a healthier choice for all involved. It also tastes better. Wild salmon has a more buttery, complex flavor than farmed salmon. When I lived in Alaska there was nothing I loved more than the taste of freshly caught wild salmon, especially when I caught it myself. Cooking up wild salmon on the same day it was caught is about as close to a spiritual experience as I've had through food.

I also understand farmed salmon is sometimes the only salmon available in markets. If you do choose to buy it, do it very sparingly. Don't make it your predominant choice at the exclusion of other fish, as many Americans currently do. And don't forget about the other species of oily wild Atlantic fish! They are just as delicious.

Flavor – buttery, full, and rich (though not nearly as much as wild salmon)

Texture – oily, moist, firm

Sustainability – choose very sparingly

Seasonality – year round (summer and early fall for wild Pacific salmon)

Best soup use – all

Other New England Fish

Many more edible fish swim in New England waters with culinary potential. Outside the fish listed previously, very few others make it to consumer markets. But things can change fast. Julia Child featured monkfish on one of her popular PBS cooking shows in the 1980s. It quickly became trendy on restaurant menus everywhere. With the prevalence of today's cooking shows and celebrity chefs, who knows what the next trend could be. I'd like to think it would be dogfish or maybe a fish like scup, both of which are abundant and delicious. Keep an eye out for the fish listed here, which are all local to New England.

Dory

Croaker

Cunner

Cusk

Ocean pout

Wreckfish

Tilefish

New England Fish Substitutes

If you live outside New England, you may be able to find some of the species listed in this chapter in your local fish markets. However, because fish are so easily interchangeable in soup recipes, it would be much better to support your local fisheries. The five ways to support US fisheries discussed in Chapter 1 apply not just to New England but throughout the country.

The table lists some of the more common species throughout the United States. There are dozens more than those listed. Get to know your local fish, especially the lesser known and undervalued ones!

	Southeast Atlantic and Gulf Coast	Pacific Coast including Alaska	Great Lakes and other freshwater species
Lean, Mild Whitefish	Croaker, Drum, Grouper, Mahi Mahi, Red snapper	Sole, Rockfish, Lingcod, Pacific Cod, Pacific Halibut	Catfish, Northern Pike, Walleye, Smallmouth Bass
Oily, Full-Flavored Fish	Cobia, King and Spanish mackerel, Pompano	Pacific mackerel, Salmon, Sablefish, Opah	Trout, Lake Whitefish

Chapter 3

The Native Shellfish of New England

Fish can certainly make some wonderful seafood soups. But shellfish can really take them to another level, because the concentrated juices held tightly inside their shells infuse soups with a pungent, briny burst of the sea. Clams and mussels are like Nature's bouillon cubes, creating instant broths full of flavor when simmered in water for just a few minutes. Oyster liquor, which is simply collected from shucked raw oysters, has the same effect when added to water. And crabs and lobsters harbor a rich complex of juices that makes for some divine stocks.

And then there's the rich, sweet, juicy meats of New England shellfish, which are among the greatest delicacies in the sea. Heck, as far as I'm concerned, they're the greatest delicacies in the world. Even better for our purposes, their flavors become heightened when combined with their respective broths and stocks into a soup.

Following are short overviews of the different native New England shellfish species that are used in the recipes of this book. Though I have not subdivided

them into different categories, try to seek out the species that are less familiar to you, and always feel free to substitute one shellfish for another, where applicable. And just like with New England fish, most New England shellfish are interchangeable in recipes, especially in medleys and stews.

It's also important to know that unlike salmon and shrimp farms, some types of farmed shellfish are actually *good for the environment.*

Why You Should Buy US Farmed Shellfish

New England has a vibrant and thriving commercial shellfish aquaculture industry. The overwhelming majority of oysters, clams, and mussels found in New England markets come from aquaculture operations. Scallops are more often wild caught, but there are farmed options too. All other shellfish are wild caught.

Because shellfish are filter feeders, they help to *improve* water quality by breaking down and expelling toxins. That doesn't mean contaminants can't build up if the shellfish are grown in heavily polluted waters. But farmed shellfish in the United States have strict water quality regulations and are famed for being among the cleanest and safest seafoods to consume.

Another benefit of farmed shellfish is that they don't require artificial feeds. In fact, they don't require *any feed.* Their diet is the same as wild shellfish—plankton from the seawater that they filter. And because their environment and diet is 100 percent natural, there's no waste buildup and no antibiotics are needed.

In some cases, farmed shellfish are *better options* than wild shellfish, the latter being frequently harvested by dredging methods that can damage the ocean floor. Many farmed shellfish are grown via suspension techniques in which they cling to ropes or mesh bags that hang in the open water, thereby avoiding the need to dredge. Not to mention, farmed shellfish, specifically mussels and clams, come precleaned to markets, saving the consumer extra work at home.

But while there are many pros to farmed shellfish, keep in mind that shellfish aquaculture is a global business. Many international companies compete with our own. Always seek out shellfish from local, US-based sources. Doing so supports a well-managed industry that helps maintain and clean our critical coastline habitats. What's more, because the shellfish are from local sources less fossil fuels are required to transport the harvest from farm to market.

Quahogs
(Hard-Shell Clams)

Quahogs, a name derived from the Indian name *poquauhock,* are also known as hard-shell clams. Quahogs are widely considered one of the great culinary clams on the planet. They are prolific, growing all along the Eastern Seaboard, but they're most abundant in New England from Cape Cod to points south. They come in many sizes and can be prepared in myriad ways. Clambakes, clam fritters, and baked clams (called stuffies in southern New England) are widely popular quahog dishes. But in my opinion, their greatest gift isn't their meat. It is their luscious ultra-briny liquor, the key ingredient in so many seafood soups including New England's most famous of all quahog dishes, clam chowder.

Quahogs (*Mercenaria mercenaria*) go by three different common names, which simply denote their size and thus growth stage. Littlenecks are the smallest (about 1 to 2 inches in diameter), cherrystones are medium-sized (2 to 3 inches), and quahogs are the largest (over 3 inches). Generally speaking, you'll get about 6 to 10 littlenecks per pound, 4 to 6 cherrystones per pound, and 1 to 2 quahogs per pound. Why the name *quahog* refers to both the generic name and their largest size is a mystery, and it's often a source of confusion. A clearer name you'll often see for the largest size is chowder clams, as these are best for making chowder.

Quahogs, in their various sizes, are

incredibly versatile in almost any clam-based recipe, but especially in soups and stews. The small size of littlenecks means they make great additions in stews and medleys where they are often served whole in their shells. Larger cherrystones and quahogs need to be steamed in a separate pot first. Then the meats are removed from the shells, chopped (or sometimes left whole), and added to soups.

Soft-Shell Clams (Steamers)

Despite their misleading name, soft-shell clams don't have a soft shell. Rather, they have a thinner, more brittle shell than

hard-shell clams. Their oval-shaped shells are an off-white color with grayish-brown streaks and/or blotches. Generally speaking, they have a bit of a rougher appearance than hard-shell clams. But what is soft about them is the ultra-tender meats inside, brimming with lush, flavorful juices. As compared to hard-shell clams, soft-shell clams are a little sweeter and their broth is less briny. Soft-shell clams are always served on the side (along with melted butter) when they're prepared in their most popular form, as a steamed appetizer. This is why they're referred to as steamers in New England.

Another distinguishing feature of steamer clams is a long muscular attachment called a siphon, which has a protective membrane that can easily harbor sand and debris. Make sure to remove this membrane after the clams are cooked. Though edible, the siphon can be tough and chewy on larger soft-shell clams. It can be easily sliced off after cooking, which also means you won't have to remove the membrane.

Soft-shell clams can be difficult to find in markets outside New England. They're not typically farm-raised nor do they keep or transport well, all of which I consider a blessing in disguise. A truly regional food! They're quite popular from Cape Cod up to Maine where they thrive in the colder waters. Though rarer in soups than quahogs, soft-shell clams and their sublime broth can make equally delicious soups.

Atlantic Blue Mussels

With a mild, sweet flavor and herbaceous, fragrant liquors, Atlantic blue mussels are not just tasty treats themselves, but they also make wonderful broths that integrate well with a wide variety of seasonings. Their glossy dark blue and black shells can easily be seen clinging to rocks, jetties, and piers. Ironically, despite its highly visible profile, only in recent decades has it become a regular feature in markets and restaurants.

Long considered a delicacy in Europe, blue mussels were historically ignored in America due to their reputation for causing sickness as a result of pollutants and red tides (rare but harmful algae blooms that make shellfish poisonous). They also require tedious cleaning from the dirt and grit that can accumulate both on and inside their shells. Their notorious "beards," a ropelike protrusion that they use to attach to rocks, can also be stringy and a bit difficult to remove. However, the advent of mussel aquaculture in

the 1970s and 1980s solved all these problems. Today, all farmed mussels come precleaned to markets and are grown in clean waters that are highly monitored. Blue mussels are now one of the most widely consumed shellfish in New England and beyond. A true aquaculture success story!

That doesn't mean wild mussels aren't good choices too. Commercial harvesting of wild mussels are also subject to strict water quality monitoring. But they may be harder to find in markets, especially supermarkets. I have noticed that wild blue mussels tend to yield more liquor than farmed mussels, which is ideal for our soup-making purposes. Unlike farmed blue mussels, which tend to be uniformly small, wild mussels can vary greatly in size. Some can be quite large with stronger hinges that keep the shells closed tightly with all the liquor inside. Mussel shells can gape open slightly when out of the water, which is natural. As a result, some of the liquor can be lost. Make sure to purchase wild mussels only from trusted sources.

Many seafood markets today only carry imported Prince Edward Island (PEI) blue mussels, which dominates the marketplace. Other types of farmed mussels, such as New Zealand green-lipped mussels, can also tempt consumers away from local options. If your only option is PEI blue mussels, that's okay. They're the same species as New England blue mussels and are quite good. But whether farmed or wild, New England blue mussels should always be your first choice.

Atlantic Sea Scallops and Bay Scallops

Like perfectly symmetrical folding fans with clear ridges and varying shades of whites, browns, reds, and purples, the scallop shell would easily win a shellfish beauty pageant. The sweet, creamy, and tender meats, sometimes called the "marshmallows of the sea," are almost universally adored. Sadly, it's rare to see them whole at markets. Unlike oysters and quahogs, their shells do not close tightly, and they lose freshness quickly after harvest. Scallops are shucked on the boat with only the adductor muscle being saved. This white, fleshy part is what most people know as a scallop. The rest, albeit edible, is discarded. This means you'll never be able to make a pure scallop broth (though there's very little liquid inside anyway). Even so, they're widely featured in seafood stews and can easily integrate with any type of seafood broth or stock.

Large Atlantic sea scallops are found year round in markets. The highly coveted and smaller New England bay scallops (sometimes called Nantucket or Martha's

Dry vs. Wet Scallops

Many sea scallops are treated with chemicals to preserve them after harvest. This treatment causes them to retain water. These "wet" scallops lose their flavor and texture. Be certain to buy only fresh "dry" or "dry pack" scallops, which just means they are untreated and in their natural state. If it's not clearly labeled, ask your fishmonger for dry scallops.

You may also see "diver" and "dayboat" scallops, which are names that describe how the scallops are caught. Diver scallops are harvested quite literally by divers who take them by hand, making them quite pricey but also rare to see at markets. Dayboat scallops refers to scallop boats that leave and return to shore within 24 hours (most stay out for days at a time) thereby bringing fresher scallops to market. Dayboat scallops are always dry scallops and never treated with chemicals.

Vineyard bay scallops), which are about the size of your thumb from the tip to the first joint, are only available from late fall to early winter. Fair warning, bay scallops can be quite pricey. But their succulent, sweet flavor is so extraordinary that you may have a hard time resisting the urge to shell out (pun intended) whatever it is they cost. I get them at least once a year and always marvel at their sublime taste. Sometimes calico scallops, which come from warmer, southern waters are mislabeled as bay scallops. They are very small, about the size of a fingertip, very cheap, and not very flavorful compared to both bay and sea scallops. Be sure to avoid them.

Eastern Oysters

Like wine grapes or coffee beans, oysters take on the flavors of where they live. And it can be argued that nothing quite takes on the flavor of the sea like oysters. The salinity of the water, the minerals in the sediment, and the type of nutrients the oysters filter are just some of the factors that affect their flavor. These environmental factors can vary dramatically from state to state, bay to bay, harbor to harbor.

Eastern oysters are the only species of oyster native to the East Coast. Generally speaking, they're brinier and have more complex flavors than West Coast oysters. But many consider, specifically, New England area oysters the best of the best on the East Coast. New England water

conditions favor oysters, and they are often brinier, plumper, and slightly bigger than oysters grown in warmer, southern East Coast waters. New England oysters can also be sweet, minerally, and/or buttery with hints of melon and cucumber.

Once decimated by pollution, disease, and overharvesting, eastern oysters have experienced a renaissance in recent years thanks to a booming aquaculture industry with hundreds of oyster farms lining the northeastern seaboard.

Longfin Squid

Abundant almost everywhere in the world, squid reproduce prodigiously, about every six months, thus making them highly resistant to fishing pressure and a very sustainable seafood. Squid is a staple in many cuisines, especially in Mediterranean and Asian cuisines. One of my favorite sights along the coasts of Asia is that of the lights of the squid boats on the horizon at night, which extend from long poles off the sides of the boats and easily attract squid. It is especially beautiful to see the lights as they first emerge in early evening, silhouetted against a fiery sky painted with orange, red, pink, and purple hues as the sun dips below the horizon.

The longfin squid is the primary species in Atlantic waters used for human

How to Shuck Oysters

If you've never shucked oysters before, it's best to have someone show you how to do it. It is very easy to puncture, or worse, seriously injure your hand. There are some good instructional videos on YouTube as well. You'll need an oyster knife and a dish towel.

Wrap the towel over one hand (to protect it) and firmly hold the oyster down by its larger, more rounded end. With the other hand (your dominant hand), place the tip of an oyster knife into the hinge (the narrower end), press firmly, twist, and pry the shell open. Carefully slide the knife along the edges, continuing to gently twist and pry, until the top shell completely releases from the bottom shell. Be careful not to spill the liquor! Once you get the hang of it, it's quite easy, though it can certainly require some elbow grease.

consumption. A similar species, shortfin squid, is primarily used as bait. But like so much of our native seafood, most is shipped overseas. The one exception of the domestic use of squid would be for its preparation as calamari (the Italian word for squid), a restaurant appetizer that has become so popular in recent decades that a viable domestic market exists because of it. However, very few people would dare purchase fresh squid or have a clue what to do with it at home.

Ironically, squid is one of the easiest seafoods to prepare and cook. Like scallops, it's almost always precleaned at markets and ready to add to any dish. The only preparation necessary might be to slice the long tubular body into rings.

Squid have a slightly sweet, buttery, tender flesh that can easily turn rubbery if improperly cooked. The general rule is to cook them for under two minutes (how calamari are cooked) or more than 20 minutes. Anything in between makes them tough, which means that squid make super simple additions to soups and stews, but especially the latter where it melds beautifully with other shellfish in countless seafood stew recipes from around the world. Another benefit of using squid is its very affordable price tag. For this reason it's a great substitute in seafood stew recipes that include pricier items such as lobster and scallops.

Maine Lobster (American Lobster)

Though dozens of species of lobsters exist throughout the world, it is the East Coast Maine lobster, also known as the American lobster, a cold-water species with two large claws full of firm but tender meat, that is the most renowned for its sweet, succulent flavor. It is arguably America's most widely beloved native seafood. Though its range extends as far south as North Carolina, the population is highly concentrated in the Gulf of Maine, where the overwhelming majority of the lobster

fishery is located. The cold waters in the Gulf of Maine create almost ideal conditions where lobsters thrive and develop their unparalleled iconic taste and texture. Those conditions have been augmented by the Maine lobster fishery, which has become one of the great seafood sustainability success stories. For about 50 years now, thousands of small-scale family-run operations have followed strict guidelines to protect breeding females to ensure an abundant and thriving population.

Ironically, up until the late 19th century lobsters were widely considered food for the poor and even used as fertilizer for livestock. That's hard to imagine today, but it wasn't until the decades following World War II that the market for Maine lobsters expanded well beyond New England.

Though fresh Maine lobsters are found in seafood markets everywhere, few people cook them regularly at home. And even fewer use them for homemade soups. But the rich, flavorful juices within the lobster shell make one of the greatest of all seafood stocks. Unlike the instant broths of the bivalves, lobster stock is more like fish stock in that the carcasses need to be simmered in water to develop flavor. In some ways, lobster stock resembles a land-based animal stock in that roasting the shells or browning them in a little oil first, similar to roasting chicken or beef bones, helps to intensify the flavor of the stock. Though pricier and more time-consuming to make than other types of seafood soups, a lobster soup made from New England

lobsters and a homemade lobster stock is a delicacy that is truly worth the time and effort required.

Jonah Crab, Atlantic Rock Crab (Peekytoe Crab), Blue Crab, Green Crab

Crabs have historically not been important commercial fisheries in New England. But that could be changing in the near future due to global warming. The southern New England lobster industry, that being all points south of Cape Cod, has suffered tremendous losses in recent decades. The reasons for the collapse are not entirely understood, but rising water temperatures, which are causing an increase in disease and predation, are thought to be the key factors. As a result, lobstermen and lobsterwomen are being forced to adapt. Ironically, one of New England's most abundant crab species, the Jonah crab, once a nuisance bycatch of lobster traps, is now being targeted.

Commercial landings of Jonah crabs have been increasing over the past 20 years, and in 2015 a federal management plan was established for the first time (including minimum sizes and prohibition of taking egg-bearing females). Though still relatively unknown, even in New England, they're slowly starting to find their way into markets. As it turns out, Jonah crabs are quite delicious! They are medium-sized, reddish-brown crabs with two large front claws, and their meat is often described as sweet, briny, and flakier than the more well-known blue crab. Chefs are starting to use them in popular dishes like crab cakes where they once used much pricier crabmeats from outside New England.

The Atlantic rock crab, another abundant coastal species, is also starting to catch on. It's very similar in appearance and flavor to the Jonah crab, albeit slightly smaller in size and with thinner front claws. It also goes by the name peekytoe crab, altered slightly from the colloquial "picked toe" of Down East Maine, to make it more marketable. It's become a fashionable food in the summer months along the New England coast, especially in Maine where most of the harvesting and processing occurs.

Another crab that could potentially see an increase in New England due to warming waters is the blue crab of Chesapeake Bay fame. Blue crabs are native to southern New England waters though they're not nearly as abundant as in the mid-Atlantic, where they thrive in warmer waters. However, in recent years there have been reports of increased blue crab populations in southern New England. Though recreational blue crab fishing prevails in southern New England, no commercial blue crab fisheries exist, at least not yet.

Finally, a non-native species to New England, the invasive green crab, also has culinary potential. These smaller crabs were introduced from Europe in the late 1800s but have been exploding in recent years due to warming waters. They are wreaking havoc on local ecosystems, destroying vital eelgrass habitat and eating native shellfish, especially soft-shell clams, a favorite food source of green crabs. Concerned parties are attempting to find markets for them. One organization, Greencrab.org (formerly the Green Crab R&D Project), is working to increase consumer awareness, partner with chefs, and develop recipes. One potential use for our purposes is Crab Stock (page 81).

That said, any local New England crab, be it Jonah, rock, blue, or green are interchangeable with each other in any crab recipes and all make excellent crab soups and stocks. Availability of New England crabs in New England markets is still somewhat scarce as compared to other, more established shellfish. But again, the future holds potential. You can be part of the change *now* by being curious, asking your local fishmonger to stock some, and/or snatching them up while the prices remain incredibly low.

Atlantic Northern Shrimp, Wild-Caught Gulf Shrimp

With a range from Greenland to the Gulf of Maine, the Atlantic northern shrimp once occupied a small but significant shrimp fishery in northern New England. They never had much of a national appeal, as they're much smaller and have a softer texture than other types of shrimp, but they carved out a small niche of devotees in New England, especially in Maine, where most of the fishery was located. Sadly, the northern shrimp fishery has been shut down since 2014 due to heavily depleted stocks. Prospects for a recovery are looking bleak as global warming is pushing their habitat outside the southernmost extent of their range.

Though local New England seafood should always be a first choice, I cannot be an idealist and, as the saying goes, "make perfect the enemy of the good." Sometimes alternatives are suitable. As explained in Chapter 1, our wild-caught shrimp fisheries need help in the face of the global farmed shrimp trade. US Gulf Coast shrimp, be it the species of browns from Texas or white and pink varieties from Louisiana to Florida, are the firm, meaty, sweet varieties most people adore. They stand up well in soups and stews. Look for US wild-raised Gulf shrimp in markets and be sure to avoid all farmed shrimp from overseas.

Other New England Shellfish and Substitutes

There are many species of New England shellfish beyond what is listed in this chapter. As of now, there's very little domestic market for them. Those that are harvested are mostly shipped to foreign markets. But perhaps domestic markets will develop more awareness. Innovative chefs will sometimes feature these lesser-known species in creative ways. This includes the many types of snails that are abundant on New England shores such as

Why You Should Buy Whole Shrimp

The best shrimp for soups are whole shrimp with their heads and shells still attached, as they harbor fats and juices that add wonderful flavors. You can cook them right in the soups and stews without de-shelling or removing the head. Yes, they'll take a little more work to peel, and this may seem awkward in the middle of a meal, but they retain more crunch and flavor when left whole. You can even suck the juices right out of the head (and weird out your fellow diners), like they do in Cajun country and other places around the world where shrimp heads are considered the best part of shrimp (like fish heads). If you can't find whole head-on shrimp, purchase shrimp with the shell on. Peeled and deveined shrimp, albeit more convenient, often lose flavor and texture.

periwinkles, slipper limpets, and whelks. It also includes other species of native clams, such as razor clams and blood clams. There's also the Atlantic deep sea red crab whose sweet meat is similar to the famed king crab of Alaska. If you see them in US markets in the coming years, be curious and adventurous! See if you can find a way to incorporate them in the recipes.

Finally, there are many types of shell-fish that thrive in other regions. You'll find plenty of options for possible substitutes. Some of the more well-known and commercially available options on the Pacific coast include Manila clams, cockle clams, geoduck clams, California mussels, Pacific oysters, Pacific squid, Dungeness crab, snow crab, king crab, and rock crab. In the southeast Atlantic and Gulf Coast, there's crawfish, blue crab, stone crab, Caribbean spiny lobster, and queen conch.

Chapter 4
The Portuguese Influence

Few people think of Portuguese food when it comes to New England cuisine. But all across New England, especially along the southern coast of Massachusetts and Rhode Island, are communities with a strong Portuguese presence and identity. Many have roots dating back as far as the early 1800s when New England whaling ships sailed across the Atlantic and brought back Portuguese men looking for new opportunities in America. A large percentage hailed from the Azores, a distinct island archipelago region of Portugal that sits almost 1,000 miles from mainland Portugal, as well as the Cape Verde islands, a Portuguese colony until the mid-20th century.

Since then, additional waves of immigration further established Portuguese communities in New England who have adapted their native cuisine to native New England foods, especially the seafood, which was already an integral part of most Portuguese diets. Even today, Portugal, with its extensive Atlantic coastline, has one of the highest rates of seafood consumption in the world, per capita. Native New England fish and shellfish were seamlessly integrated into traditional Portuguese dishes. It's the other ingredients of Portuguese cuisine where more distinct differences lie.

Stemming from a long history of seafaring and exploration, Portuguese cuisine consists of both exotic herbs and spices from the East, like cumin, cloves, and cinnamon as well as foods from western voyages to the Americas, such as tomatoes, potatoes, green peppers, and a variety of hot chile peppers. Other identifying features of Portuguese cuisine are a liberal use of onions, garlic, leafy greens, rice, wheat, beans, olive oil, vinegar, and wine. All of these ingredients are fused in countless ways to create a unique national cuisine that is often richer and spicier than that of its European neighbors.

In bringing this cuisine to New England, Portuguese communities created their own regional cuisine within a broader regional cuisine, fusing it with New England ingredients but still retaining a unique Portuguese identity.

And nowhere does that identity shine more than in their seafood soups and stews. This is, in my highly biased opinion, the ultimate way to experience Portuguese cuisine in New England. In the *Provincetown Seafood Cookbook,* Howard Mitcham writes of the Azores islanders, "An acute and permanent shortage of fuel led them to become masters of 'the simmer'—a long, slow cook that never boils or bubbles, and consumes a minimum of fuel and is ideal for thick soups, stews and sauces." He goes on to say, "Their lack of beef, lamb and other meats forced them to become the world's greatest seafood cooks and the things they do with fish and shellfish is almost miraculous."[6]

It might sound odd to say, but one of the best clam chowders I've ever had in New England is Portuguese Clam Chowder (page 115). As you can see in the recipe, it resembles little of what people think of when it comes to New England clam chowder. There's no dairy or bacon. No chowder clams. Not even potatoes. Rather, it features sausage, whole littleneck clams, and tomatoes. A tomato-based chowder may seem sacrilegious to many New Englanders, yet it *is* a style of New England clam chowder. What's more,

it resembles little of the tomato-based Manhattan clam chowder that most New Englanders scoff at.

Furthermore, the absolute best seafood stews I've ever had in New England are Portuguese seafood stews. Caldeirada (a fish stew), mariscada (a shellfish stew), shrimp Mozambique (a shrimp stew), Portuguese-style paellas, or any of the variety of spicy stews that use individual species such as salt cod, squid, or clams are almost indescribably delicious.

My Experience

To be clear, I am not a scholar of Portuguese food or culture. I have never been to Portugal. I barely knew anything about Portuguese food until I moved to Massachusetts in 2008. It was only then I learned about the Portuguese communities on the southeastern coast. And I fell in love with the food. But the more I learn, the more I realize how little I know.

I still remember my first Portuguese meal in New England like it was yesterday. It was a Portuguese clam boil. And the thing that stood out more than anything was the broth. My god, how flavorful it was! All the juices from the clams, the spicy chourico sausage (similar to the more well-known Spanish chorizo), and the vegetables combined to make an utterly divine tonic. After the feast, I remember my host and friend, who prepared the meal, was about to dump the leftover broth from the main pot down the drain. I literally jumped out of my seat screaming, "Whoa, whoa, whoa! I want that!" I saved all of it in containers and brought it home.

After that initial meal I started trying more and more Portuguese cuisine, but the more I tried, the more I gravitated to the soups and stews. In fact, these days, I rarely order anything else because I know I'll be in heaven with every sip and slurp. It's for this very reason that half of the recipes you'll find in Chapter 9, Classic Seafood Medleys and Stews, are of Portuguese origin.

I should also mention that my experience is reflected purely in the Portuguese cuisine of southern New England, which is heavily influenced from the Azores of Portugal, more so than other regions of Portugal. As with all countries, there are different regional styles and variations, which are constantly changing and evolving. Portuguese food in New England may not be reflective of the more cosmopolitan and trendy cuisine of modern-day Portugal. Many of the Portuguese immigrants who came to New England in the middle decades of the 20th century did so to escape political turmoil, poverty, and even more specifically, a series of volcanic eruptions in the Azores from 1957–1958 that covered the islands in ash, forcing thousands to flee. From my research and understanding, the Portuguese immigrants of that time came with a much

more rustic, hearty cuisine than what developed later in Portugal in the 20th and 21st centuries.

As a result, the Portuguese recipes you'll find here may not be what many people consider to be "authentic." Also, while I did try to stay true to my experience of Portuguese cuisine in New England, I did take some small creative liberties in some of the recipes. For example, I found a squeeze of lime in some of the richer tomato-based stews to be a perfect finishing touch to brighten the stew and bring out a little pop of acidic sweetness. I have not found much evidence of lime juice in Portuguese seafood stews. Rather, it was my affinity for Southeast Asian cuisine with its liberal use of lime juice in soups and stews that inclined me to try it. And I loved it.

I actually find there's an interesting symmetry between Southeast Asian cuisine (a cuisine I've experienced in multiple trips to Thailand, Burma, Indonesia, and Cambodia) and Portuguese cuisine. After all, in the 16th century it was the Portuguese who introduced Thailand to the tiny bird's eye chile from their voyages to Latin America. This small chile, also called the Thai chile, has become an essential and iconic part of Thai cuisine. There are many more culinary lines of connection among Southeast Asia, Latin America, and Portugal, few of which I can pinpoint historically, but that my taste buds suggest to me are interconnected.

At the very least, the Portuguese recipes

in this book provide some interesting colors and contrasts to many of the other recipes. For example, Portugal's two famous sausages, linguica and chourico, as well as cumin, cilantro, vinegar, and hot sauces, are common features that are not often found in other types of New England soups and stews.

Personally speaking, these were some of my favorite recipes in the book. Many of my friends who gave me feedback when I was creating and testing the recipes thoroughly agreed. I take no personal credit for this, but rather I tip my cap to the ingenuity and creativity of the Portuguese cooks and chefs through the ages who inspired the soup and stew recipes herein. I hope you find them as deeply delicious and nourishing as I do.

Finally, if you happen to find yourself in the areas of southern New England with sizeable Portguese populations, such as Fall River, New Bedford, and Taunton in Massachusetts and East Providence, Bristol, and Warren in Rhode Island, don't miss out on the opportunity to sample the many wonderful Portuguese restaurants found there. Many of these places are located outside more well-known touristy places like downtown Newport. But they're only a short drive away. Seek them out for a side of New England cuisine that still remains somewhat unknown. And if it's not obvious already, I'd highly recommend ordering a seafood stew. I promise you won't be disappointed!

Section 2

The Key Foundation of All New England Soups from the Sea

Chapter 5

Stocks and Broths

Seafood stocks and broths provide a solid foundation to any type of seafood soup. They create unity, background flavors, and support for the bolder flavors of a dish. Fish stock greatly enhances the flavor of any fish soup, fish chowder, or seafood stew. Lobster stock is the key ingredient that makes lobster bisque taste more like lobster than lobster itself. And a clam chowder made from the broth of freshly steamed clams will elevate it far beyond what most restaurants serve. These homemade stocks and broths are essential to creating balanced, rounded, and truly sublime seafood soups.

This is why I urge you to never substitute boxed seafood broths. The last thing that should be done with seafood simmered in water, especially fish, is package it. Not only do all the aromas and flavors get lost, but they also turn flat and fishy, and added flavorings such as salt and preservatives can't hide the lack of freshness.

But I understand that sometimes we just need something quick and simple. Work, family, and other time commitments can make cooking challenging. There are some shortcuts you can take if you don't have the time to make a stock or broth from scratch. I share some time-saving techniques at the end of this chapter, but I encourage you not to rely on them too much.

Truth is, seafood stocks and broths are the easiest and cheapest stocks and broths to make at home. Most people are familiar with chicken and beef stock, the two most common homemade bone stocks. Compared to seafood, the dense bones and tough fibers of land animals require much longer simmering periods to break them down and extract their flavor and nutrients. Chicken stock can be simmered as long as 24 hours, and beef stock can be simmered for over two days. But, as you'll find in the next few pages, seafood stocks and broths are rarely simmered for more than an hour and are therefore much quicker to make.

And unlike bones from land animals, the low demand for fish carcasses means you can get them for extremely cheap and enjoy all their nutrients at a low price. It's the other ingredients in fish stock, namely the vegetables and herbs, that will cost you more than the carcasses themselves. And that is just insane.

Ultimately, I argue for homemade broths and stocks because I want you to make soup that will make you weak in the knees. Every single recipe in this book made me do that. And it's not because I'm a trained chef. I simply adhere to the two most important principles for making truly outstanding seafood soups: use good-quality seafood and make your own stocks and broths. Anyone can do this. It's not difficult.

Stocks vs. Broths Terminology

Generally speaking, the words *stock* and *broth* are used interchangeably to describe the same thing—an infusion of vegetables, bones, meat, shells, and often other herbs and seasonings. In the culinary world, fish infusions are referred to as fish stocks. Same for lobster and other crustaceans with thick, hard shells—lobster stock, crab stock, and so forth. But in recent years, the term *bone broth* has become sort of an

umbrella term, used mostly by health and food bloggers, for all types of broths and stocks. You'll now see the term *fish broth* as much as *fish stock*.

Then there's the bivalve molluscs, like clams and mussels, which have flavorful liquids inside their shells that make for some delicious broths too. Though they're referred to as broths, they're not really true stocks or broths, since no bones or carcasses are involved. Nor are they simmered with vegetables, herbs, and seasonings. Rather, clam and mussel broths are made by simply steaming these molluscs in water. The heat opens the shells and releases the briny juices that lie inside, instantly creating an intensely flavored sea-tinged broth.

Seafood Stocks and Broths Are Often Interchangeable

Sometimes you might have some extra stock on hand and don't want to make the stock that a recipe calls for. Typically, it's not that big of a deal. For example, I've used lobster stock when recipes called for fish stock and vice versa. I've used clam broth in countless recipes that call for another type of broth or stock. But for the most part, each type of stock goes best with recipes that feature the seafood used in that stock. Sure, you can use fish stock in a clam chowder, but clam broth

Gelatin and Its Benefits in Fish Stock

It's interesting to note that many cultures around the world prize fish heads in soups. For example, fish head curries have many different incarnations all around Asia. In other parts of the world, certain parts of the fish head are considered delicacies, such as the cheeks, the meat along the jawbones, and even the eyes. They're all packed with nutrients, but especially extra fat which is rich in omega-3s.

While I understand that most of us in America have not been raised to eat fish heads, there's a middle ground: we can use them in homemade fish stocks. All the nutrients from the heads will leach out into your stock, including perhaps its best kept nutritional secret: collagen.

There's *a lot* of collagen in fish heads. It's the most abundant protein in animals and you can see evidence of it when a stock cools. It will thicken and form gelatin. Gelatin is basically cooked collagen. The more gelatin a stock contains, the more it will jiggle after cooling—just like Jell-O. This is why collagen-rich parts of land animals, like feet, heads and backs, are included along with bones when making gelatin-rich bone broth. And this is why fish heads are needed to make a gelatin-rich fish stock.

Gelatin has a unique amino acid profile that is particularly concentrated in three potent anti-inflammatory amino acids: glycine, proline, and glutamine. Various studies have shown that they help with a wide variety of gut issues. Before the rise of pharmaceutical drugs, many doctors used gelatin therapeutically to treat a wide assortment of digestive problems. Beyond gut issues, gelatin has also been shown to benefit our joints, skin, and our immune health, to name a few.[7]

Is this perhaps why for centuries, grandmothers have prescribed simple broth-based soups for things like the common cold and digestive issues? Anecdotal evidence of its medicinal powers abounds, which comes from people who report immediate and noticeable health benefits when consuming stock and broth-based soups. I count myself among them.

Common reactions include a feeling of nourishment, ease and digestive wellness. I know how good fish stock and fish stock-based soups make me feel and I don't need to wait around for evidence-based studies to prove it. Our ancestors could not identify omega-3s, vitamins, and minerals but they had the passed down wisdom of knowing how to prepare foods in nutrient-dense ways. Fish stocks and soups were certainly an essential part of that.

is a much better choice. At the end of the day, know that almost any type of homemade seafood stock or broth will improve upon the flavor of your seafood soups. It's always a better option than using just water as a base or, god forbid, boxed seafood broths.

FISH STOCK

Making a fish stock is like a meditation. It requires your full attention and presence because you can easily overcook fish stock. It's those pesky, fragile polyunsaturated fats in fish that are to blame. Unlike the more heat-stable fats in land animals, polyunsaturated fats go rancid when exposed to heat for a prolonged period of time.

It was for this reason that my first venture into making fish stocks did not go well. I was following a recipe in a well-respected cookbook in which the author said to simmer the fish carcasses for up to 24 hours. Although I am not 100 percent sure, I believe this author, who is not a chef, and who writes about food and nutrition more from an agrarian perspective, wrongly assumed the simmering times for fish would be the same as for chicken and beef stocks. To put it mildly, simmering fish for 24 hours will make your stock (as well as your house) overly fishy.

As any chef will tell you, you never want to cook fish stock for more than an hour. Some chefs even cap it at 40 minutes. When prepared in this manner, fish stock will smell *pleasantly fresh* and have a delicate and palatable taste of the sea. Your tongue may not be able to identify the flavor of fish stock in a seafood soup. After all, it should blend into the background and not overpower the other flavors; but it will complement them in a way that lets you know it's there. In many ways that is the true test of a great fish stock. And best of all, it is so very easy to make at home.

Recipes follow for Basic Fish Stock (page 73) and Robust Fish Stock (page 74).

Guidelines for Making Fish Stock

Use Carcasses from Nonoily Whitefish (Mostly)

By "carcasses" I mean the parts of a fish that remain after it has been gutted and filleted, namely the heads, bones, tails, and trimmings. Members of the cod family are good choices. But really, any nonoily fish works fine. Black sea bass, blackfish, and monkfish are great choices too. However, contrary to popular belief, oily fish can be used for fish stocks too. Many chefs, cookbooks, and online recipes will tell you not to use oily fish. But this is a myth.

I've made fish stocks from bluefish and salmon, and they've been nothing short of fantastic. A colleague of mine who lived in

Alaska had a fish stock company for many years that used wild salmon carcasses. Her stocks were some of the best I've ever tasted. Yes, using oily fish will result in a stronger flavor, but it works well with soups that favor bolder flavors, such as a bluefish chowder, a salmon chowder, or a brothy soup that utilizes an oily fish. You would not want to use a strong-flavored fish stock in soups with more delicate flavors, such as those that include lean, mild whitefish. That said, without question, the majority of your fish stocks will be made from nonoily fish.

Where to Find Fish Carcasses Locally and How to Prepare Them

When searching for the right fish for a stock or broth, go to your local fisherman and see if he or she can reserve some carcasses for you. A more likely go-to will be your local fishmonger. They often purchase whole fish and fillet them right in their shop. Ask them to save some carcasses for you.

My fish stock recipes yield approximately 2½ quarts, which translates to 3 pounds of carcasses per recipe. This usually equates to two medium or three smaller carcasses. This is very manageable for most home cooks who use standard size stockpots. If you want to make double, triple, or even more than my stock recipes, simply adjust the ingredients proportionately, except for the water volume, which may need to be reduced slightly.

Because locally caught fish can vary so much in size, I don't recommend using a set number of fish. The size of the carcass you buy from local fishmongers or fisherwomen will simply be what they have that day. Some carcasses and heads can be quite large! Others, much smaller. So measure the fish you buy in weight according to how much stock you want to make. It's fine to use just one carcass, if it's big enough.

If you get a large carcass or two from your fishmonger or local fisherman, ask them to cut it into smaller pieces for you. Because of the short simmer time, smaller pieces increase the surface area exposed to the water, which in turn creates a more flavorful stock.

Seek out carcasses with the heads included. The heads create bolder flavors and a more gelatinous texture (and therefore greater nutrient density). Before adding your carcasses to your stockpot, rinse them thoroughly with water to remove any blood and slime. Finally, make sure the gills are removed when purchasing carcasses. The blood in the gills can impart a bitter flavor to fish stocks.

Dice the Veggies Finer than You Would for a Chicken or Beef Stock

Slice your carrots, celery, and onion into thin slices, about a quarter inch or less. This will increase their surface area and allow for a quicker extraction of flavors due to the short simmering time.

Add Just Enough Water to Cover Your Stock Ingredients

This is a rough but basic guideline. A more specific guideline is about 1 quart of water for every pound of carcasses. It might be a little less. Trust your eyes. Make sure everything is barely submerged under water in the stockpot but don't overfill the pot, which can dilute the flavors. Remember, fish stocks cook for a very short time which means *less water* will better concentrate the flavors. It's better to underfill it slightly because you can always add more water later.

The size and shape of your stockpot also can affect how much water to add. A tall and narrow stockpot, as opposed to a shorter and wider one, is preferred because the water will better cover the carcasses.

Skim the Scum and Don't Boil the Stock

When bringing your stock to a simmer, you can initially turn the heat to high. As the water starts to heat up, scum will form on the surface. The same thing happens with chicken and beef stocks. The scum contains impurities that can affect the flavor of the stock (though it's quite subtle). Simply skim it off. Keep a careful eye on the water at the same time. Make sure it doesn't come to a boil. Boiling can quickly damage the delicate fats and turn your stock bitter and fishy. Just before it starts to boil, turn down the heat to a very gentle simmer. By a "gentle simmer" I mean

a barely perceptible simmer. You should see some bubbles rising to the surface here and there, but the surface itself should be fairly still.

Gently Press the Heads Apart

Once the carcasses start to cook, you can use a kitchen utensil like a wooden stirring spoon to press the heads. They will easily break apart and further release their nutrients, especially the collagen. This is especially helpful if you're using carcasses with large heads. Whenever I do this I find the result is a more gelatinous stock.

Cool Your Stock Quickly and Store It

Once you strain your stock, you want to cool it down as quickly as possible to better preserve its flavor. This can sometimes be tricky for home cooks. Chefs in restaurants often have big ice machines and big industrial sinks for making a simple ice bath. Many also have a large cylinder-like tool made from strong, durable plastic that can be filled with water and frozen. It can be placed directly in the stock to chill it quickly. You can purchase one of these from online retailers. Search for *chiller wand* or *cooling paddle*. This is not a small device, so you'll need some additional space in your freezer to store it.

If you have enough ice in your freezer, you can use it to make an ice bath in your sink and put the pot right in it. Another tip: If it's wintertime and you live in a cold region, put the stock outside. Better yet, if there's snow on the ground, put the pot right in it. I always do this in winter! Once chilled, seafood stocks can last up to three days in your fridge and about three months in your freezer.

Don't Stress If You Don't Have All the Ingredients

The standard trio of vegetables for most fish stocks, sometimes referred to as a mirepoix, is carrots, onions, and celery. Thyme, bay leaves, whole black peppercorns, dry white wine, and parsley are also fairly standard because they all work together so beautifully. You can never go wrong with this formula. I rarely deviate from it. But if, for whatever reason, you don't have one or two of the ingredients, don't stress it. A little extra of this or a little less of that won't make dramatic differences. On occasion, I've forgotten to buy white wine and didn't want to run out to the store. The stock still tasted great.

Salt Is the Key Ingredient

Salting your fish stock is the last step and an important one. It really perks up the overall flavor and puts the finishing touches on it. But be careful when salting your stock! There will be a natural salinity to fish stocks, so you don't need a lot. Lightly salt it, taste it, and add a little more, if needed.

Experiment with Different Veggies, Herbs, and Spices

There are many other ingredients that can be used in fish stocks. Fennel, with its anise flavor and sweet aroma, is a great choice and can be substituted for celery. Herbs like rosemary, tarragon, and marjoram work well. Spices like cloves, mace, star anise, juniper berries, and allspice add subtly different flavors and aromas too. Don't be afraid to improvise and experiment with different combinations to your fish stocks.

Basic Fish Stock

MAKES ABOUT 2½ QUARTS

Generally speaking, there are two ways to make fish stock: basic stock and Robust Fish Stock (page 74). This recipe is for what I call a basic fish stock. The method for making this stock is simple and quite similar to making a basic chicken stock. The result is a delicate yet pronounced *fresh* fish flavor. Basic fish stocks and robust fish stocks are interchangeable in soup recipes but basic fish stocks are best utilized in dishes that include other seafood, such as a seafood stew.

Ingredients

3 pounds fish carcasses (bones, heads, tails, and trimmings) from any nonoily whitefish, cut into smaller pieces

1 cup dry white wine

2½ to 3 quarts water, or until carcasses are completely covered

1 large onion, thinly sliced

2 carrots, sliced into ¼-inch rounds

2 celery stalks, sliced into ¼-inch pieces

1 bay leaf

1 cup loosely packed parsley with stems

5 or 6 fresh thyme sprigs

1 tablespoon black peppercorns

Salt

Instructions

1. Rinse the carcasses of any blood or slime. If the gills are included, make sure to cut them out.

2. Add the fish carcasses, wine, and water to a medium stockpot. Make sure the water just barely covers the carcasses.

3. Turn the heat to high. As the water starts to heat up, skim off any scum that forms on the surface.

4. Just before the water comes to a boil, turn down the heat until the water comes to a very gentle, but barely perceptible simmer. Add the remaining ingredients (except the salt) and keep it at a very gentle simmer, uncovered, for 40 minutes.

5. Remove the stockpot from the heat and let it rest for about 10 minutes.

6. Strain the stock through a fine mesh strainer and lightly salt to taste.

7. Chill whatever you won't be immediately using. Store in the fridge for up to 3 days or in the freezer for up to 3 months.

Robust Fish Stock

MAKES ABOUT 2½ QUARTS

A robust fish stock brings out some additional depths of flavor in both the vegetables and the fish. It creates a slightly stronger tasting stock than a Basic Fish Stock (page 73). The veggies are first sautéed in butter and then the fish carcasses are placed on top, without adding any water, and then cooked for another 10 to 15 minutes. This process is sometimes referred to as sweating, because juices start to release from the fish. It's these juices, full of flavor compounds, that bring out the stronger flavors. After the fish sweats, water is added. Robust fish stocks tend to pair well with soups that feature only fish, for example a brothy fish soup or a fish chowder.

Ingredients

3 pounds fish carcasses (bones, heads, tails, and trimmings) from nonoily whitefish

2 to 3 tablespoons butter

1 large onion, thinly sliced

2 celery stalks, sliced into ¼-inch pieces

2 carrots, sliced into ¼-inch rounds

1 bay leaf

1 cup loosely packed parsley with stems

5 or 6 thyme sprigs

1 tablespoon black peppercorns

1 cup dry white wine

3 quarts water, or until carcasses are completely covered

Salt

Instructions

1. Rinse the carcasses of any blood or slime. If the gills are included, make sure to cut them out.

2. In a medium stockpot, melt 2 tablespoons butter over medium heat. Add the veggies, herbs, and peppercorns and simmer for 7 to 10 minutes, or until the veggies are softened and fragrant. Add another tablespoon butter, if needed. Stir frequently and be careful not to brown.

3. Add the wine and simmer for a few more minutes or until it's slightly reduced. Add the fish carcasses and cover tightly. Cook for 10 to 15 minutes. Add the water, making sure to cover the carcasses completely.

4. Turn the heat to high. As the water starts to heat up, skim off any scum that forms on the surface.

5. Turn down the heat to medium-low to medium before the water boils and keep at a very gentle but barely perceptible simmer, uncovered, for 20 to 30 minutes.

6. Remove the stock from the heat and let it rest for about 10 minutes. Strain the stock through a fine mesh strainer and lightly salt to taste.

7. Chill whatever you won't be immediately using. Store in the fridge for up to 3 days or in the freezer for up to 3 months.

LOBSTER STOCK

Richer than fish stock and slightly sweet, lobster stock is the perfect base for dishes like Lobster Corn Chowder (page 134) and Lobster Bisque (page 221). Lobster stock is quite versatile, however, and you can substitute it in dishes that use other types of stocks and broths.

Those juicy crustaceans are expensive, and making a lobster stock probably won't be a regular part of your kitchen routine. And that's even more reason to save those shells, because they make an incredible tasting stock!

If you order lobster in a restaurant, ask the server to package up the shells so that you can bring them home. If a local café or seafood shack makes fresh lobster rolls or any sort of dishes with fresh lobster meat, ask if they have extra shells you can have. Sometimes your fishmonger might make special preparations with lobster meat like lobster salad. If so, ask for the extra shells.

Recipes follow for Basic Lobster Stock (page 78) and Robust Lobster Stock (page 79).

Guidelines for Making Lobster Stock

Steam Whole Lobsters Instead of Boiling Them

It's certainly easiest to use lobster shells from a previous lobster meal. But if you're making a soup from scratch with whole uncooked lobsters, you'll need to boil or steam the lobsters first and remove the meat from the shells. Steaming is much better for our purposes, because the lobsters will leach some of their juices as they cook. The steaming water will better concentrate those juices than a big pot of boiling water. You can then reserve the steaming water and add it to your stock water.

Remove the Head Sac

Whether you're using carcasses or whole lobsters, make sure to remove the head sac (also called the grain sac or sand sac), which sits just behind the eyes. The head sac is actually the stomach of the lobster and contains some gritty parts like bones and pieces of shells. It's about an inch long and a half inch wide. Simply take a sharp knife to split the head open, lengthwise, and remove the head sac.

Include the Tomalley, if Possible

Don't be intimidated by the tomalley, the green pasty substance inside the body of cooked lobsters. It doesn't look particularly appetizing, but truth be told, the tomalley is actually considered a delicacy. It's not essential to include it, but it will add some nice subtle flavors. If you include it, I promise your lobster stock won't turn green.

Use Fresh Tomatoes Instead of Canned Tomatoes or Tomato Paste

Fresh tomatoes add some nice color and subtle sweetness to your lobster stock, but they're not totally necessary. Just be sure not to use canned tomatoes or tomato paste. Countless lobster stock recipes use them, but I find that they're way too rich and sweet and can often obscure the lobster flavor.

Simmer Assertively

The shells of lobsters can handle a little more heat than a fish stock. You don't want to aggressively boil it, but you want a slightly more assertive simmer than a fish stock. This will also evaporate some of the liquid and concentrate the flavors. Similar to fish stock, cover the carcasses completely. If after an hour of simmering it's not flavorful enough, keep simmering it down. You can reduce it by up to half, if needed. If you find the water has reduced too much, simply add more.

Basic Lobster Stock

MAKES ABOUT 1½ TO 2 QUARTS

This basic lobster stock has a delicate but pronounced lobster flavor, compared to the robust stock (Robust Lobster Stock, page 79). Use this basic stock in soups that have many other flavors, such as a Lobster Corn Chowder (page 134) or a seafood medley like Cioppino (page 253). You could also use it as a substitute for fish stock.

Ingredients

Two 1¼- to 1½-pound live lobsters or the carcasses from 2 previously cooked lobsters

2 to 3 quarts water, or until carcasses are covered

1½ cups fresh tomatoes, chopped (optional)

1 cup dry white wine

1 large onion, thinly sliced

1 fennel bulb, thinly sliced

2 carrots, sliced into ¼-inch rounds

3 to 4 garlic cloves, sliced thinly

4 or 5 fresh thyme sprigs

1 bay leaf

2 teaspoons whole black peppercorns

Salt

Instructions

1. For live lobsters: Steam them first following the steps in How to Steam and Prepare Live Lobsters (page 80). Otherwise, proceed to the next step.

2. Place the lobster carcasses in a medium stockpot and add the 2 to 3 quarts water, reserved steaming water, and any reserved juices, making sure to fully cover the carcasses.

3. Turn the heat to high. As the water starts to heat up, skim off any scum that forms on the surface.

4. Add all the other ingredients (except the salt), cover, and simmer for about 1 hour. Taste the stock; if more flavor is desired, continue simmering for at least another 20 minutes, with the cover off, and let the stock cook down by about a third.

5. Taste it again. If it's still too watered down, continue simmering with the lid off for another 15 to 20 minutes, or until the desired flavor is achieved.

6. Strain the stock through a fine mesh strainer and lightly salt to taste.

7. Chill whatever you won't be immediately using. Store in the fridge for up to 3 days or in the freezer for up to 3 months.

Robust Lobster Stock

This robust stock has a richer lobster flavor, as compared to Basic Lobster Stock (page 78). Robust stock is meant for soups where a strong lobster flavor predominates. It is the foundation for the perfect Lobster Bisque (page 221). In addition to a bisque, Maine Lobster Stew (page 200) is also a great place to use this stock.

Ingredients

Two 1¼- to 1½-pound live lobsters or the carcasses from 2 previously cooked lobsters

2 to 3 tablespoons unsalted butter, more if needed

2 to 3 tablespoons olive oil, more if needed

1 large onion, roughly chopped

1 fennel bulb, roughly chopped

2 carrots, sliced into ½-inch rounds

3 to 4 garlic cloves, roughly chopped

4 or 5 fresh thyme sprigs

1 bay leaf

2 teaspoons whole black peppercorns

1 cup dry white wine

1½ cups fresh tomatoes, chopped (optional)

3 to 4 quarts water, or enough to cover carcasses

Salt

Instructions

1. For live lobsters: Steam them first following the steps in How to Steam and Prepare Live Lobsters (page 80). Otherwise, proceed to the next step.

2. Take the lobster carcasses and further break the tail and claws into smaller pieces. To do this you can wrap the carcasses in a kitchen towel and use a meat pounder or a rolling pin to crush them. You could also use a strong pair of scissors or a mortar and pestle. Cut the spindly legs into smaller pieces too.

3. Heat the butter and olive oil over medium heat in a large stockpot. Add the lobster carcasses and sauté for 5 to 10 minutes, stirring frequently, until the color darkens, but be careful not to burn.

4. Add the vegetables (and a little more oil or butter if necessary) and sauté for about 5 minutes, or until the veggies are softened and fragrant. Stir frequently.

5. Add the thyme, bay leaf, black peppercorns, white wine, and optional tomatoes and simmer a few minutes more or until the wine is slightly reduced.

6. Add the 3 to 4 quarts water to cover the carcasses and turn the heat to high. Include any lobster juices that were collected from steaming and/or breaking apart the shells. As the water starts to heat up, skim off any scum that forms on the surface.

(continued)

7. Turn down the heat and simmer, uncovered, for about 1 hour. Keep the cover off and let the water evaporate and the stock cook down by about a third.

8. Taste it again. If it's still too watered down, continue simmering with the lid off for another 15 to 20 minutes, or until the desired flavor is achieved.

9. Strain the stock through a fine mesh strainer and lightly salt to taste.

10. Chill whatever you won't be immediately using. Store in the fridge for up to 3 days or in the freezer for up to 3 months.

How to Steam and Prepare Live Lobsters

Fill a large pot with about 2 inches of water. Bring the water to a rolling boil, add the lobsters, cover the pot and steam for about 7 to 10 minutes. Remove the lobsters from the water and add them to an ice bath to cool them quickly. Otherwise, they'll continue to cook and can easily turn tough and chewy. Reserve the steaming water.

Next, crack the shells with a nut or lobster cracker. Remove the head sac (see page 80). Pick out the meat from the lobster, being sure to catch and save all the juices over a large bowl. Reserve the meat for any lobster soup recipes and save the juices and carcasses for the stock. You'll get approximately 1 to 1½ cups of loosely packed meat (or about 4 to 6 ounces) per 1¼- to 1½-pound lobster.

CRAB STOCK

Similar to a lobster stock, you can make a crab stock from the shells and carcasses leftover from a crab meal, or you can use whole crabs. Without question, using crab carcasses is a lot easier than using whole crabs. Whole crabs need to be boiled or steamed first, cooled, and then cracked open so that all the little bits of meat can be removed. This can be a time-consuming and tedious process. However, since you'll need crabmeat to make a crab soup, some form of whole crabs will be necessary if you want to avoid using canned crabmeat (which is mostly imported from Asia).

In this case, you can use precooked frozen crab claws, which are commonly available in most seafood markets. All you need to do is gently reheat the claws, crack the shells, and pick out the meat. The meat in the claws is much easier to pick out than the legs and bodies. You'll then use the shells to make the stock. Another benefit of just using the claws is that you get a lot more meat per pound. In New England–area crabs, such as the Jonah crab, most of the meat is located in the claws (as opposed to other crab species that have very meaty legs).

Another alternative is to steam or boil some whole crabs and not even bother with picking out the meat. One benefit of using whole crabs is that the bodies harbor some nice flavors. Once cooked, slice and/or crush them up into smaller pieces (making sure to catch and save the juices), and then make your stock. This is a great way to use the pesky and invasive green crabs, if you can find them, because they are so small and have so little meat in them.

How to Steam and Prepare Live Crab

Fill a large pot with about 1 inch of water. Bring the water to a rolling boil, add the crabs, cover the pot, and steam for 4 to 6 minutes. Remove the crabs from the water and add them to an ice bath to cool them quickly. Otherwise, they'll continue to cook and can easily turn tough and chewy. Reserve the steaming water.

Next, crack and open the shells, being sure to catch and save all the juices over a large bowl, and pick out the meat. Reserve the meat for any of the crab soup recipes and save the juices and shells for the stock.

Basic Crab Stock

MAKES ABOUT 1 TO 1½ QUARTS STOCK

This the ideal stock for using in Crab, Bacon, and Cheddar Corn Chowder (page 140), New England Jonah Crab Stew (page 203), New England Summer Crab Soup (page 204), and New England Jonah Crab Bisque (page 224). You can also use it as a substitute for lobster stock and vice versa, as the flavors are so similar.

Ingredients

4 pounds precooked New England Jonah crab claws or 2 pounds New England crab carcasses (any combo of shells, legs, claws, and bodies), crushed and/or cut into smaller pieces

2 quarts water, or enough to cover carcasses

1½ cups fresh tomatoes, chopped (optional)

1 medium yellow onion, roughly chopped

2 celery stalks, roughly chopped

3 to 4 garlic cloves, roughly chopped

3 or 4 fresh thyme sprigs

1 bay leaf

1 teaspoon whole black peppercorns

Salt

Instructions

1. For whole crab claws (or whole crabs): Steam them first following the steps in How to Steam and Prepare Live Crab (page 81). Otherwise, proceed to the next step.

2. Place the shells and crab carcasses in a medium stockpot and add the 2 quarts water (if you steamed the crabs, add the reserved steaming water and any reserved juices), making sure to fully cover the carcasses. Optional step: For a more robust crab stock, first place the shells on a roasting pan and roast at 400°F for 10 minutes.

3. Turn the heat to high. As the water starts to heat up, skim off any scum that forms on the surface.

4. Add all the other ingredients (except the salt), cover, and simmer gently for about 1 hour. Taste the stock; if more flavor is desired, continue simmering for at least another 20 minutes, with the cover off, and let the stock cook down by about a third.

5. Taste it again. If it's still too watered down, continue simmering with the lid off for another 15 to 20 minutes or until the desired flavor is achieved.

6. Strain the stock through a fine mesh strainer and lightly salt to taste.

7. Chill whatever you won't be immediately using. Store in the fridge for up to 3 days or in the freezer for up to 3 months.

CLAM BROTH

If I had to choose just one seafood stock or broth that I could not live without, it would undoubtedly be clam broth. For me, it's the heart and soul of the sea, so intensely briny and so very invigorating, like a cool, refreshing ocean breeze on a hot summer day. Making clam broth is as easy as steaming clams in water. The pungent liquor held tightly inside the shells is released when the clams open, infusing the water and immediately creating the broth. Nothing else is needed.

In the process, you'll also get freshly cooked clam meats, which are vastly superior in flavor and texture to rubbery minced canned clams. That said, clam broths can retain their flavors quite well when bottled. Some recipes in this book recommend clam broth as a substitute for another broth or stock or as a way to enhance the briny flavor of a recipe. In that case, it's good to have some bottled clam broth around.

I include recipes for Hard-Shell Clam Broth (page 86) and Soft-Shell Clam Broth (page 87) to follow.

Guidelines for Making Clam Broth

For a Hard-Shell Clam Broth, Seek Out Fresh Cherrystones or Quahogs

Ideally, quahogs should be prepared as soon as possible. They will lose freshness over time, including some of their wonderful liquors. If it's unavoidable, store them in the coldest part of your fridge for up to two days. Transfer them to a nonplastic bowl or any open container and cover it with a damp towel. Don't submerge them in water, which will kill them.

You can also make a good clam broth from littleneck clams, but it'll be quite a bit more expensive. Also, because you'll need considerably more of them per pound, littlenecks can be a bit unwieldy in a stockpot.

At the market, they should be stored on ice at all times. Make sure the shells are tightly closed. They should have a dark grayish color with clearly visible lines in the shells. Many have brownish hues with both brown and black streaks. Avoid any that are a dullish light gray or white in appearance without clear lines in the shells, as these are signs of a lack of freshness.

For a Soft-Shell Clam Broth, Clean the Clams Well

As opposed to hard-shell clams, soft-shell clams acquire a good bit of sand and debris inside their shells. To clean this debris, put them in a pot and cover them with cold, salted water (at an approximate ratio of ¼ cup salt to 2 quarts of water). Soak them for at least 20 minutes, stir them around gently once or twice, drain the water, and then repeat this a few times as needed, until there's no debris left. If you plan ahead, an extended soaking of several hours or even overnight (in the fridge to keep them cold) is even better. Discard any clams with cracked or damaged shells.

Use a Large, Wide Stockpot

You'll want a stockpot that is wider than it is tall so that the clams don't overly stack on top of each other, which makes it harder for them to open and harder for you to see when they open.

Shoot for a Ratio of 3 Cups of Water to 1 Cup of Clam Liquor

Seven to 8 pounds of hard-shell clams will release 1 to 2 cups of clam liquor. But that's a very general estimate. Some clams have a lot more liquor than others. It's hard to say exactly how much liquor will be released. Regardless, steaming 7 to 8 pounds of hard-shell clams in 3 cups of water will yield a pretty fantastic tasting clam broth every time. If your broth turns out super salty, just add some water to dilute it.

Clam Broth Should Have a Cloudy Gray Appearance

That's normal! It shouldn't look too clear, otherwise it won't be flavorful enough. That rule applies for both hard-shell and soft-shell clam broths.

Hard-Shell Clam Broth

MAKES ABOUT 1 QUART

Crisp, aromatic, strong, and salty, clam broth perhaps captures the spirit of the ocean more than any other seafood stock or broth, as it has both soothing and energizing qualities. This may sound strange, but the next time you're feeling depleted, sluggish, or even a little hungover, try a little clam broth as a tonic. It was actually considered a common remedy in America in the early 20th century. It has some seriously good juju to it, like one of those ancient Chinese recipes passed down for thousands of years, with benefits that modern science can't explain but everyone knows just works. More importantly, for our purposes, it creates the perfect foundation for any clam-based chowder, soup, or stew.

~~~~~~

Ingredients

7 to 8 pounds littleneck, cherrystone or quahog clams

3 cups water

Instructions

1. Clean the clam shells of any grit by rinsing and scrubbing in cold running water. If there's a lot of dirt on the shells, soak them in cold water for 5 to 10 minutes then rinse and scrub them thoroughly with a sturdy brush.

2. Bring the 3 cups of water to a rolling boil in a large, wide stockpot.

3. Add the clams and cover the pot. Boil for 5 to 10 minutes, or until the shells open. The shells will open at different times. Remove the clams with tongs as they open and set aside to prevent the meats from overcooking.

4. Let the broth sit for about 10 minutes to allow any grit or pieces of shell to settle to the bottom.

5. While the broth sits, remove the meats from their shells and refrigerate if not using them right away. You'll get about 2 cups, or 1 pound, of clam meats.

6. Slowly strain the broth through a fine mesh strainer, but not the last few ounces, which contain the grit.

7. Chill whatever you won't be immediately using. Store in the fridge for up to 3 days or in the freezer for up to 3 months.

Soft-Shell Clam Broth

MAKES ABOUT 1 QUART

A soft-shell clam broth is slightly sweeter and not as intensely briny as a Hard-Shell Clam Broth (page 86) but is equally flavorful in its own way. There are about 12 to 15 soft-shell clams in a pound.

Ingredients

4 to 5 pounds soft-shell clams

3 cups water

Instructions

1. Clean the soft-shell clams according to the directions on page 84.

2. Bring the 3 cups water to a rolling boil in a large, wide stockpot.

3. Add the clams and cover. Boil for 5 minutes. Remove any clams that have opened with tongs. Carefully stir the rest of the clams to allow them to cook evenly. Put the cover back on and boil for several more minutes or until all the shells open. Remove the remaining clams and set them aside.

4. Let the broth sit for about 10 minutes to allow any grit or pieces of shell to settle to the bottom.

5. While the broth sits, remove the meats from their shells. Remove the black membranes from the siphons or, alternatively, slice off the siphons entirely. Refrigerate the meats if not using them right away. You'll get about 2 cups, or 1 pound, of clam meats.

6. Slowly strain the broth through a fine mesh strainer, but not the last few ounces, which contain the grit.

7. Chill whatever you won't be immediately using. Store in the fridge for up to 3 days or in the freezer for up to 3 months.

Mussel Broth

The technique for making mussel broth is almost identical to clam broth. It's not nearly as salty, but it has a wonderful flavor all its own. Generally speaking, 1 pound of mussels will release about a ½ cup of liquor. Similar to clams, mussels can differ in size and the amount of liquid they hold, so you might get a little more or less. There are 20 to 25 blue mussels in a pound, so a fairly large, wide stockpot is needed.

Ingredients

4 to 5 pounds New England blue mussels

2 cups water

Instructions

1. Most farmed mussels come pre-cleaned to markets. Simply clean the mussels of any remaining grit by rinsing in cold running water. Wild mussels may need more thorough cleaning. In this case, soak them in cold water for 20 to 30 minutes, changing the water and repeating this process until the soaking water is relatively clear. Then rinse the mussels under cold water, scrub the outer shells thoroughly, and remove the beards: Pinch them with your thumb and forefinger, twist slightly, and then pull toward the hinge.

2. Bring the 2 cups water to a rolling boil in a large 10- to 12-quart stockpot.

3. Add the mussels and cover the pot. Steam for a few minutes. Remove the cover and stir gently with a wooden spoon to distribute the heat throughout the stacked mussels. Put the cover back on and continue steaming for a few more minutes until all the shells open.

4. Remove the stockpot from the heat. With a large, slotted spoon, transfer some of the mussels to a large serving bowl to make the process of straining a little easier.

5. Strain the broth into a container through a large colander to catch the remaining mussels. Set the remaining mussels aside. Let the broth sit for about 10 minutes to allow any grit or pieces of shell to settle to the bottom.

6. Slowly strain the broth again through a fine mesh strainer, but not the last few ounces, which contain the grit.

7. Chill whatever you won't be immediately using. Store in the fridge for up to 3 days or in the freezer for up to 3 months.

SHORTCUTS AND SUBSTITUTES

If you don't have time to make a seafood stock or broth from scratch, consider any of the following options:

Bottled Clam Broth

The only shellfish broth that is widely available in stores across the country is clam broth. For reasons that escape me, it's typically labeled as clam juice. Considering America's squeamishness with seafood, maybe a marketing term that doesn't sound totally gross would make more sense? But hey, at least they don't market fish stocks as fish juice.

Unlike packaged seafood stocks, some brands of bottled clam broth are quite good. In particular, a Maine-based seafood company, Bar Harbor Foods, makes a very good clam broth from New England clams.

Bottled clam broth can be substituted for any recipe that uses a homemade clam broth. It can also be used to enhance the flavor of any seafood soup or stew, be it a few tablespoons or a few bottles. I often add liberal amounts of clam broth to soups that feature scallops or squid since neither of those have shells that contain liquor. I might add a moderate amount to boost the flavor of some seafood stews. And I might add just a tad (or none at all) to soups with milder flavored stocks, such as fish stock.

Finally, you can dilute clam broth with water and use that as a substitute for almost any seafood broth or stock. To what degree you dilute the clam broth is up to you and the soup recipe you're making.

Homemade Chicken Broth or Good-Quality Boxed Chicken Broth

Chicken broth is surprisingly versatile, and it's a suitable substitute for fish stock and clam broth. You will find it in countless seafood soup recipes. It adds a nice background umami flavor without overpowering the other flavors. Making a homemade chicken broth is almost identical to the process of making a basic fish stock. You'll find countless chicken broth recipes online. Or you can follow the instructions in my recipe for Basic Fish Stock (page 73) with the following changes: Substitute about 4 to 5 pounds of chicken carcasses (or any combination of leftover chicken parts like wings, legs, backs, and so forth) for the fish carcasses. Skip the white wine. Add one more carrot, celery stalk, and onion. Chop the veggies roughly into 1 to 2 inch pieces. Simmer the broth for two to three hours. Double up the parsley and only add it in the last 20 minutes or so of simmering. Store the chicken broth in the fridge for up to five days or six months in the freezer.

A good-quality boxed chicken broth

is even more useful when you're short on time. There are a variety of good brands in stores that use pasture-raised chickens and other organic ingredients.

Seagreens Broth

If you've ever had a miso soup in a Japanese restaurant, chances are you've had a dashi broth, which is made from dried bonito flakes and kombu, a type of seagreen. Seagreen broths have a delicate umami and sea tang flavor that can be used as a substitute for fish stock.

You can use many types of dried seagreens. Seek out a North Atlantic kombu product, if possible. Many companies from Maine harvest and sell dried kombu and other seagreens.

To make a quick seagreens broth, take about an ounce (about three or four 3- to 4-inch pieces) of dried seagreens and soak it in a quart of water for 20 to 30 minutes. (A longer soaking period of at least two to three hours is preferred, as the broth will develop more flavor.) Transfer the water and seagreens to a saucepan on the stovetop and bring the water to a gentle simmer. Just before the water boils remove the seagreens with tongs. Lightly salt to taste. That's it!

You can also soak seagreens overnight in the fridge. Longer soaking periods (a method known as cold brewing) is all that's needed to make the broth. You don't even need to heat it. Simply strain out the seagreens and it's done.

Section 3

New England Soups and Stews

Chapter 6

Chowders

Chowder, New England's most iconic meal, in its most basic form is no more than six ingredients: bacon or salt pork, onions, potatoes, stock or broth, fish or shellfish, and milk or cream. The formula for making it is so simple that even the most rudimentary cook could whip up a delicious pot in under 30 minutes.

Though opinions and recipes differ, the universal beauty of chowder is its rustic simplicity.

Chowders were originally created by fishermen, hundreds of years ago, for long sea voyages, and adapted by common folk for both household meals and communal gatherings. Harriet Adams in her 1941 cookbook, *Vittles for the Captain: A Cape Cod Cookbook*, writes that chowder is "not one of those fine, thin fugitive soups that you delicately toy with in a genteel ladies' tea room."[8] Louis De Gouy in *The Soup Book* writes that chowder is "one of the most indelicate of our national dishes. It is rude, rugged, a food of body and substance."[9]

Ironically, today, chowders are consumed in restaurants more than at home, and more as an appetizer than a main dish. Nobody wants to make soup as an appetizer when they come home from work on a weeknight. But chowder, in its original incarnation, was meant to be consumed as a full meal. It is hearty, nourishing, and, contrary to popular belief, perfectly healthful when made with real ingredients. It can be made quickly without sacrificing quality, and it can be made in large amounts for easy leftovers. And get this—leftovers taste *better*. That's not an exaggeration (more on that in the section Additional Chowder Tips, see page 102).

And yet a brief survey of recipes, be it from print cookbooks or online, can quickly disorient the newbie chowder maker, like a gentle snowfall turned wind-whipping whiteout nor'easter. All of a sudden one can find oneself submerged in a highly contentious and confusing realm of widely divergent opinions, techniques, and even ingredients.

Some swear by milk, others cream, and some swear by no dairy at all. Some say to never use bacon but rather salt pork, bacon's historical predecessor. Some use flour to thicken chowders, some use crackers, others use potatoes. Some say to never use thickeners. Some swear by using spices and herbs, some say to never use either.

Having tried every possible New England chowder variation, I'm here to tell you that everybody's opinions are right. They're right because all chowders, no matter the regional variation, are delicious if they're made from scratch with fresh ingredients! It's simply a matter of personal preference.

I love anyone who has strong opinions about food. I love to hear the passion in their voice, see the veins pop out in their forehead, their brows furrow, lips quiver, and arms wave wildly as they proudly and defiantly declare their chowder to be the best, the purest, the most original, or the most authentic. But a brief foray into the history of New England chowder shows that chowder, like all foods, is never static, always evolving, mixing with other cultures and continuously reinventing different versions of itself.

A Brief History of Chowder

18th Century: Before Potatoes, Dairy, and Clams

The early chowders of the 18th century probably resembled little of what we've come to know as New England chowder today. They were made by layering salt pork, onions, fish, and crackers, often in repeating layers, in cauldrons and cooking the mixture over an open flame. Spices were used quite liberally, and recipes sometimes included marjoram, nutmeg, mace, cayenne pepper, and even curry powder. Water or sometimes wine (or both) was added to distribute the heat for even cooking and not as a brothy base. Thus, the early chowders were much thicker than today. Large cauldrons of chowder could feed a lot of people and were conducive to community settings. Chowder parties on beaches, sailing boats, at churches, and other social gatherings became common and helped spread its popularity around New England and even beyond.

19th Century: Chowder Evolves

As chowder became even more fashionable, recipes started appearing in print publications, including cookbooks, most of which were written by women for women, at a time when women had few opportunities outside their expected roles as mother and housewife, and of course, full-time cook. Many creative touches and refinements were added, such as fish stock in place of water. Recipes differed widely, but the second half of the 19th century saw the convergence of what most people think of as chowder today.

Potatoes replaced crackers, though the latter remains a staple as a chowder accompaniment. Milk and cream became popular additions in northern New England and tomatoes in southern New England. And clams started to gain wider acceptance in place of fish, though it would take another hundred years before they supplanted fish as the dominant chowder protein.

1900–1949: The Golden Age of Chowder

The accounts of the abundance and variety of seafood in this era are almost hard to believe compared to today. Along our eastern coastline, people embraced the bounty of the sea in all its myriad shapes, sizes, and species. And it all went into the chowder pot.

In *The Book of Chowder,* Richard Hooker writes of this time, "The great Delmonico's in New York City, for nearly a century the country's model of excellence, made chowders of freshwater fish—eels, perch or wallyeye pike—and saltwater fish—sea bass, sheepshead, blackfish or kingfish."[10]

Cookbooks from this era present an astounding variety of recipes. *The Soup Book,* published in 1949 by Chef Louis De Gouy, features not one, not two, but one hundred different chowder recipes, which include the likes of blackfish, carp, catfish, crabs, eel, fish roe, flounder, frogs legs, fluke, halibut, mussels, oysters, perch, pike, snapper, sturgeon, and turtle.

However, little did most people know that this abundance had its roots in overfishing and overharvesting. Combined with increasing industrial pollution of our coastal waterways, the coming decades would see a shocking decline in fish stocks and shellfish beds. But for a brief time, in this era, fish chowder and clam chowder stood as equals.

1950–1999: Clam Chowder Reigns Supreme

With victory in World War II, America shifted its industrial power to economic development at home. Millions moved to the suburbs to raise baby boomers. The laborious task of food production was meanwhile turned over to giant corporations. Small family farms and small community fishing fleets were slowly consolidated or put out of business by government policies that favored everything on a large scale. Family cooking traditions faded and the supermarket age of highly processed foods took hold. No food was immune to the unstoppable force of convenience and "progress," not even chowder.

Chowder became homogenized by canned soup companies and fast-food chains. In his book *50 Chowders,* Chef Jasper White cleverly called it the howardjohnsonization effect.[11] Restaurant franchises like Howard Johnson's brought New England–style chowder to the masses, and with it two changes that became somewhat universal, especially outside of New England.

First, within industrial food factories and fast-food kitchen environments, canned clams were now more cost effective. They also retained their texture better and were much easier to make into chowder compared to canned (or frozen) fish. Second, most of these chowders were now universally flour-thickened, often to the point of excess. Thick, pasty New England clam chowder became America's favorite chowder.

Chowder purists lamented the rubbery canned clams and the gloopy, thick texture. However, for the millions exposed to chowder for the first time, it was a soul-satisfying rich and creamy elixir of the land and the sea. And that included myself.

Years later, with hundreds of bowls of chowder under my belt, including chowders made using the recipes in this chapter, I was better able to differentiate between good and not-so-good chowder. My love of homemade stocks and broths, fresh seafood, and good-quality dairy taught me how much better chowder is when those things are emphasized. It's made me more appreciative of fresh food and of the time, love, and care it takes to really make nutrient-dense, delicious food.

This era played an important role in redefining what chowder was, even to New Englanders, and it moved chowder away from being a home-cooked meal and more toward being a restaurant indulgence or a quick and easy canned good.

Chowder and Sustainability in the 21st Century

Thick and creamy New England clam chowder still dominates the chowder landscape, but I think we're entering a new era for chowder, one that combines the great diversity of seafood that was embraced in the first half of the 20th century with the growing consciousness from the first half of the 21st century on where our seafood comes from.

I see the roots of this awareness starting to take place everywhere. Many chefs and restaurants are trying to offer more local and creative fare, and they're putting their own unique spin on chowder while using good-quality ingredients.

I'd like to think that in the coming years, more and more Americans will embrace chowder not just as an appetizer at a chain restaurant, but as a nourishing homemade meal. It is my hope they will walk into a locally owned fish market, pick up a piece of in-season fish caught by a small-scale sustainable fishery, and happily add it to the chowder pot. Likewise, I hope they will support a local restaurant that sources its seafood locally and creates new and inventive chowder recipes! There's nothing wrong with a bowl of real, creamy New England clam chowder. It will always be my favorite type of chowder. But chowder can and should be so much more.

Keep an open mind with the chowder recipes here. Let go of your regional bias. Let go of your expectation of what chowder should taste like. Try the recipes that are unfamiliar! When fresh, locally sourced ingredients are used, it's almost impossible to make a bad tasting bowl of chowder, no matter the regional style.

Basic Chowder Ingredients

Salt Pork or Bacon

Every chowder recipe starts out by dicing salt pork or bacon into smaller pieces and then heating it in a stockpot over medium-low heat until the fat renders out. This fat serves two purposes. One, for flavor. And two, for a cooking fat to sauté onions (and sometimes other vegetables). Salt pork and bacon are interchangeable in any chowder recipe. But a few distinctions should be noted.

Salt pork is, quite simply, pork fat that is salt cured. It typically comes from the pork belly and is fattier than bacon. Prior to refrigeration technology, many foods were salted as a preservative, including pork. But despite it being less common today, salt pork still enjoys some popularity in New England. Many old-school New Englanders feel the smoky flavor of bacon is too intense in chowder and overpowers other more subtle flavors. That said, salt pork is saltier than bacon and can be a bit much for some folks, especially if your chowder is made with an already salty clam broth.

Personally, I do prefer the flavor of salt pork. However, I have not had a lot of success finding a good-quality product. And, due to different preservation methods today, modern salt pork products often don't release a lot of fat. If you can find a good source of artisan-made salt pork, that would be ideal, but don't stress it.

If you do choose bacon, be sure to avoid super lean bacon strips. Remember, you want fattier pieces, which will render into cooking fat. Seek out slab bacon or fattier cuts or strips.

Finally, as the fat renders out, the meatier portions will crisp up. Be careful not to overcook and burn these pieces, which is easy to do. If using salt pork, you'll get some wonderful, browned pieces of pork cracklings, which you can remove and save for later. You can then reheat them and add them as a topping. Same for the bacon, which can be diced into bacon bits.

Onions and Potatoes

Onions add an earthy, astringent, slightly sweet flavor to chowder (or any soup). Your best choice is any type of yellow onion. Make sure your onions are fresh and firm. Shallots and leeks, both members of the onion family, are sometimes used in chowders too. They impart a slightly milder flavor than onions. You'll also see chives and green onions (scallions) in chowders, but their delicate nature means they're better used as garnishes.

Potatoes add body, substance, and their own subtle flavors to chowder. The best varieties are those that both hold their shape after cooking and retain a firm but tender texture. Medium-starch potatoes, often called all-purpose potatoes (such as white and Yukon Gold), are your best choice. Avoid high-starch potatoes like russets, which easily fall apart during cooking.

The Whole Dairy Story

Another important ingredient in chowder is a controversial one. Many old-school New Englanders lament the overly pasty restaurant chowders of today and blame the thickening for obscuring the flavor of the clams and dairy. But not all thickened chowder is bad chowder. I think there's a much bigger culprit, one that inhabits almost every bowl of restaurant chowder, thickened or not: modern dairy.

There is a world of difference between modern and traditional dairy. Today, most restaurants use modern dairy in their chowder because it's cheaper. But using traditional dairy may just set your homemade chowder apart from all the rest.

In the 1967 gem of a little "book" (more like an in-depth pamphlet), *Clam Shack Cookery*, a collection of old Cape Cod recipes, fisherman Cap'n Phil Schwind says this about milk.

> *For the benefit of those who can't remember back before milk came in cardboard or plastic containers, all pasteurized, homogenized and preserved, there was a time when milk came in round, glass 'milk bottles', and if allowed to set, the cream would rise to the top of the bottle. This "top" milk, nearly cream, was what my grandma was referring to when she spoke of "whole" milk. The rest, the skim milk she used to feed our cat, Old Tiger.*[12]

He's referring to traditional raw milk here, and throughout the book he asks the reader to use "rich milk" in many of the recipes. Rich cream, along with fresh, whole quahog clams (and their liquor) are the two pillars for making really superb tasting chowder. The first time I tasted traditional raw milk I couldn't believe how delicious it was compared to modern milk. It was so rich and creamy and so full of flavor. It was one of those foods that instantly felt restorative and life-giving. Unlike modern milk, which tastes the same across state lines and milk brands, traditional milk has variations in taste that depend on many natural factors like rainfall, geography, the types of grasses the cows eat, and the time of year in which those grasses are most nutrient-dense.

In addition to its unmatched flavor, traditional dairies also provide other benefits. To name a few, they are *almost always* small-scale dairies, they feed their cows a natural diet, and they contribute to a self-sustaining system that promotes soil integrity and complexity. This is in contrast to large-scale industrialized dairies that we're all becoming more aware of.

Unfortunately, traditional milk dairies are not accessible to the majority of Americans. Moreover, traditional raw milk, which is unpasteurized, is a highly contentious topic. If you're interested in learning more, I recommend you read up on it. The website Real Milk (www.realmilk.com) has dozens of well-researched articles and links to many resources.

But the bottom line is this: Supporting small-scale dairies is similar to supporting small-scale fisheries. They are better for the planet and better for us. The good news is that many people are now aware of the problems with modern dairy, and better choices are more available than ever, even in conventional supermarkets. I highly encourage you to get the best-quality dairy you can that is as close to 100 percent traditional milk as possible. It will make such a difference in how your chowder tastes. So let's look at the different options as they pertain to chowder.

Best Option: Cream

Back in the days when small family farms thrived and traditional milk was common, cream was just cream. It was the creamy fat-rich portion of milk that rose to the surface. When people drank traditional milk, they'd shake or stir the bottle to resuspend the fat back into the more liquid portion of milk. And when they skimmed off the cream, they used it for other purposes such as making butter.

If you ever have the fortunate opportunity to purchase raw cream, consider yourself very lucky. It is what I'd consider the crème de la crème of cream (a most fitting use of this French phrase if ever there was). Its sweet, soulfully satisfying rich flavor has to be experienced to be believed. Nothing in stores can compare.

Today, cream is sold and labeled according to the percentage of its fat content.

For the most part, you'll see three types of cream in stores: light cream, whipping cream, and heavy cream.

Light cream usually contains somewhere between 18 percent to 30 percent fat. Whipping cream contains somewhere between 30 to 36 percent fat. And heavy cream, the richest of all three, contains at least 36 percent fat. You can use any of these three for chowders. However, I would highly recommend heavy cream.

Because heavy cream is so rich and flavorful, you don't need a lot per recipe. In my recipes I use about 4 cups of broth or stock for a six-person serving. To that amount I would only add 1 to 2 cups of heavy cream.

The second advantage to using heavy cream is that your chowder will never curdle. Curdling in soups happens when the high heat causes the milk proteins to clump together. If this ever happens, it doesn't mean your soup has gone bad. It just won't look very good. But the higher the fat content, the less the chance this will happen, so it's not an issue with heavy cream!

Second Best Option: Half-and-Half

Half-and-half is pretty much what it says it is—half cream and half whole milk. Its fat content is around 12 percent to 18 percent fat. Half-and-half is a much closer approximation to rich, traditional whole milk.

I have only one recipe that calls exclusively for half-and-half instead of cream, a Maine-style chowder. However, all of my recipes give you the option to use half-and-half or cream.

If you really prefer the taste and consistency of half-and-half, go for it. Because it has a lower fat content than cream, you might need to add a little more. This can add to the liquid base of your chowder, thereby thinning out the consistency and possibly some of the flavor. Some people prefer a thinner texture. It's your chowder, so do whatever you like best.

Third Best Option: Whole Milk

I don't recommend using whole milk for the reasons already stated. It's too thin, especially modern conventional brands, and the fat content, which is about 4 percent, just doesn't make the final product creamy enough. It's also more prone to curdling. However, rich raw milk may be suitable.

Not an Option: Low-Fat Milk

Low-fat milk in chowder is like the flute in rock music. It's not against the law, but in my opinion, it should be (no offense, Jethro Tull fans). It never works. Ever. Please don't even think about making chowder with low-fat milk. It's not healthier and it will just result in a bland, watered-down chowder.

The Great Tomato Chowder Debate

It is the ultimate chowder debate that pits New Englanders against New Yorkers. Perhaps only the Red Sox-Yankees rivalry can stir regional passions more than the great chowder debate.

Contrary to popular belief, New England didn't always abhor tomatoes in chowder. From the mid-1800s into the 20th century, tomatoes were featured in chowder recipes throughout New England. Though not as common as their dairy counterparts, they coexisted for many decades without folks getting all bent out of shape. The highly influential *Boston Cooking-School Cookbook* by Fannie Farmer, originally published in 1896, includes a recipe for a chowder that replaces milk with tomatoes. Nothing is mentioned of tomatoes being an offensive interloper.

In *The Soup Book*, renowned chef Louis De Gouy claims that Manhattan clam chowder has its origins not from Manhattan but "from Gloucester, Nahant, Cohasset, Scituate, all around the Cape, and up and down Narragansett Bay from the Point to Providence."[13] His recipe for New England clam chowder includes three peeled large tomatoes. Go figure.

I don't know when or why the rivalry became so intense, but sometime after World War II tomatoes virtually disappeared from New England–style chowders, especially from Massachusetts to Maine, and the classic creamy New England–stye chowders became an increasing source of regional identity and pride.

But if you were from New York or parts of Connecticut, you embraced red chowder. In the *Long Island Seafood Cookbook,* it's written: "In New York and Long Island, clam chowder was developed more as a soup course, which therefore was not desired to be so substantial as to clog the appetite for other courses. The restaurants of New York, in particular, were not patronized in earlier days by those who wanted to dine only on clam chowder. They wanted a soup which would fulfill what French masters of cookery have always allotted to soup as its proper function, namely to *whet,* rather than to completely satisfy the desire for food."[14]

Others have postulated that Italian immigrants adapted their many varieties of native tomato-based seafood soups (zuppa di pesce) into clam chowder. Some claim Portuguese immigrants, who embraced tomatoes long before New Englanders did, helped spread their inclusion in chowder.

Whatever the clouded history, keep in mind that before the mid-1800s very few New Englanders would've thought to include clams, dairy, or tomatoes in chowder. Who knows what strange twists and turns chowder will take in the next 150 years. One thing is for certain: It will change.

But the beauty of clams is that their flavor, especially their liquor, melds equally well with cream as it does with tomatoes. Both types of chowders are fantastic! And though tomatoes are not a regular part of New England chowders, they do live on in some places. The little-known Portuguese clam chowder is perhaps New England's best kept chowder secret. And Manhattan clam chowder is still a popular choice along the coast of Connecticut and Rhode Island. You'll find recipes for both here, as well as a fun hybrid chowder, Connecticut Clam Chowder (page 117), which is my attempt to give Connecticut its own chowder identity.

Additional Chowder Tips

1. Cool Chowder Properly

If there are leftovers, allow your chowder to cool for a few hours before transferring it to the fridge. Put it on a surface where air can circulate underneath and leave the lid off to facilitate cooling. This includes when you transfer it to the fridge. If it hasn't completely cooled to room temperature, condensation will form on the inside of the lid and then drip back into the chowder. This can negatively alter the flavor. Once the entire chowder has thoroughly cooled, you can put the lid back on. It's okay to leave the lid off overnight and put it back on in the morning.

2. Leftovers Taste Better

It's strange to think that leftovers will taste better, but in the case of chowder, and many other soups, it is true. The flavors amalgamate and mature over time. This is known as curing or aging chowder. That doesn't mean you can't eat chowder right away. But even letting it cure on the stovetop for an hour or two will improve the flavor.

When discussing the old chowder-making methods on Long Island, J. George Frederick, in the *Long Island Seafood Cookbook* writes, "To eat a chowder within a few hours after making it—or even on the same day it was made—sounds like sacrilege to these old men of the chowder pots of Long Island."[15]

3. The Pros and Cons of Crackers

Crackers have always been a part of New England chowders. Hardtack, or "ship's biscuit," a very dense, nonperishable cracker, was used as a thickener in the early chowders of the 18th century, especially on long sea voyages. Potatoes eventually replaced hardtack when chowder gained widespread appeal in the 19th century. But other types of crispy crackers became popular accompaniments. Common crackers, pilot crackers, and oyster crackers (probably the most popular today) all make excellent additions to a bowl of chowder.

But it's important to note that oyster crackers are highly processed and made with poor-quality, genetically modified oils (GMOs) like soybean or canola oil. Will the occasional bag of oyster crackers harm you? Probably not. But as someone who is passionate about supporting good-quality food, I simply want to point this out to you and let you decide. If you'd like to avoid GMOs and other highly processed ingredients, there are some good-quality organic cracker products in health food stores.

4. The Pros and Cons of Bread

Similar to crackers, different types of bread make a great complement to chowder. A warm piece of toasted bread dipped into chowder can be a heart-stopping moment of pure heaven. Almost any type of bread will work—French, Italian, Portuguese, sourdough, biscuits, corn bread, garlic bread, and so on. Use whatever type you like. But like conventional cracker products, conventional bread products are full of poor-quality ingredients too, including GMO oils. Ideally, choose a good-quality bread from a local bakery that uses organic, real ingredients. Health food stores have a variety of good breads too, including gluten-free choices.

5. Don't Freeze Chowder

The cream is more likely to curdle, the vegetables will turn mushy, clams can turn extremely rubbery, and the overall flavors will get muted. It's always best to consume all of your chowder within three to four days.

CLAM CHOWDERS

Classic Creamy New England Clam Chowder

SERVES 6

This is a standard classic and creamy chowder. Simple and straightforward, there's nothing crazy or unusual about it. But when you use fresh quahogs and steam them yourself to make the broth, you allow the ocean-fresh aromas and flavors to work their magic. Just let the magic happen on its own. The salty, pungent elixir is, as far as I'm concerned, the heart and soul of clam chowder. And with just a little thickening, you can create a nice texture that doesn't obscure the very essence of the broth.

A ratio of 1 tablespoon flour to 1 tablespoon cooking fat to 1 cup of clam broth is ideal for a roux that creates a light but not overly sludgy consistency. Thickening is of course always optional! But if you grew up like I did, expecting New England clam chowder to be thick and creamy, well, this version should satisfy that expectation but far exceed other versions in flavor.

As far as I'm concerned, this chowder delivers a total zen type of experience. Time slows down. Worries ease. And inner contentment is achieved. *That* is the true measure of a good-quality, classic, creamy New England clam chowder.

Ingredients

4 cups Hard-Shell Clam Broth (page 86)

7 to 8 pounds large cherrystones or small quahog clams

4 ounces fatty slab bacon (about 4 large strips) or salt pork, roughly diced into ½-inch pieces

¼ cup unsalted butter plus additional 2 to 3 tablespoons, if needed

1 large or 2 medium yellow onions, roughly diced into ½-inch pieces

4 to 5 thyme sprigs, leaves removed and stems discarded

1 dried bay leaf

1 pound potatoes, roughly chopped into ½-inch cubes

¼ cup all-purpose flour

1 to 2 cups heavy cream or half-and-half

Optional seasonings, to taste

Freshly ground black pepper

Salt pork cracklings or bacon bits

Fresh chives, chopped

Fresh parsley, chopped

(continued)

Instructions

1. To make the clam broth: Use the clams and make the broth following the instructions on page 86. Reserve the cooked clam meats from the prepared broth in the fridge until it's time to chop them and add them to the chowder.

2. Heat the bacon in a medium stockpot over low heat until a few tablespoons of fat render out. Raise the heat to medium and brown the meatier pieces, being careful not to burn them. Remove and reserve the browned pieces but leave the fat in the pot. Before serving the chowder, you can reheat the crispy browned cracklings from the salt pork or the bits from the bacon and add them as a topping.

3. Add 2 to 3 tablespoons butter, if needed, for additional cooking fat. Add the onions, thyme, and bay leaf. Sauté about 5 minutes until the onions are softened.

4. Add the clam broth and bring to a boil.

5. Add the potatoes, cover the pot, and simmer for 10 to 12 minutes, or until the potatoes are cooked through.

6. While the potatoes are cooking, make a roux in a separate pot. Melt ¼ cup butter over medium heat, add the flour, and stir continuously for 3 to 5 minutes. It should bubble and thicken as you stir it. Remove from the heat and let it cool slightly.

7. When the potatoes are cooked through, whisk in the roux and continue stirring until the chowder thickens slightly.

8. Add 1 cup heavy cream and taste. Add up to 1 more cup of heavy cream to desired taste. Remove the pot from the heat.

9. Chop the clams roughly, into quarters or halves, and stir into the chowder. Leave a few of the smaller clams whole, if desired.

10. Ladle into individual bowls and add optional seasonings to taste.

Rhode Island Clam Chowder

SERVES 6

When it comes to regional chowder wars, everyone tends to think their regional version is the original or most authentic. But the dairy-free version found in Rhode Island (and parts of coastal Connecticut) may in fact be closest to the original chowders of the 18th century. We know that dairy wasn't added to chowders until somewhere in the middle of the 19th century. Perhaps when this dairy trend started, parts of Rhode Island were insulated from it, resisted it, or just maintained the tradition of dairy-free chowders. Whatever the clouded history, today, on the southern coast of Rhode Island, a clear broth chowder is the preferred style. And it is just as delicious as white or red chowders!

   It should also be noted that Rhode Island clam chowders are the only clam chowders that are just as good with either a clam broth or a fish stock. You can use either one. Because my recipes use fresh whole clams and the broth from steaming them, your first choice will probably be a clam broth. But if you do want to try a fish stock instead, make a Robust Fish Stock (page 74). The more pronounced flavor in a robust fish stock compared to a basic fish stock will really shine through in this recipe.

Ingredients

4 cups Hard-Shell Clam Broth (page 86) or Robust Fish Stock (page 74) or combination of both

7 to 8 pounds pounds large cherrystones or small quahog clams

4 ounces fatty slab bacon (about 4 large strips) or salt pork, roughly diced into ½-inch pieces

2 to 3 tablespoons unsalted butter, if needed

1 large yellow onion, roughly diced into ½-inch pieces

3 celery stalks, roughly diced into ½-inch pieces

4 fresh thyme sprigs, leaves removed and stems discarded

2 bay leaves

3 to 4 garlic cloves, roughly chopped

1 pound potatoes, roughly chopped into ½-inch cubes

Optional seasonings, to taste

Freshly ground black pepper

Salt pork cracklings or bacon bits

Fresh chives, chopped

Fresh parsley, chopped

(continued)

Instructions

1. To make the clam broth: Use the clams and make the clam broth following the instructionson page 86. Reserve the cooked clam meats from the prepared broth in the fridge until it's time to chop them and add them to the chowder.

2. Heat the bacon in a medium stockpot over low heat until a few tablespoons of fat render out. Raise the heat to medium and brown the meatier pieces, being careful not to burn them. Remove and reserve the browned pieces but leave the fat in the pot. Before serving the chowder, you can reheat the crispy browned cracklings from the salt pork or the bits from the bacon and add them as a topping.

3. Add the butter, if needed, for additional cooking fat. Add the onion, celery, thyme, and bay leaves. Sauté about 5 minutes, until the vegetables are softened. Add the garlic in the last minute.

4. Add the clam broth or fish stock and bring to a boil.

5. Add the potatoes, cover the pot, and simmer for 10 to 12 minutes, or until the potatoes are cooked through.

6. Chop the clams roughly, into quarters or halves, and stir into the chowder. Leave a few of the smaller clams whole, if desired.

7. Ladle into individual bowls and add optional seasonings to taste.

Milky Maine Steamer Clam Chowder

SERVES 6

The defining characteristic of Maine-style chowders is that traditionally, they were made with milk and never thickened with flour, so they are on the brothier side of the chowder spectrum.

They are also known to use soft-shell clams. I took a few creative liberties with this version of a milky Maine chowder. First, I used half and half instead of milk, which is a closer approximation to traditional rich whole milk. Second, I only used butter as the cooking fat and I used a liberal amount. I felt salt pork or bacon would interfere with the sweet briny flavor of the broth. And lastly, I love the addition of lemon juice to round it out. As a result, this recipe is a bit of a hybrid between a chowder and a bowl of steamers, which are always served with a side of butter, broth, and lemon wedges.

Ingredients

4 cups Soft-Shell Clam Broth (page 87)

5 pounds soft-shell clams

8 tablespoons (1 stick) unsalted butter

1 large yellow onion, roughly diced into ½-inch pieces

2 celery stalks, roughly diced into ½-inch pieces

3 to 4 fresh thyme sprigs, leaves removed and stems discarded

1 bay leaf

1 pound potatoes, roughly chopped into ½-inch cubes

1 to 2 cups half-and-half or rich whole milk

Optional seasonings, to taste

Freshly ground black pepper

Fresh lemon juice (*highly* recommended)

Fresh parsley, chopped

Fresh chives, chopped

Instructions

1. To make the clam broth: Use the clams and make the broth following the instructions on page 87. Reserve the cooked clam meats from the prepared broth in the fridge until it's time to chop them and add them to the chowder.

2. Heat the butter in a medium stockpot over medium heat. Add the onions, celery, thyme, and bay leaf. Sauté until the vegetables are softened, about 5 minutes.

3. Add the clam broth and bring to a boil.

4. Add the potatoes, cover the pot, and simmer for 10 to 12 minutes, until the potatoes are cooked through.

5. Add 1 cup of half-and-half and taste. Add up to 1 more cup of cream to desired taste. Remove the pot from the heat.

6. Add the steamer clam meats and stir in.

7. Ladle into individual bowls and add optional seasonings to taste.

Manhattan Clam Chowder

SERVES 6

Though more associated with New York, Manhattan clam chowder is a staple on menus in southern New England, especially coastal Connecticut. Contrary to what most residents of New England believe, tomatoes and clams can make a truly harmonious union in a Manhattan clam chowder. Here, I set out to make what I believe is a purer, more restrained version of this dish, one without excessive vegetables and one that highlights the natural symmetry of tomatoes and, of course, *clams*. That means using fresh clams and their beautiful broth.

I exclude typical Manhattan clam chowder ingredients like green peppers, carrots, and celery. I also add some tomato paste for a slightly thicker consistency and richer tomato flavor. This may be an unusual interpretation, but to be quite honest it's the best version I've ever had. So if you're the tomatoes-in-chowder-is-anathema-to-chowder type of person, I ask one thing: Don't judge this recipe until you try it! I bet you'll have a newfound respect for Manhattan clam chowder.

Ingredients

2½ cups Hard-Shell Clam Broth (page 86)

7 to 8 pounds large cherrystones or small quahog clams

3 tablespoons olive oil

1 large or 2 medium yellow onions, roughly diced into ½-inch pieces

4 to 5 fresh thyme sprigs, leaves removed and stems discarded

2 teaspoons dried oregano

½ teaspoon red pepper flakes, plus more to taste

1 dried bay leaf

4 to 5 garlic cloves, roughly diced

1 pound potatoes, roughly chopped into ½-inch cubes

One 28-ounce can San Marzano tomatoes

2 tablespoons tomato paste

1 cup parsley, loosely packed

Optional seasonings, to taste

Freshly ground black pepper

Fresh parsley, chopped

Fresh chives, chopped

Hot sauce of your choice

Instructions

1. To make the clam broth: Use the clams and make the clam broth following the instructions on page 86. Reserve the cooked clam meats from the prepared broth in the fridge until you're ready to chop them and add them to the chowder.

2. Heat the olive oil in a medium stockpot over medium heat. Add the onion, thyme, oregano, red pepper flakes, and bay leaf. Sauté about 5 minutes, until the onions soften. Add the garlic in the last minute.

3. Add the clam broth and bring to a boil.

4. Add the potatoes, cover the pot, and simmer for 10 to 12 minutes, or until the potatoes are cooked through.

5. When the potatoes are done, add the tomatoes, tomato paste, and parsley. Stir in and simmer another few minutes.

6. Chop the clams roughly, into quarters or halves, and stir into the chowder. Leave a few of the smaller clams whole, if desired.

7. Ladle into individual bowls and add optional seasonings to taste.

Portuguese Clam Chowder

SERVES 4 OR 5

It's been suggested that the many styles of tomato-based Portuguese soups and stews were the precursor to the famed Manhattan clam chowder. Tomatoes started showing up in chowder recipes in Rhode Island and Connecticut in the late 19th and early 20th centuries where Portuguese immigrant communities were established. Though tomatoes in chowder mostly faded away in New England in the second half of the 20th century, it's thought that they found a more welcoming home in the New York area, where it eventually became the standardized dish we know today as Manhattan clam chowder. For my version, see the recipe for Manhattan Clam Chowder (page 112).

Regardless of the murky history, here's what I can say *without a doubt:* This Portuguese clam chowder is one of the most fantastic chowders I've ever tasted. Compared to Manhattan clam chowder, it's more piquant, richer, smokier, and spicier with *whole* littleneck clams that infuse the tomato base with a salty sea essence.

I don't care what side of the chowder debate you're on, red or white, you gotta try it to believe it.

My version is a fusion between a chowder and a Portuguese dish known as *ameijoas na cataplana* (clams in a cataplana pan), which utilizes a special rounded copper cooking pan with a hinged lid (it actually looks like a giant clam) to steam clams. A regular flat sauté pan with a lid is perfectly fine for this recipe though. If four dozen littleneck clams don't all fit in your sauté pan, simply steam the rest in a separate pot and add them back in, with the broth included of course!

Ingredients

4 dozen littleneck clams

4 tablespoons olive oil

1 large yellow onion, roughly diced into ½-inch pieces

1 large green pepper, roughly diced into ½-inch pieces

2 links chourico or linguica sausage (about 2 cups), sliced into ¼-inch rounds

4 to 5 garlic cloves, roughly diced

½ teaspoon fennel seeds

1 bay leaf

4 to 5 fresh thyme sprigs, leaves removed and stems discarded

½ teaspoon paprika

½ teaspoon red pepper flakes

2 tablespoons tomato paste

One 28-ounce can fire-roasted tomatoes

½ to 1 cup bottled clam broth, plus more as needed

2 tablespoons apple cider vinegar or red wine vinegar

1 cup tarragon leaves, loosely packed

(continued)

Optional seasonings,
to taste

Fresh parsley, cilantro,
and/or tarragon, chopped

Pinch or two of red pepper
flakes

Hot sauce of your choice

Splash of apple cider
vinegar

Instructions

1. Rinse and scrub the littleneck clams.

2. Heat the olive oil in a large heavy-bottom stockpot or sauté pan. Add the onion, green pepper, and sausage. Sauté about 5 minutes, until the vegetables are softened. Add the garlic, herbs, and spices and sauté another 2 to 3 minutes, stirring frequently.

3. Add the tomato paste and sauté another 2 to 3 minutes, stirring frequently. Add the canned tomatoes and bring to a simmer. Cover and cook for about 10 minutes.

4. Add the clams, cover, and simmer until all the shells open, 7 to 10 minutes. Add additional bottled clam broth, if necessary.

5. Add the vinegar and tarragon and stir in.

6. Ladle into individual bowls and add optional seasonings to taste.

Connecticut Clam Chowder

SERVES 6

Poor Connecticut. It gets the least respect of all the New England states. Most people rarely see more of Connecticut than what they see from behind a windshield on their way to more well-known New England destinations. But Connecticut has a significant coastline bordering the Long Island Sound, and it has lots of great seafood.

Because Connecticut sits between New York to the west and Rhode Island to the east, most establishments serve both the tomato-based Manhattan-style chowder and the clear broth Rhode Island–style chowder. Connecticut is the only New England state with a long coastline that doesn't have its own chowder. But I want to change that.

Now, truth be told, this recipe actually is inspired from a mysterious chowder known as a Long Island chowder. It's a pink-colored chowder that's a blend between a tomato-based Manhattan chowder and a dairy-based white New England chowder. But this recipe seemed more fitting for Connecticut, which is more of a fusion between these two regions than Long Island.

This recipe is really just as simple as making a Manhattan chowder base (though keeping the veggies to a minimum) and finishing it off with cream. It's actually quite delicious! Especially when you use fresh whole clams, fresh clam broth, good-quality tomatoes, and good-quality dairy. Maybe it will catch on, maybe it won't, but regardless Connecticut needs some love and respect too!

Ingredients

3 cups Hard-Shell Clam Broth (page 86)

7 to 8 pounds large cherrystones or small quahog clams

4 ounces fatty slab bacon (about 4 large strips) or salt pork, roughly diced into ½-inch pieces

2 to 3 tablespoons unsalted butter, if needed

1 large or 2 medium yellow onions, roughly diced into ½-inch pieces

2 celery stalks, roughly diced into ½-inch pieces

4 fresh thyme sprigs, leaves removed and stems discarded

1 bay leaf

2 teaspoons dried oregano

½ teaspoon red pepper flakes

2 garlic cloves, roughly diced

One 14-ounce can diced tomatoes in juices

2 tablespoons tomato paste

1 pound potatoes, roughly chopped into ½-inch cubes

1 to 2 cups heavy cream or half-and-half

Salt and freshly ground black pepper

(continued)

*Optional seasonings,
to taste*

**Freshly ground black
pepper**

**Salt pork cracklings or
bacon bits**

Fresh parsley, chopped

Fresh chives, chopped

Hot sauce of your choice

Instructions

1. To make the clam broth: Use the clams and make the broth following the instructions on page 86. Reserve the cooked clam meats from the prepared broth in the fridge until it's time to chop them and add them to the chowder.

2. Heat the bacon in a medium stockpot over low heat until a few tablespoons of fat render out. Raise the heat to medium and brown the meatier pieces, being careful not to burn them. Remove and reserve the browned pieces but leave the fat in the pot. Before serving the chowder, you can reheat the crispy browned cracklings from the salt pork or the bits from the bacon and add them as a topping.

3. Add the butter, if needed, for additional cooking fat. Add the onion, celery, thyme, bay leaf, oregano, and red pepper flakes. Sauté 5 to 7 minutes over medium heat, until the vegetables are softened. Add the garlic in the last minute.

4. Add 3 cups of of the clam broth, tomatoes, and tomato paste and bring to a boil.

5. Add the potatoes, cover the pot, and simmer for 10 to 12 minutes, or until the potatoes are cooked through.

6. Add 1 cup of the heavy cream and taste. Add up to 1 more cup of heavy cream to desired taste. Remove the pot from the heat.

7. Chop the clams roughly into quarters or halves and stir into chowder. Leave a few of the smaller clams whole, if desired.

8. Ladle into individual bowls and add optional seasonings to taste.

FISH CHOWDERS

Classic New England Whitefish Chowder

SERVES 6

For centuries this recipe has been the basic formula for the classic fish chowders of New England. Fish chowders actually predate clam chowders and were the first types of chowders in colonial days. Back in the days when the cod family was the backbone of New England's fishing economy, it was also the backbone of most fish chowders. As chowder's popularity spread, so did the inclusion of other types of fish, though cod and haddock are still the most common choices today. They certainly make great fish chowders but *any type* of lean, mild whitefish is perfectly suitable for this recipe. Try to use one of the undervalued whitefish species, if possible. Black sea bass, blackfish, and dogfish make sublime fish chowders too.

Ingredients

4 ounces fatty slab bacon (about 4 large strips) or salt pork, roughly diced into ½-inch pieces

2 tablespoons unsalted butter, if needed

1 large or 2 medium yellow onions, roughly diced into ½-inch pieces

4 to 5 fresh thyme sprigs, leaves removed and stems discarded

2 dried bay leaves

4 cups Robust Fish Stock (page 74)

1 pound potatoes, roughly chopped into ½-inch cubes

Salt

2 pounds any lean, mild whitefish fillets (see Chapter 2 for all options)

1 to 2 cups heavy cream or half-and-half

Optional seasonings, to taste

Salt and freshly ground black pepper

Salt pork cracklings or bacon bits

Fresh chives, chopped

Fresh parsley, chopped

(continued)

Instructions

1. Heat the bacon in a medium stockpot over low heat until a few tablespoons of fat render out. Raise the heat to medium and brown the meatier pieces, being careful not to burn them. Remove the browned pieces with a slotted spoon but leave the fat in the pot. Before serving the chowder, you can reheat the crispy browned cracklings from the salt pork or the bits from the bacon and add them as a topping.

2. Add the butter, if needed, for additional cooking fat. Add the onions, thyme, and bay leaves. Sauté about 5 minutes, until the onions are softened.

3. Add the fish stock and bring to a boil.

4. Add the potatoes, cover the pot, and simmer for 10 to 12 minutes, until the potatoes are cooked through.

5. Add salt to taste.

6. Add the fish and simmer gently for a few minutes. Remove the pot from the heat, cover, and let the chowder sit until the fish is cooked through. Thicker and denser pieces of fish will need a little more time to cook than thinner and flakier pieces.

7. Once the fish is cooked, add 1 cup of the heavy cream, stir gently, and taste. Add up to 1 more cup of heavy cream to desired taste.

8. Ladle into individual bowls and add optional seasonings to taste.

Wild Salmon Chowder

Red, yellow, and green. It's not too often you get such unique colors in a chowder. But yellow corn, green peas, and the deep rich red flesh of a wild-caught salmon (as opposed to the pale pink of farm-raised salmon) make for a striking presentation.

And I really do encourage you to buy wild-caught salmon. As discussed in Chapter 2, any salmon labeled Atlantic is farm raised, which is a practice that has negative environmental impacts. Wild Atlantic salmon are an endangered species and are forbidden from any commercial or recreational fishing. With so many people eating salmon today, it's important to shift our awareness to the difference between farm raised and wild caught, and to support our wild salmon fisheries on the West Coast.

Even though this recipe isn't a true New England chowder, wild salmon is so delicious that an exception needs to be made. It makes a unique chowder both in its colors and flavors, especially with dill and a little sour cream. The latter may seem unusual, but it adds a nice touch of extra rich flavor. If you're not sure about it, don't add it to the main pot. Rather, scoop out a small amount of chowder to a bowl and mix in just a dab of sour cream to get a sense of its flavor. If you like it, you can then add it back to the main pot. Alternatively, let each person add it to taste in their individual bowl.

Ingredients

4 ounces fatty slab bacon (about 4 large strips) or salt pork, roughly diced into ½-inch pieces

2 tablespoons unsalted butter, if needed

1 large leek, white part only, cut in half lengthwise, diced into ½-inch pieces

1 bay leaf

3 to 4 fresh thyme sprigs, leaves removed and stems discarded

½ cup dry white wine

4 cups Robust Fish Stock (page 74)

1 pound potatoes, chopped into ½-inch cubes

½ cup peas

½ cup corn kernels

Salt

2 pounds wild salmon fillets, cut into 3- to 4-inch pieces

1 to 2 cups heavy cream or half-and-half

¼ cup sour cream, plus more to taste (optional)

1 cup fresh dill, loosely packed, plus more to taste

Optional seasonings, to taste

Salt and freshly ground black pepper

Salt pork cracklings or bacon bits

Sour cream

Fresh dill, chopped

Fresh chives, chopped

(continued)

Instructions

1. Heat the bacon in a medium stockpot over low heat until a few tablespoons of fat render out. Raise the heat to medium and brown the meatier pieces, being careful not to burn them. Remove the browned pieces with a slotted spoon but leave the fat in the pot. Before serving the chowder, you can reheat the crispy browned cracklings from the salt pork or the bits from the bacon and add them as a topping.

2. Add the butter, if needed, for additional cooking fat. Add the leeks, bay leaf, and thyme. Sauté about 5 minutes, until the leeks are softened.

3. Add the wine, raise the heat, and simmer for a few minutes or until it's slightly reduced.

4. Add the fish stock and bring to a boil.

5. Add the potatoes, cover the pot, and simmer for 10 to 12 minutes, until the potatoes are cooked through.

6. Add the peas and corn and simmer another 3 to 4 minutes. Add salt to taste.

7. Add the salmon and simmer gently for a few minutes. Remove the pot from the heat, cover, and let it sit for 5 to 10 more minutes, or until the salmon is cooked through and flakes easily. Gently break apart the salmon and mix into the chowder.

8. Add 1 cup of the heavy cream, the optional sour cream, and dill, and taste. Add up to 1 more cup of heavy cream and additional sour cream and dill to desired taste.

9. Ladle into individual bowls and add optional seasonings to taste.

Portuguese Fish Chowder

SERVES 6

This chowder is a natural fusion between classic New England whitefish chowders and the many varieties of traditional tomato-based Portuguese seafood stews. Zesty spices and chourico sausage combine to infuse the base of fish stock and tomatoes, which further heightens the flavor of any lean mild whitefish. It's a great contrast to the more familiar cream-based New England fish chowders and one that will equally satisfy and enliven the taste buds.

Ingredients

2 tablespoons olive oil

1 large or 2 medium yellow onions, roughly diced into ½-inch pieces

1 fennel bulb, core removed, roughly diced into ½-inch pieces

2 chourico links, about 2 cups, sliced into ¼-inch-thick rounds

1 bay leaf

4 fresh thyme sprigs, leaves removed and stems discarded

2 whole allspice berries or ¼ teaspoon ground allspice

½ teaspoon chili powder or slightly more

2 teaspoons smoked paprika

3 to 4 garlic cloves, diced

4 cups Robust Fish Stock (page 74)

1 pound potatoes, roughly chopped into ½-inch cubes

One 28-ounce can whole tomatoes in juice, roughly chopped into small pieces, juice reserved

Sea salt

2 pounds any lean, mild whitefish fillets (see Chapter 2 for all options)

½ cup fresh parsley, chopped and packed

Optional seasonings, to taste

Sea salt and freshly ground black pepper

Fresh parsley, chopped

Apple cider vinegar

Red pepper flakes or hot sauce of your choice

Instructions

1. Heat the olive oil over medium heat in a medium stockpot.

2. Add the onions, fennel, chourico, bay leaf, thyme, allspice, chili powder, and paprika. Sauté about 10 minutes, or until the onions and fennel are softened. Add the garlic in the last few minutes.

3. Add the fish stock and bring to a boil.

4. Add the potatoes, cover the pot, and simmer for 10 to 12 minutes, until the potatoes are cooked through.

5. Add the tomatoes and juice and simmer for 5 more minutes. If there's too much liquid, continue simmering until the liquid is reduced.

6. Add the sea salt to taste.

7. Add the fish and simmer gently for a few minutes. Remove the pot from the heat, cover, and let the chowder sit until the fish is cooked through. Thicker and denser pieces of fish will need a little more time to cook than thinner and flakier pieces.

8. Add the parsley and stir in.

9. Ladle into individual bowls and add optional seasonings to taste.

Tips for the Perfect Fish Chowder

Flaky fillets like those in the cod family can be added whole to chowder. They will cook in the hot chowder and then will easily flake apart when they're done. Firmer fillets, such as halibut and monkfish, won't flake apart as easily and are best cut into smaller 1- to 2-inch chunks.

I'd highly recommend not using a thickener for fish chowders. Fish stock is not as intensely flavored as clam broth, so you don't want to obscure its more delicate flavors. The beauty of a classic New England fish chowder is the fresh ocean flavors of fish! And a homemade fish stock is an important part of that.

Bluefish Chowder with Cherry Tomatoes, Basil, and Tarragon

SERVES 6

I was tempted to name this recipe something like Full-Flavored New England Fish Chowder and make it all-inclusive for any oily, full-flavored fish. But bluefish holds a special place in my heart.

As a kid, there was nothing I loved more than the thrill of catching bluefish. Yet it's only recently that I learned to appreciate them for their culinary potential. Bluefish have a high oil content, which means they're fantastic eating when they're fresh and in season from late spring through fall. They have a meaty but tender flesh that is rich and light at the same time. They also make a great fish stock and a luscious chowder.

Ideally, this recipe should be made in late summer, when bluefish season is at its height and when sweet juicy cherry tomatoes are popping off their vines. Fresh summer basil and tarragon, with its anise, notes make it all the more fantastic. I like to add the cherry tomatoes at the end with the cream and herbs. This keeps them from cooking too much and preserves their fresh, sweet flavor.

The best place to find bluefish is at a fish market that specializes in locally caught fish. Supermarket fish departments are less likely to carry bluefish. However, with the demand for more local and sustainable seafood, it is possible that some supermarket fish counters will stock them on a more regular basis. If you can't find bluefish, you can substitute wild salmon, swordfish, mackerel, or striped bass.

Ingredients

4 ounces fatty slab bacon (about 4 large strips) or salt pork, roughly diced into ½-inch pieces

2 tablespoons unsalted butter, if needed

1 large or 2 medium yellow onions, roughly diced into ½-inch pieces

2 celery stalks, roughly diced into ½-inch pieces

2 garlic cloves, roughly diced

4 cups Robust Fish Stock (page 74)

1 pound potatoes, roughly chopped into ½-inch cubes

Salt

2 pounds bluefish fillets, cut into large chunks, 3- to 4-inch pieces

1 to 2 cups heavy cream or half-and-half

2 cups cherry tomatoes, sliced in half

1 cup basil leaves, loosely packed

1 cup tarragon leaves, loosely packed

Optional seasonings,
to taste

Salt and freshly ground
black pepper

Salt pork cracklings or
bacon bits

Fresh lemon juice

Fresh basil, chopped

Fresh tarragon, chopped

Instructions

1. Heat the bacon in a medium stockpot over low heat until a few tablespoons render out. Raise the heat to medium and brown the meatier pieces, being careful not to burn them. Remove the browned pieces with a slotted spoon but leave the fat in the pot. Before serving the chowder, you can reheat the crispy browned cracklings from the salt pork or the bits from the bacon and add them as a topping.

2. Add the butter, if needed, for additional cooking fat. Add the onions and celery. Sauté about 5 minutes, until the onions are softened. Add the garlic in the last minute.

3. Add the fish stock and bring to a boil.

4. Add the potatoes, cover the pot, and simmer for 10 to 12 minutes, until the potatoes are cooked through.

5. Add salt to taste.

6. Add the bluefish and simmer gently for a few minutes. Remove the pot from the heat, cover, and let it sit for 5 to 10 more minutes. Push into the fillets or chunks with a kitchen utensil until they easily flake apart. Gently break apart the bluefish and mix into the chowder.

7. Add 1 cup of the heavy cream, the cherry tomatoes, basil, and tarragon. Stir gently and taste. Add up to 1 more cup of heavy cream to desired taste.

8. Ladle into individual bowls and add optional seasonings to taste.

Smoked Haddock Chowder with a Poached Egg

SERVES 6

A poached egg in a chowder? Oh yes indeed! A runny yolk in a bowl of soup is a staple in many types of Asian cuisine, and though it sounds a little weird in a chowder, it works really well with the distinct flavor of smoked fish. Smoking fish was once a method for preserving it, but today it's done more for its unique and strong taste. It makes an unmistakable but still magnificent bowl of chowder. Not all seafood markets carry smoked haddock, but you might find finnan haddie, which is a popular lightly smoked haddock from a method that originated in Scotland. Other types of smoked fish are suitable substitutes. You might also check with your local fishmonger, especially those who specialize in smoking fish such as bluefish or mackerel.

Ingredients

4 ounces fatty slab bacon (about 4 large strips) or salt pork, roughly diced into ½-inch pieces

2 to 3 tablespoons unsalted butter, if needed

1 medium onion, diced into ½-inch pieces

1 small leek, white part only, cut in half lengthwise, diced into ½-inch pieces

1 bay leaf

3 to 4 fresh thyme sprigs, leaves removed and stems discarded

2 garlic cloves, roughly diced

½ cup dry white wine

4 cups Robust Fish Stock (page 74)

1 pound potatoes, roughly chopped into ½-inch cubes

6 eggs

Salt

2 pounds smoked haddock fillets

1 to 2 cups heavy cream or half-and-half

1 cup chives, loosely packed, diced

Optional seasonings, to taste

Salt and freshly ground black pepper

Fresh chives, chopped

Fresh parsley, chopped

Worcestershire sauce

Instructions

1. Heat the bacon in a medium stockpot over low heat until a few tablespoons of fat render out. Raise the heat to medium and brown the meatier pieces, being careful not to burn them. Remove the browned pieces with a slotted spoon but leave the fat in the pot. Before serving the chowder, you can reheat the crispy browned cracklings from the salt pork or the bits from the bacon and add them as a topping.

2. Add the butter, if needed, for additional cooking fat. Add the onion, leek, bay leaf, and thyme. Sauté for about 5 minutes, until the vegetables are softened. Add the garlic in the last minute.

3. Add the wine and simmer for another 4 to 5 minutes, or until the wine is slightly reduced.

4. Add the fish stock and bring to a boil.

5. Add the potatoes, cover the pot, and simmer for 10 to 12 minutes, until the potatoes are cooked through.

6. While the potatoes are cooking, bring another small pot of water to a gentle boil. Stir the water in a clockwise motion with a kitchen utensil and crack the eggs into the water. This motion keeps the white part of the eggs from overly fraying. Poach for 3 to 4 minutes, until the white parts cook but the yolks remain runny. Remove the eggs with a slotted spoon and set aside.

7. When the potatoes are done, add salt to taste.

8. Add the smoked haddock and simmer gently for a few minutes. Remove the pot from the heat, cover, and let the chowder sit for 5 to 10 minutes, until the haddock is cooked through and flakes easily.

9. Add 1 cup of the heavy cream and chives, stir gently, and taste. Add up to 1 more cup of heavy cream to desired taste.

10. Ladle into individual bowls and add optional seasonings to taste. Add a poached egg on top and press into it gently to let the yolk ooze out.

Hake and Skate Chowder

SERVES 6

This recipe comes courtesy of my passionate seafoodie friend, Amanda Grace-Davies. She's created a nonprofit called Our Wicked Fish (www.ourwickedfish.com), which serves to educate and connect more New England residents to local and sustainable sources of New England seafood. Much of this information centers on raising awareness about the importance of consuming more undervalued fish. Like skate!

Amanda brought a pot of this chowder to one of the many soup tasting parties I hosted when I was creating the recipes for this book. I loved the tender chunks of skate wing and hake along with the sweet corn. You could easily substitute another member of the cod family for hake.

I also loved that Amanda pureed a small portion of the chowder, which created a fantastic creamy texture. I've included it in the recipe as an optional thickening method at the end. Thickened or not, this is a classic fish chowder that pairs an undervalued fish (skate) with a more common one (hake). It's a good example of the many types of chowders that mix multiple types of seafood. Always feel free to experiment and add different types of seafood to chowders, especially the undervalued fish species mentioned in Chapter 2.

Ingredients

3 tablespoons unsalted butter, more if needed

1 large or 2 medium yellow onions, roughly diced into ½-inch pieces

2 to 3 celery stalks, roughly diced into ½-inch pieces

4 or 5 fresh thyme sprigs, leaves removed and stems discarded

2 bay leaves

1 teaspoon celery seeds

4 cups Robust Fish Stock (page 74)

1 cup sweet corn kernels

1 pound potatoes, roughly cut into ½-inch cubes

Sea salt

1 pound hake fillets

1 pound skate wing

1 to 2 cups heavy cream or half-and-half

Optional seasonings, to taste

Salt and freshly ground black pepper

Fresh chives, chopped

Fresh parsley, chopped

Instructions

1. Heat the butter in a medium stockpot over medium heat. Add the onions, celery, thyme, bay leaves, and celery seeds. Sauté until the vegetables are softened, about 5 minutes. Add more butter, if needed.

2. Add the fish stock and bring to a boil.

3. Add the corn and potatoes, cover the pot, and simmer for 10 to 12 minutes, until the potatoes are cooked through.

4. Add the sea salt to taste.

5. Add the hake and skate wing and simmer gently for a few minutes. Remove the pot from the heat, cover, and let the chowder sit until the fish is cooked through.

6. Add 1 cup of the heavy cream, stir gently, and taste. Add up to 1 more cup of heavy cream to desired taste.

7. Optional thickening method: Scoop out about one-quarter of the chowder and transfer it to a blender. Press the top down firmly with a small kitchen towel to prevent splattering. Puree the chowder until smooth and thickened then pour it back into the main pot and stir it all together.

8. Ladle into individual bowls and add optional seasonings to taste.

SHELLFISH CHOWDERS

Lobster Corn Chowder

SERVES 5 OR 6

Lobster bisque may feature prominently on menus, but a lobster corn chowder could easily rival a lobster bisque, especially in summer when fresh, sweet New England corn is in season. Tender chunks of juicy lobster, hearty chunks of onion, corn, potato, and bacon, melding together in a briny lobster broth simmered with white wine, fennel, and herbs that's finished off with heavy cream is about the most divine lobstery thing you'll ever taste.

Ingredients

4 cups Basic Lobster Stock, (page 78)

Two 1¼- to 1½-pound lobsters

4 ounces fatty slab bacon (about 4 large strips) or salt pork, roughly diced into ½-inch pieces

2 tablespoons unsalted butter, if needed

1 large yellow onion, roughly diced into ½-inch pieces

1 fennel bulb, core removed, roughly diced into ½-inch pieces

4 or 5 fresh thyme sprigs, leaves removed and stems discarded

½ cup dry white wine

1 pound potatoes, roughly chopped into ½-inch cubes

One 10-ounce bag frozen corn or kernels removed from 3 ears of fresh whole corn

1 to 2 cups heavy cream or half-and-half

Salt

Optional seasonings, to taste

Salt and freshly ground black pepper

Fresh parsley, chopped

Fresh chives, chopped

(continued)

Instructions

1. To make the lobster stock: Use the lobsters to make the stock following the instructions on page 78. Reserve the cooked lobster meat from the prepared stock in the fridge until it's time to add it to the chowder. You'll get about 2 to 3 cups of meat total. If possible, do this 1 day ahead. Alternatively, make a lobster stock from leftover carcasses (or use a lobster stock you previously made) and purchase fresh lobster meat.

2. Heat the bacon in a medium stockpot over low heat until a few tablespoons of fat render out. Raise the heat to medium and brown the meatier pieces, being careful not to burn them. Remove the browned pieces with a slotted spoon but leave the fat in the pot. Before serving the chowder, you can reheat the crispy browned cracklings from the salt pork or the bits from the bacon and add them as a topping.

3. Add the butter, if needed, for additional cooking fat. Add the onions, fennel, and thyme. Sauté 7 to 10 minutes, until the onions and fennel are softened.

4. Add the wine, raise the heat, and simmer for a few minutes or until it's slightly reduced.

5. Add the lobster stock and bring to a boil.

6. Add the potatoes, cover the pot, and simmer for 10 to 12 minutes, until the potatoes are cooked through.

7. Add the corn and simmer until tender. Frozen corn will take 2 to 3 minutes. Fresh corn kernels will take 5 to 7 minutes.

8. Add the lobster chunks and 1 cup of the heavy cream, stir, and taste. Add up to 1 more cup of heavy cream to desired taste.

9. Add salt to taste.

10. Ladle into individual bowls and add optional seasonings to taste.

Mussel Chowder with Fennel

SERVES 6

You never see a mussel chowder on menus. Other shellfish—lobster, crab, and scallop—make a very occasional appearance in chowders, but not mussels.

A mussel chowder is just not something people are accustomed to, perhaps because mussels only gained widespread acceptance as a food with the advent of mussel aquaculture in the 1970s. But mussels can be just as well-suited to chowder as clams. Even better, because mussel chowder hasn't been standardized with regional variations, there's no preconceived expectation of exactly what it should taste like. And that means you have an open invitation to try different ingredients and be creative.

Enter fennel. Fennel is a perfect complement to mussels. Its subtle anise flavor adds a dimension to mussel chowder that is unlike anything you'll find in more typical clam chowders.

Ingredients

4 cups Mussel Broth (page 88), if you get less than 4 cups from steaming the mussels, add clam or fish stock, if needed, to measure 4 cups total

4 pounds blue mussels

4 ounces fatty slab bacon (about 4 large strips) or salt pork, roughly diced into ½-inch pieces

2 tablespoons butter, if needed

1 medium yellow onion, roughly diced into ½-inch pieces

1 fennel bulb, core removed, roughly diced into ½-inch pieces

1 red pepper, roughly diced into ½-inch pieces

¼ teaspoon fennel seeds

1 pound potatoes, roughly chopped into ½-inch cubes

1 to 2 cups heavy cream or half-and-half

Salt

Optional seasonings, to taste

Sea salt and freshly ground pepper

Salt pork cracklings or bacon bits

Fennel fronds, finely chopped

Fresh basil, finely chopped

(continued)

Instructions

1. To make the mussel broth: Use the mussels to make the broth following the instructions on page 88.

2. You should get about 3 to 4 cups of mussels broth. You'll also gct about 2 to 3 cups of mussel meats. It will help to have someone assisting you remove all the meats from the shells. Put the meats in the fridge until you're ready to add them to the chowder.

3. Heat the bacon in a medium stockpot over low heat until a few tablespoons of fat render out. Raise the heat to medium and brown the meatier pieces, being careful not to burn them. Remove the browned pieces with a slotted spoon but leave the fat in the pot. Before serving the chowder, you can reheat the crispy browned cracklings from the salt pork or the bits from the bacon and add them as a topping.

4. Add the butter, if needed, for additional cooking fat. Add the onions, fennel, red pepper, and fennel seeds. Sauté 7 to 10 minutes, until the vegetables are softened.

5. Add the 4 cups of mussel broth and bring to a boil.

6. Add the potatoes, cover the pot, and simmer for 10 to 12 minutes, or until the potatoes are cooked through.

7. Add 1 cup of the heavy cream and taste. Add up to 1 more cup of heavy cream to desired taste. Remove the pot from the heat.

8. Add the whole mussel meats and stir in.

9. Add salt to taste.

10. Ladle into individual bowls and add optional seasonings to taste.

Crab, Bacon, and Cheddar Corn Chowder

SERVES 6 TO 8

This recipe was inspired from a bacon-cheddar-corn chowder I made years ago. The simple addition of sweet, juicy crabmeat and crab stock made it that much more seductive. Not for the faint of heart, this chowder is rich, creamy, smoky, sweet, and cheesy.

Don't let your saturated fat and cholesterol-fearing friends convince you that this recipe is "artery clogging." Many people, especially older folks, are still conditioned by the theory that saturated fat and cholesterol cause heart disease and weight gain, a theory that has been thoroughly disproven by science in the past decade. We now know that the "bad" cholesterol, the kind that can accumulate in arteries, ironically, does not come from animal foods, but rather from highly processed inflammatory foods that are typically high in sugar and poor-quality fats (like processed vegetable oils).

With a chowder, good-quality ingredients—a homemade stock, real crabmeat, pastured bacon, grass-fed dairy, and organic vegetables—are the key to making it healthy. That doesn't mean one should eat it at every meal. Healthy, real foods like this need to be balanced with other healthy, real foods. Dietary needs are, of course, highly dependent on the constitution and health of each individual, but chowder can, and should, be nourishing to the body. Hard as it may be to believe for some, even a main course that includes crab, bacon, cheese, and cream can be a source of sustenance. At the very least, it can't be argued that this recipe is deeply soulful, hearty, and satisfying.

Ingredients

4 cups Basic Crab Stock (page 82)

4 pounds Jonah crab claws or 2 pounds New England crab carcasses

4 ounces fatty slab bacon (about 4 large strips), roughly diced into ½-inch pieces

2 tablespoons butter, if needed

1 large yellow onion, roughly diced into ½-inch pieces

2 celery stalks, roughly diced into ½-inch pieces

1 pound potatoes, roughly chopped into ½-inch cubes

One 10-ounce bag frozen corn or kernels removed from 3 fresh corn on the cob

4 or 5 fresh thyme sprigs, leaves removed and stems discarded

12 to 16 ounces cheddar cheese

1 to 2 cups heavy cream or half-and-half

Sea salt

Optional seasonings, to taste

Sea salt and freshly ground pepper

Fresh parsley, chopped

Fresh chives, chopped

Old Bay or similar seafood seasoning blend

Instructions

1. To make the crab stock: Use the crab claws or carcasses and make the stock following the instructions on page 88. Reserve the cooked crab from the prepared stock in the fridge until it's time to add it to the chowder. You should get at least a quart of crab stock and 2 cups of crab meat. If possible, do this 1 day ahead.

2. Heat the bacon in a medium stockpot over low heat until a few tablespoons of fat render out. Raise the heat to medium and brown the meatier pieces, being careful not to burn them. Remove the browned pieces with a slotted spoon but leave the fat in the pot.

3. Add the butter, if needed, for additional cooking fat. Add the onions and celery. Sauté about 5 minutes until softened.

4. Add the crab stock, potatoes, corn, and thyme. Bring to a boil, reduce heat, and simmer gently, 10 to 12 minutes, or until the potatoes are cooked through.

5. While the potatoes are cooking, chop the reserved bacon further and grate the cheddar cheese. Set the bacon and cheese aside.

6. Add the crabmeat and stir in. Simmer for a minute or two.

7. Add 1 cup of the heavy cream and taste. Add up to 1 more cup of heavy cream to desired taste. Remove the pot from the heat.

8. Add the sea salt to taste. Be careful not to overdo it here because the cheese, which is added in the next step, will also add some salty flavor.

9. Ladle into individual bowls and let each person add however much bacon and cheese he or she wants. Add optional seasonings to taste.

Scallop and Wild Mushroom Chowder with Chives

SERVES 6

Though you can certainly use common store-bought mushrooms in this recipe, I highly encourage you to seek out wild mushrooms instead. Wild mushrooms have much more varied and interesting flavors.

Learning to forage and identify edible wild mushrooms is something I've only recently become interested in. With the help of guided walks from local experts, guidebooks, and online foraging communities, I've been able to clearly identify many types of edible mushrooms, such as black trumpets, chanterelles, hen of the woods, and more. But if foraging for wild mushrooms is not on your agenda anytime soon, do not worry. Many edible wild mushrooms are harvested by enthusiastic foragers and sold at farmers' markets and other types of specialty markets. Try any type of wild mushroom in this recipe or use combinations of them.

If there are few options for wild mushrooms where you live, there's a simple solution: use shiitake mushrooms. They have a rich, bold flavor that works really well in chowders, and their meaty texture is actually similar to scallops.

As for the scallops, small and sweet bay scallops or the much larger sea scallops are both fine to use. Because scallops don't have their own broth, I'd recommend clam broth for a stronger seafood flavor. Fish stock or lobster stock is certainly usable too.

Ingredients

4 ounces fatty slab bacon (about 4 large strips), roughly diced into ½-inch pieces

2 tablespoons unsalted butter, if needed

1 large yellow onion, roughly diced into ½-inch pieces

8 ounces wild mushrooms, roughly chopped into ½-inch pieces

4 or 5 fresh thyme sprigs, leaves removed and stems discarded

1 bay leaf

3 garlic cloves, roughly diced

4 cups Hard-Shell Clam Broth (page 86) or bottled, or any other seafood stock

1 pound potatoes, roughly chopped into ½-inch cubes

1½ pounds bay or sea scallops, cut into quarters and/or halves

1 to 2 cups heavy cream or half-and-half

1 cup chives, chopped, plus more to taste

Sea salt

Optional seasonings, to taste

Salt and freshly ground black pepper

Bacon bits

Fresh parsley, chopped

Fresh chives, chopped

Hot sauce of your choice

Instructions

1. Heat the bacon in a medium stockpot over low heat until a few tablespoons of fat render out. Raise the heat to medium and brown the meatier pieces, being careful not to burn them. Remove the browned pieces with a slotted spoon but leave the fat in the pot. Before serving the chowder, you can reheat the browned bits from the bacon and add them as a topping.

2. Add the butter, if needed, for additional cooking fat. Add the onion, mushrooms, thyme, and bay leaf. Sauté for 7 to 10 minutes, until the onions and mushrooms are softened. Add the garlic in the last minute.

3. Add the clam broth and bring to a boil.

4. Add the potatoes, cover the pot, and simmer for 10 to 12 minutes, or until the potatoes are cooked through.

5. Add the scallops and simmer for a few minutes until they are cooked through.

6. Add 1 cup of the heavy cream and taste. Add up to 1 more cup of heavy cream to desired taste.

7. Add the chives and gently stir in.

8. Add salt to taste.

9. Ladle the chowder into individual bowls and add optional seasonings to taste.

Oyster Spinach Chowder

SERVES 6

Unlike the bold flavors of a clam chowder, I think an oyster chowder does better with more muted flavors. Butter instead of bacon, leeks instead of onions, fennel instead of celery, and some lemon zest complement oysters nicely in a chowder. And baby spinach is more tender and sweeter than regular spinach.

The real challenge can be the broth. You want a pronounced oyster flavor to come through. This can be a little tricky because it's easy to dilute the flavor of the oyster liquor when you're adding additional liquid. The salinity and amount of the oyster liquor can also be highly variable depending on the type of oysters you purchase and the time of year they're harvested. I recommend starting out by adding your reserved oyster liquor to fish stock or water to make 2 cups total. Taste it. You'll get a sense of what type of additional liquid you should add. I like to keep a strong briny flavor and add 2 cups of clam broth. You might choose fish stock or water instead. Adjust things accordingly to your desired taste.

Ingredients

3 dozen oysters, shucked, liquor reserved (½ to 1 cup)

1 to 1½ cups Basic or Robust Fish Stock (pages 73 and 74) or water plus additional 2 cups Hard-Shell Clam Broth (page 86) or bottled, fish stock, or water (3 to 3½ cups total)

3 tablespoons unsalted butter

1 medium leek, white part only, cut in half lengthwise, diced into ½-inch pieces

1 fennel bulb, roughly diced into ½-inch pieces

2 garlic cloves, roughly diced

1 pound potatoes, roughly chopped into ½-inch cubes

Zest of 1 lemon (optional)

1 to 2 cups heavy cream or half-and-half

8 ounces baby spinach, thicker stems discarded

Optional seasonings, to taste

Freshly ground black pepper

Fresh chives, chopped

Fresh parsley, chopped

Fresh lemon juice

Hot sauce of your choice

Instructions

1. Set the shucked oysters aside. Add the ½ to 1 cup reserved oyster liquor to 1 to 1½ cups fish stock or water to make 2 cups. Taste it and add 2 more cups of clam broth, fish stock, or water to make 4 cups of broth total. Set the broth aside.

2. Melt the butter over medium heat and sauté the leek and fennel for 7 to 10 minutes until softened. Add the garlic in the last minute.

3. Add the 4 cups of broth and bring to a boil. Reduce the heat and add the potatoes and lemon zest. Cover and simmer for 10 to 12 minutes, or until the potatoes are cooked through.

4. Add 1 cup of the heavy cream and taste. Add up to 1 more cup of heavy cream to desired taste.

5. Add the spinach and gently stir it in. Simmer just a minute or two until the spinach wilts.

6. Add the oysters and simmer until the edges curl, 2 to 3 more minutes.

7. Ladle into individual bowls and add optional seasonings to taste.

Curried Butternut Squash Squid Chowder

SERVES 6 TO 8

This is, by far, the most unusual chowder of any in this chapter. I wanted to create something well beyond the standard concept of a chowder but one that still retains the key elements of a chowder. Squid felt like the perfect choice for branching out and experimenting since it's so rarely found in chowders.

I thought of the many varieties of squid curries I've had in Southeast Asia and how closely some of them resemble the texture of a chowder. However, most Southeast Asian curries contain things like chiles, lemongrass, galangal, and kaffir lime leaves, which have the potential to overpower a chowder. I thought a dried curry powder, much milder in taste, might work.

But I didn't want to just create a chowder with added curry powder. I chose to add butternut squash to this recipe, as it has a pleasantly soft texture that easily absorbs the flavorful spices. It also contributes its own sweet, nutty flavor that melds perfectly with the other ingredients. But it's the clam broth, squid, and cream that fused this chowder together and made it work. It also kept it firmly in the realm of a New England chowder, albeit a very unique one! Finally, bacon's smokiness can be a bit much for this recipe, though it won't ruin it in any way. If you choose to use it, remove the meatier portions after rendering the fat. Salt pork is definitely preferable.

Ingredients

4 ounces fatty slab bacon (about 4 large strips) or salt pork, roughly diced into ½-inch pieces

1 to 2 tablespoons butter, if needed

1 medium yellow onion, roughly diced into ½-inch pieces

1 pound squid, rings and tentacles

3 to 4 garlic cloves, roughly diced

4 to 5 Roma tomatoes, quartered, cored, deseeded, and roughly chopped into ½-inch pieces

1 tablespoon curry powder

5 cups Hard-Shell Clam Broth (page 86) or bottled

3 or 4 fresh thyme sprigs, leaves removed and stems discarded

Zest from 1 lemon

1 pound butternut squash, peeled, deseeded, and roughly chopped into ½-inch cubes

1 pound potatoes, roughly chopped into ½-inch cubes

1 to 2 cups heavy cream or half-and-half

Salt

Optional seasonings, to taste

Sea salt and freshly ground pepper

Fresh cilantro, chopped

Fresh parsley, chopped

Instructions

1. Heat the bacon in a medium stockpot over low heat until a few tablespoons of fat render out. Raise the heat to medium and brown the meatier pieces, being careful not to burn them. Remove the browned pieces with a slotted spoon but leave the fat in the pot.

2. Add the butter, if needed, for additional cooking fat. Add the onions and sauté about 5 minutes until softened. Add the squid, garlic, and tomatoes and sauté for another 3 to 5 more minutes, stirring frequently.

3. Add the curry powder and stir well for another minute.

4. Add the clam broth, thyme, lemon zest, butternut squash, and potatoes and bring to a boil. Reduce the heat and simmer gently, 10 to 15 minutes, until the potatoes and butternut squash are cooked through.

5. Add 1 cup of the heavy cream and taste. Add up to 1 more cup of heavy cream to desired taste.

6. Add salt to taste.

7. Ladle into individual bowls and add optional seasonings to taste.

Chapter 7

Brothy Soups

Brothy soups and stews have not gained a foothold in our soup consciousness as much as New England clam chowder or lobster bisque. And yet, in times past, brothy concoctions were common household creations in coastal New England when fresh shellfish was more abundant (and cheaper) and when whole fish were embraced, not just for their fillets but also their carcasses, to make fish stock.

A good example would be oyster stew. Although it's called a stew, it's really more of a brothy soup. Any pre-World War II New England cookbook most likely has a recipe. It became so popular on the East Coast that it spread well beyond New England and evolved into regional variations in both the South and the Midwest. Sadly, the rapid decline of Eastern oyster populations after World War II (more on page 190) meant it would also decline as a common household meal.

The difference between a soup and a stew is really just the amount of liquid. Soups are brothier and stews are thicker, the latter coming from a higher ratio of meat and vegetables to broth and/or an extended simmering to reduce the broth to a thicker consistency.

You can find many examples of brothy soups and stews in New England cookbooks published prior to World War II. But, as opposed to clam chowder or bisque, which don't venture too far from somewhat standardized recipes, a brothy soup recipe from one cookbook would be completely different from a brothy soup recipe in another. I consider this a good thing! That means there's more room for creativity and improvisation with these recipes. There's no standardized versions of these recipes to judge them by. So have no fear! Have fun with these recipes and allow your taste buds to be the true judge. If you feel the need to add or subtract something, by all means, follow your intuition.

FISH SOUPS

It was the summer of 1999 and I was on an epic cross-country trip. A few weeks before heading to Alaska I was on the Pacific coast with a college buddy. We were driving up scenic Route 101 and decided to stop for a meal in Newport, Oregon. We took a wrong turn off the highway and found ourselves not in the touristy downtown area but near the fishing docks. Now, at first, we didn't see the fishing docks. But man, could we smell them. The scent of fish was so strong that it was unmistakable. Many people would undoubtedly describe it as "fishy" and "gross." But to me, it smelled beautiful, like a salty sea breeze that carries with it all those mysterious scents of muddy marshes and the creeping creatures that lurk within when the tide rolls out.

The lap of the water on the piers, the setting sun, the call of seagulls, and that alluring smell of the sea made me want to stay forever in that moment. I wondered how much of the fish that was caught there really wound up in the tourist restaurants on the other side of town. I wondered why the other side of town, with nary a view of the water, and so many seafood restaurants, was so separate from this place that seemed more connected to the sea. Why couldn't there be at least one fish shack, one little café serving whatever it was those rusty, worn fishing boats caught? I'd take an old-time shanty serving up fresh seafood anyday.

In *Provincetown Seafood Cookbook*, Howard Mitcham writes, "Modern packaging and the supermarket have really murdered the nice smells which gave glamour, mystery and seductiveness to the old-time grocery store."[16] I think it's done the same to many of our once-thriving fishing communities, too. Modern supermarkets have harmed many other aspects of our seafood. For example, they've also done away with the popularity of the whole fish.

Rarely does anyone purchase a whole fish in America anymore. Their nutrient-rich heads, bones, tails, and trimmings, which provide the basis for a good fish stock and therefore a good fish soup, are just thrown away. How crazy is that?!

But in many countries, vibrant early morning seafood markets still thrive. Fishing boats roar in before the sun rises, and people buy their seafood *direct* from the fishermen and fisherwomen. Freshly caught fish, often still thrashing in buckets, are sold in whole form. The fishermen or a family member who's part of the business may fillet the fish for a customer, but the customer will also get the carcass.

There are countless examples of traditional brothy fish soup recipes from around the world. In New England, the early chowders were actually made with fish and fish stock. Rustic whitefish soups like cod soups, haddock soups, and flounder soups never caught on like chowders, but creative home cooks learned to embellish them with different combinations of herbs, spices, fruit, wine, and even beer. Besides making your own fish stock, you can draw some inspiration from these cooks to add creative touches that bring out additional depths of flavor. Making a good fish soup is a bit of a lost art form, but it can be revived one pot at a time.

Adding some potatoes or rice to fish soups is optional, but these ingredients will make a heartier, fuller meal. Feel free to add either when you see fit in any of these recipes. Personally, I prefer the texture and flavor of rice with brothy seafood soups. I find that potatoes edge a recipe a little more toward a chowder-like soup than a brothy soup.

Finally, most of the recipe titles in this section include two fish. The first ones listed are those that tend to be available year-round. The second ones, those in parentheses, are more undervalued and thus tend to be less commercially available, or they're just more seasonal in their availability. They're simply suggested but highly recommended alternative choices. But really, you can substitute any lean mild whitefish or any full-flavored fatty fish in any of these recipes and the soups will still be delicious. Seek out whatever is in season and, of course, try different species to expand your knowledge and taste buds.

Monkfish (or Dogfish) Soup with Ginger, Lemongrass, and Lime

SERVES 4 TO 6

In Barton Seaver's brilliant seafood cookbook, *Two If By Sea*, he recommends a squeeze of lime with fresh oysters instead of lemon. The acidity and sweetness of lime can enhance the flavor of oysters just as well, if not better than, lemon.

I always have *both* lime and lemon in my fridge so that I can taste which one I prefer in my soups. In this recipe, lime was the clear winner. When paired with ginger, lemongrass, and cilantro, it gives the broth a Southeast Asian–inspired feel without it venturing too far into the realm of a true Southeast Asian soup. The mild sweetness of both the butternut squash and the monkfish are perfect with lime. Start with 2 tablespoons of lime juice, taste, and add more to your liking. I think 4 tablespoons (about the juice of a 1 lime) is just about right for this recipe.

If the monkfish fillet is covered with a gray membrane (this is normal), be sure to remove it. Otherwise, the meat will shrink and toughen when cooked. Also, know that the lemongrass is meant to infuse the soup—it's too fibrous to eat. You can remove it before serving or leave it in to improve the flavor of the soup over time. Finally, though still rare to find, dogfish, with its meaty, dense fillets would be a fantastic alternative to monkfish.

Ingredients

1 tablespoon olive oil

1 small to medium leek or ½ large leek, white part only, cut in half lengthwise, diced into ½-inch pieces

One 1-inch piece ginger, peeled and diced

2 to 3 garlic cloves, diced

½ cup dry white wine

1 lemongrass stalk, bottom half only, sliced into ¼-inch rings

1 quart Robust Fish Stock (page 74)

2 cups butternut squash, peeled and chopped into bite-sized cubes

2 to 4 tablespoons lime juice

1½ pounds monkfish, gray membrane removed, or dogfish, cut into 1-inch chunks or substitute another lean, mild whitefish (see Chapter 2)

1 cup cilantro leaves, chopped and tightly packed, and/or ¼ cup mint leaves, chopped and loosely packed

Salt

Optional seasonings, to taste

Salt and freshly ground black pepper

Fresh cilantro and/or mint leaves, chopped

Crushed red pepper flakes

Fresh lime juice

(continued)

Instructions

1. Heat the olive oil over medium heat in a medium stockpot. Sauté the leeks and ginger for 5 minutes, or until
the leeks soften. Add the garlic in the last minute.

2. Add the wine, raise the heat, and simmer for a few minutes or until it's slightly reduced. Then add the lemongrass and fish stock. Bring to a gentle boil, reduce the
heat, and simmer for about 10 minutes.

3. Add the butternut squash and simmer for another 10
to 15 minutes, or until the squash is tender.

4. Add 2 tablespoons of the lime juice and the monkfish.
Simmer very gently a few minutes more until the fish
is cooked through.

5. Taste and add another 1 to 2 tablespoons lime juice, if
desired.

6. Stir in the cilantro and simmer 1 more minute.

7. Add salt to taste.

8. Ladle into individual bowls and add optional seasonings to taste.

Lemony Haddock (or Black Sea Bass) Soup

SERVES 4 TO 6

This recipe is a good example of how both salt and citrus can transform a soup. Before adding either at the end, give the soup a taste. You'll probably notice it tastes good but not out-of-this-world good. Then add the lemon and salt to taste. Almost instantly, the anise flavor of the fennel and tarragon, the light creaminess, and all the spices meld into a magical elixir of soup heaven.

You can't go wrong with haddock in this recipe. Its mild sweetness is a nice complement to the other flavors. However, if you can find black sea bass in markets, it makes an even better choice. Its texture is a little firmer and it has a slightly more complex flavor profile.

Also, there's a reason that the word *lemony* is in the title of this recipe. Start with 2 tablespoons, taste, and add more, as needed. Personally, I think 2 tablespoons is the perfect amount, giving the soup a pronounced lemony flavor without being overly lemony.

Ingredients

2 tablespoons olive oil

½ medium yellow onion, diced into ½-inch pieces

½ fennel bulb, core removed, diced into ½-inch pieces

2 to 3 garlic cloves, diced

½ cup white wine

1 quart Robust Fish Stock (page 74)

1 bay leaf

Pinch of saffron threads, crushed (about 20)

¼ teaspoon ground allspice

1 to 1½ cups heavy cream or half-and-half

1½ pounds haddock fillets, cut into 3- to 4-inch chunks, or substitute any other whitefish (see Chapter 2)

1 cup loosely packed fresh tarragon leaves, plus more to taste

2 tablespoons lemon juice, plus more to taste

Salt

Optional seasonings, to taste

Salt and freshly ground black pepper

Fresh lemon juice

Pinch of paprika or cayenne

Hot sauce of your choice

Old Bay or another seafood seasoning blend

Fresh parsley, chopped

Instructions

1. Heat the olive oil over medium heat in a medium stock-pot. Sauté the onions and fennel for 5 minutes or until softened. Add the garlic in the last minute.

2. Add the white wine, raise the heat, and simmer for several minutes or until it's slightly reduced.

3. Add the fish stock, bay leaf, saffron, and allspice and bring to a gentle simmer. Simmer for 10 minutes with the lid on.

4. Add 1 cup of the cream and stir in. Taste and add another ½ cup cream, if desired.

5. Add the haddock and simmer very gently for a few minutes, or until it's cooked through.

6. Add the tarragon leaves and stir in.

7. Turn the heat off and then add 2 tablespoons lemon juice slowly, stirring it well, to prevent the cream from curdling. Taste and add more lemon juice or tarragon leaves to taste.

8. Add salt to taste.

9. Ladle into individual bowls and add optional seasonings to taste.

Portuguese Two Fish Soup

SERVES 4 TO 6

If you've never made a Portuguese recipe before, this is a great one to start with. It's quite simple and will introduce you (and probably hook you) to the unique flavors of Portuguese cuisine. In particular, the broth is infused with the smoky, slightly spicy flavor of chourico, one of Portugal's most iconic foods. Canned diced tomatoes give the soup an extra burst of robust richness, and the white wine adds a bright, acidic background flavor. The cumin, saffron, and parsley, which are common Portuguese spices and herbs, add further depths that rouse the flavor of any fish, lean or not. But in this recipe, it's great to try both!

In *Provincetown Seafood Cookbook,* Howard Mitcham quotes a chef who says when making a fish soup to always "use two different species of fish, one white and lean and the other fatter and richer. This way they'll counterbalance one another and add zip to your 'zoop.'"[17] I like that advice very much. For a lean, mild whitefish, it's hard to go wrong with cod because it's quintessential to Portuguese cuisine. However, Atlantic pollock would certainly be a more sustainable choice. For an oily, full-flavored fish I recommend mackerel or swordfish. In the end, there are so many wonderful Portuguese flavors comingling together that you really can't go wrong with whatever two fish you choose.

Ingredients

1 tablespoon olive oil

1 yellow onion, diced into ½-inch pieces

1 link chourico sausage, sliced into ¼-inch rounds

2 garlic cloves, diced

½ cup dry white wine

One 14-ounce can diced tomatoes

1 quart Robust Fish Stock (page 74)

Pinch of saffron threads, crushed (about 20)

½ teaspoon ground cumin

1 cup chopped parsley, loosely packed

1 pound any lean, mild whitefish (see all options in Chapter 2)

1 pound any oily, full-flavored fish (see all options in Chapter 2)

Salt

Optional seasonings, to taste

Salt and freshly ground black pepper

Fresh parsley, chopped

Crushed red pepper flakes

Hot sauce of your choice

Fresh lemon juice

(continued)

Instructions

1. Heat the olive oil over medium heat in a medium stock-pot. Sauté the onion and chourico for 5 minutes, or until the onions are softened. Add the garlic in the last minute.

2. Add the wine, raise the heat, and simmer for a few minutes or until it's slightly reduced.

3. Add the tomatoes, fish stock, saffron, and cumin. Raise the heat and simmer for about 10 minutes.

4. Add the parsley, stir well, and simmer 1 more minute.

5. Turn off the heat, add the fish and let it sit for a few minutes, or until cooked through. Depending on the thickness of the fillets, the fattier fish may need to be added to the soup first as it will take a little longer to cook.

6. Add salt to taste.

7. Ladle into individual bowls and add optional seasonings to taste.

Pesto Noodle Soup with Striped Bass (or Halibut)

SERVES 4

I love this soup in summer when striped bass are running wild along the coasts. Their mild but full flavor and flaky but dense texture is a great fit in this soup, and the nice meaty chunks pair wonderfully with the tender rice noodles. Striped bass are also the least oily of the oily, full-flavored fish, making it a nice complement to the olive oil–based pesto. Halibut is my second choice here if it's outside striped bass season. If you'd like to simplify this recipe, I won't fault you for using a store-bought pesto. However, just know that nothing can beat the vibrant flavor of a homemade pesto from fresh summer basil. Another reason to make this soup in the summer!

Ingredients

For the pesto (makes about 1 cup)

2 cups fresh basil, packed

½ cup pine nuts, walnuts, or cashews

¼ cup grated Parmesan cheese

¼ teaspoon salt

2 garlic cloves, roughly chopped

½ cup olive oil

For the soup

1 tablespoon olive oil

1 medium yellow onion, diced into ½-inch pieces

1 red bell pepper, diced into ½-inch pieces

2 to 3 garlic cloves, diced

¾ cup sun-dried tomatoes

1 quart Robust Fish Stock (page 74)

¼ cup dry white wine

1 package rice noodles, vermicelli or rice stick

1½ pounds striped bass or halibut, cut into 1-inch chunks, or another dense but nonoily fish (see Chapter 2)

Salt

Optional seasonings, to taste

Salt and freshly ground black pepper

Dollop of pesto

Grated parmesan cheese

Fresh lemon or lime juice

(continued)

Instructions

To Make the Pesto

1. Add all the pesto ingredients, except the ½ cup olive oil, to a food processor. Pulse until thoroughly blended.
2. With the blade running, add the olive oil in a slow, steady stream until it forms a paste. Set aside.

To Make the Soup

1. Heat the 1 tablespoon olive oil over medium heat in a medium stockpot. Sauté the onion and red pepper for 5 minutes, or until softened.
2. Add the garlic and sun-dried tomatoes and sauté another 2 to 3 minutes, stirring frequently.
3. Add the fish stock and wine, raise the heat to a gentle boil, and simmer for about 10 minutes.
4. While the broth is simmering, prepare the vermicelli rice noodles according to the package directions.
5. Add the fish and simmer for about 5 minutes, or until tender and cooked through.
6. Add ¼ cup of the pesto and swirl in. Taste. Add more pesto, if desired.
7. Add salt to taste.
8. Add a handful of noodles to individual bowls and ladle soup over the noodles. Add optional seasonings to taste.

Tomato Swordfish (or Mackerel) Soup with Fresh Italian Herbs

SERVES 4

My first version of this recipe was a tomato-mackerel soup. Mackerel's dense, swordfish-like texture and flavor is just fantastic in a hot brothy soup. But getting a pound of mackerel fillets can take some work, as most whole Atlantic mackerel yields only a small amount of meat. By all means, try it if you can. Swordfish, with its thick, large fillets is certainly an easier choice. And it's just as delicious as mackerel. I just love a meaty, rich chomp of swordfish in every spoonful. Fresh, in-season bluefish or striped bass would also be great choices here. In this recipe, tomato paste, as opposed to canned tomatoes, keeps the soup rich in tomato flavor while still retaining a brothy, soupy feel. Finishing it off with fresh sage, parsley, and liberal amounts of fresh basil brings it all together. Add additional fresh leafy herbs to individual bowls as your tastebuds desire. Though optional, adding some white rice can make this a more filling meal.

Ingredients

1 tablespoon olive oil

½ medium yellow onion, diced into ½-inch pieces

2 to 3 garlic cloves, diced

5 to 6 tablespoons tomato paste

1 quart Robust Fish Stock (page 74)

½ cup dry white wine

1 bay leaf

½ tablespoon dried oregano

4 fresh thyme sprigs, leaves removed and stems discarded

1 tablespoon fresh rosemary leaves, chopped

1½ pounds swordfish or mackerel, cut into 1-inch chunks, or substitute another full-flavored, oily fish (see Chapter 2)

1 cup fresh basil, loosely packed, plus more to taste

1 tablespoon fresh sage, chopped, plus more to taste

6 fresh parsley sprigs

Salt

2 cups precooked white rice (optional)

Optional seasonings, to taste

Salt and freshly ground black pepper

Fresh basil, chopped

Fresh parsley, chopped

Fresh sage, chopped

Red pepper flakes

Instructions

1. Heat the olive oil over medium heat in a medium stock-pot. Sauté the onion for 5 minutes, or until softened. Add the garlic in the last minute.

2. Add the tomato paste and stir frequently for 5 minutes, allowing the paste to brown slightly. Be careful not to burn it.

3. Add the fish stock, white wine, bay leaf, oregano, thyme, and rosemary and simmer for about 10 minutes.

4. Add the swordfish and gently simmer for 7 to 10 minutes, or until cooked through.

5. Add the basil, sage, and parsley and stir into the soup.

6. Add salt to taste.

7. Add the optional precooked white rice and gently stir into soup. Alternatively, add the rice to the individual bowls.

8. Ladle into individual bowls and add optional seasonings to taste.

Wild Salmon (or Bluefish) and Dill Soup

SERVES 4 TO 6

Certain herbs have a mysterious, almost mystical way of perfectly pairing with a specific food—like tomatoes and basil or watermelon and mint. I think the same could be said for salmon and dill. Bluefish makes a surprisingly good pairing with dill too, though its availability in markets is more limited.

Ingredients

4 tablespoons unsalted butter

1 leek, white part only, cut in half lengthwise, diced into ½-inch pieces

2 carrots, peeled, sliced into ¼-inch rounds

1 quart Robust Fish Stock (page 74)

Pinch of saffron threads, crushed (about 20)

Zest of 1 lemon

1 cup frozen peas

1 cup heavy cream

1 cup dill, chopped and tightly packed, plus more to taste

1½ pounds wild salmon or bluefish fillet, cut into 1-inch chunks, or substitute another full-flavored oily fish (see Chapter 2)

Salt

Optional seasonings, to taste

Fresh dill, chopped

Fresh lemon juice

Salt and freshly ground black pepper

Instructions

1. Heat the butter over medium heat in a medium stockpot. Sauté the leeks and carrots for 5 minutes, or until the leeks soften.

2. Add the fish stock, saffron threads, and lemon zest and simmer for 5 to 10 more minutes, until the carrots are cooked through. Add the peas and simmer for a few more minutes.

3. Add the heavy cream and dill and stir into soup.

4. Add the salmon and simmer very gently for a few minutes, or until cooked through.

5. Add salt to taste. Add more dill, if desired.

6. Ladle into individual bowls and add optional seasonings to taste.

CLAM SOUPS

In *Fish and Shellfish,* author and chef James Peterson writes, "The purpose of clam soup—chowder or otherwise—is to show off the flavor of clams while stretching and accenting their flavor with other ingredients."[18]

One of the best vehicles for this is milk or cream, though because of the way we process milk today, cream is a better choice (please see the Whole Dairy Story on page 99). Our national obsession with New England clam chowder is a pretty good indication of how well clams and cream go together. In particular, it is the clam liquor, held tightly inside the shells, that creates such a pleasing symmetry with cream. But before clam chowder claimed the throne of clam soup supremacy, other incarnations of clams and cream could be found. The most common would be a traditional clam stew, which is basically a brothier stripped-down version of clam chowder.

The first time I made it was one of those magical *aha!* moments when the truth of something is revealed with such clarity that it leaves no doubt. For me, it was the crystal clear understanding of why clam broth (not water, fish stock, or chicken stock) and cream (not milk) should form the foundation of clam chowder. Without any bacon, potatoes, herbs, or flour to interfere, its briny-creamy essence is unmistakable and downright delicious in its own right.

Clam soups can also be made without cream by simply adding stock and/or clam broth in place of cream. These brothy brews have a character all their own that showcases the pure salty sea spirit of clam broth. In contrast to oyster and mussel soups, you do not need to worry about diluting a clam broth with too much stock. Typically, you need to worry about the opposite: a too salty and strongly flavored broth. Depending on the salinity of your clam broth, brothy clam soups can range from mildly briny to mouth-puckering briny. In the case of the latter, adding some water, fish stock, or chicken stock can help mellow it out.

Traditional Clam Stew

SERVES 2 OR 3

Compared to the longer time needed to prepare a clam chowder, a traditional clam stew can be whipped up in a matter of minutes. All you need besides clams is something in the onion family, some butter, and some cream. With so few ingredients, it's the bright briny flavor of fresh clams, clam broth, and good-quality cream that should predominate. The flavor is so hauntingly sublime that it is a wonder that clam stew has gone out of fashion. Make this recipe just once and you'll have a newfound appreciation for why New Englanders started adding clams and broth to cream hundreds of years ago.

A 2:1 ratio of cream to clam broth is a pretty reliable marker for a consistently great flavor. I also recommend using whole clams, as opposed to chopping them up. There's something about slurping up a big juicy whole clam in a salty spoonful of cream and broth that makes the experience of eating a traditional clam stew that much more extraordinary.

Ingredients

2 dozen cherrystone clams or 3 dozen littleneck clams

2 cups water

1 cup Hard-Shell Clam Broth (page 86)

1 tablespoon butter

½ cup onion, leeks, or shallots, diced into ½-inch pieces

2 cups heavy cream

Optional seasonings, to taste

Fresh parsley, chopped

Freshly ground black pepper

Seafood seasoning blend

Fresh lemon juice

Dollop of butter

Hot sauce of your choice

Instructions

1. To make the clam broth: Clean the clams of any grit by rinsing in cold, running water and scrubbing clean.

2. Add the 2 cups of water to a large stock pot and bring it to a rolling boil. Add the 2 dozen cherrystone or 3 dozen littleneck clams and make the clam broth according to the instructions on page 86 (ignore the small discrepancies in the amounts of water and clams). You should get about 2½ to 3 cups broth total.

3. Let the clams cool down for a few minutes and then remove the clam meats from their shells. Set aside.

4. Melt the butter over medium heat in a small stockpot. Add the onions and sauté 5 minutes, or until softened.

5. Add the cream, 1 cup clam broth, and clam meats. Heat to just below boiling and serve immediately.

6. Ladle into individual bowls and add optional seasonings to taste.

Spinach-Tarragon Clam Soup

SERVES 3 OR 4

Whole littlenecks submerged in their own broth is a wonderful and underappreciated way to consume them. It really brings out their salty sea essence and allows for creative combinations of other herbs, spices, and vegetables. In this recipe, the tarragon infuses the broth with a wonderful anise flavor, so don't be afraid to add it in generous amounts. I also *highly* recommend adding some additional lemon juice and seafood seasoning at the end.

Ingredients

3 dozen littleneck clams

2 cups water

3 cups Hard-Shell Clam Broth (page 86)

2 tablespoons olive oil

1 small yellow onion, diced into ½-inch pieces

1 cup plum tomatoes, quartered lengthwise and sliced into ½-inch pieces

2 to 3 garlic cloves, diced

½ cup dry white wine

1 bag loose-leaf spinach, about 8 ounces

1 cup tarragon leaves, loosely packed, chopped

1 tablespoon fresh lemon juice

Optional seasonings, to taste

Old Bay or a similar seafood seasoning blend (*highly* recommended)

Fresh lemon juice (*highly* recommended)

Tarragon leaves, chopped

Hot sauce of your choice

Salt and freshly ground black pepper

Instructions

1. To make the clam broth: Clean the clams of any grit by rinsing in cold, running water and scrubbing clean.

2. Add the 2 cups of water to a large stock pot and bring it to a rolling boil. Add the 3 dozen littleneck clams and make the broth according to the instructions on page 86 (ignore the small discrepancies in the amounts of water and clams). You should get about 2½ to 3 cups

(continued)

broth total. Add ½ cup water to measure 3 cups broth total, if needed.

3. Let the clams cool down for a few minutes. Leave them whole in their shells and set aside.

4. Heat the olive oil over medium heat in a medium stockpot. Add the onion and sauté for about 5 minutes, or until softened.

5. Add the tomatoes and sauté 2 to 3 more minutes. Add the garlic and sauté 1 more minute.

6. Add the wine and simmer for a few more minutes until slightly reduced. Add the clam broth and bring to a gentle simmer.

7. Add the spinach and tarragon and stir until the spinach wilts, 1 to 2 minutes. Add the reserved whole clams and lemon juice.

8. Ladle into individual bowls and add optional seasonings to taste.

Clams Newburg Soup

SERVES 2 OR 3

A classic seafood Newburg sauce, often served over lobster, is typically made with butter, cream, paprika, sherry, and thickened with flour and egg yolks. However, it can be easily adapted into a luscious soup by replacing the flour with an equal mix of cream and broth. Stirring in a few egg yolks will help to maintain an element of thickness. As good as that foundation may be, the true moment of metamorphosis occurs at the end when the savory tang of the Worcestershire sauce and the bright acidity of the lemon juice gel with the sweetness of the wine, the smoky heat of the cayenne, and the briny-rich base of the clams and cream. It may make you wonder, as it did me, why something this good never caught on in soup form.

Ingredients

2 dozen cherrystone or 3 dozen littleneck clams

2 cups water

1 cup Hard-Shell Clam Broth (page 86), or slightly more

3 tablespoons butter

Pinch of cayenne pepper

2 tablespoons sherry or Madeira wine

1 cup heavy cream, plus more to taste

2 egg yolks, beaten

¼ cup fresh chives, chopped, plus more to taste

1 tablespoon Worcestershire sauce, plus more to taste

1 tablespoon fresh lemon juice, plus more to taste

Optional seasonings, to taste

Freshly ground black pepper

Fresh lemon juice

Fresh chives, chopped

Worcestershire sauce

Paprika

Old Bay or other seafood seasoning blend

Hot sauce of your choice

Instructions

1. To make the clam broth: Clean the clams of any grit by rinsing in cold, running water and scrubbing clean.

2. Add the 2 cups of water to a large stock pot and bring it to a rolling boil. Add the 2 dozen cherrystone or 3 dozen littleneck clams and make the broth according to the instructions on page 86 (ignore the small discrepancies in the amounts of water and clams). You should get about 2½ to 3 cups broth total.

3. Let the clams cool down for a few minutes and then remove the clam meats from their shells. Chop the larger clams into smaller pieces, if desired. Set aside.

4. Melt 3 tablespoons of the butter in a small to medium stockpot. Add the cayenne and wine and simmer for a few minutes until the wine is slightly reduced.

5. Add the 1 cup of clam broth and heavy cream and heat to just below a steady simmer.

6. Scoop out a few tablespoons of the soup broth, blow on it to cool it slightly, and whisk it with the egg yolks in a small bowl. Continue to add small amounts of broth to the yolks and continue whisking until you have about a cup and then add it back into the stockpot, stirring it in.

7. Add the clam meats and stir in.

8. Add the chives, Worcestershire sauce, and lemon juice and stir. Taste and add more of each, if desired.

9. If more broth and cream are desired, add a little more of each to taste.

10. Ladle into individual bowls and add optional seasonings to taste.

TWO SOFT-SHELL CLAM SOUPS

There is nothing that makes my mouth water in anticipation more than a bowl of freshly steamed soft-shell clams (also called steamers) with a side of dipping broth and butter. My favorite place for steamers is Mac's on the Pier in Wellfleet on Cape Cod. It's a classic, unpretentious old-time seafood shack set right next to the fishing docks. Watching the sunset over the water in the summer months with good friends and some wine and beer while slurping down those juicy meats with a scoop of melted butter followed by a scoop of salty broth is pure bliss. Doesn't get any better than that in my book (no pun intended), with one exception. You can probably guess what that is. Steamers in a brothy soup!

Admittedly, consuming them in a soup form is highly unusual. Unlike hardshell clams, soft shell clam meats are not easy to neatly remove from their shells after steaming. Their delicate texture can easily fray and tear. Be gentle when removing them and try to keep them whole. But if some fall apart, it's no big deal. Their sublime flavor will infuse the soup and make it that much more delicious.

Steamer Clam Soup in a Tomato-Basil-Lemon Broth

SERVES 2 OR 3

This first Steamer Clam Soup recipe is a good example of how a few basic but contrasting ingredients can complement each other so well in a brothy soup. The sweetness of the tomatoes, the peppery anise-flavored basil, and the acidic lemon juice are a tried-and-true trio that never fails to please.

Ingredients

2 dozen soft-shell clams

1½ cups water

2 cups Soft-Shell Clam Broth (page 87)

3 tablespoons butter

2 medium shallots, diced

2 to 3 garlic cloves, diced

12 to 15 cherry or grape tomatoes, cut in half

½ cup dry white wine or 2 tablespoons Madeira or sherry

1 cup fresh basil leaves, loosely packed, chopped , plus more to taste

1 tablespoon fresh lemon juice, plus more to taste

Optional seasonings, to taste

Freshly ground black pepper

Fresh lemon juice

Fresh basil, chopped

Instructions

1. To make the clam broth: Clean the clams according to the directions on page 84.

2. Add the water to a medium-sized stock pot and bring it to a rolling boil. Add the 2 dozen soft-shell clams and make the broth according to the instructions on page 87 (ignore the small discrepancies in the amounts of water and clams). You should get about 2 cups broth total.

3. Let the clams cool down for a few minutes and then remove the clam meat from the shells. Pull off the black covering from the siphon or slice off the siphon entirely, if you prefer. Set the clam meats aside.

4. Melt the butter in a medium stockpot over medium heat. Add the shallots and sauté for about 5 minutes, or until softened.

5. Add the garlic and tomatoes and sauté another 2 to 3 minutes. Add the wine and simmer a few more minutes until slightly reduced.

6. Add the clam meats and clam broth. Heat to just below boiling. Add the basil and lemon juice and stir in. Taste and add more of each, if desired.

7. Ladle into individual bowls and add optional seasonings to taste.

Steamer Clam Soup in a Ginger-Garlic-Tarragon-Lime Broth

SERVES 2 OR 3

In Southeast Asia, the four classic "S" flavors—salty, sour, sweet, and spicy—often feature in strongly flavored ingredients like superhot chiles or ultrasalty soy sauce. This recipe integrates all four flavors, but in a subtle way to keep the taste buds focused on the true stars of the show: the juicy clams and the delectable broth.

Ingredients

2 dozen soft-shell clams

1½ cups water

2 cups Soft-Shell Clam Broth (page 87)

3 tablespoons butter

½ cup chives, diced

2 to 3 garlic cloves, diced

One 1-inch piece ginger, peeled and julienned

1 cup fresh tarragon, loosely packed, chopped, plus more to taste

1 tablespoon fresh lime juice, plus more to taste

Pinch of red pepper flakes, plus more to taste (optional)

Optional seasonings, to taste

Freshly ground pepper

Fresh lime juice

Fresh tarragon leaves, chopped

Instructions

1. To make the clam broth: Clean the clams according to the directions on page 84.

2. Add the 1½ cups of water to a medium-sized stock pot and bring it to a rolling boil. Add the 2 dozen soft-shell clams and make the broth according to the instructions on page 87 (ignore the small discrepancies in the amounts of water and clams). You should get about 2 cups broth total.

3. Let the clams cool down for a few minutes and then remove the clam meat from the shells. Pull off the black covering from the siphon or slice off the siphon entirely, if you prefer. Set the clam meats aside.

4. Melt the butter in a medium stockpot over medium heat. Add the chives, garlic, and ginger and sauté for a few minutes, stirring frequently.

5. Add the clam broth and clam meats. Heat to just below boiling.

6. Add the tarragon, lime juice, and optional red pepper flakes. Taste and add more of each, if desired.

7. Ladle into individual bowls and add optional seasonings to taste.

MUSSEL SOUPS

Long Island Seafood Cookbook, written by J. George Frederick and published in 1939, could very well have been written about New England. Jutting out into the Atlantic from Manhattan and paralleling the coast of Connecticut for over 100 miles, Long Island is nestled just south of New England and harbors almost identical species of fish and shellfish, and most of the recipes in *Long Island Seafood Cookbook* have similar incarnations in New England cooking. But what makes the book so fascinating and applicable to New England as well is what I call the "hyper-regional" variations in recipes. Frederick captures what eating local was like before eating local was hip and, of course, important. His recipes are named for different towns around Long Island that had developed their own take on recipes that were similar but unique from neighboring communities. But it wasn't written to educate or inspire anyone to eat local. It's just the way it was back then. I'm certain the same hyper-regional dynamic existed in New England, too.

Almost 100 years later, we're only beginning to understand why we need to return to a more local way of eating. Although the hyper-regional food described by Frederick may be a thing of the past, we can at least turn to these old recipes for inspiration, and through them we can relearn simple ways of working with seafood. A good example would be mussels! They're cheap, abundant, and super easy to work with.

Frederick's chapter on mussels includes five different types of brothy mussel soups, something you rarely see anymore. Today, most of us consume mussels in one form, as a steamed appetizer. And there's a reason why steamed mussels are more popular as an appetizer than as a soup. The broth that is released when steaming mussels has a more concentrated mussel flavor compared to a soup. This is because a soup requires the addition of more liquid. Mussel liquor is not as briny as clams and even oysters, and so diluting the mussel liquor with too much liquid can dilute the mussel flavor. However, that doesn't mean it shouldn't be attempted. When that right balance of mussel-flavored broth is achieved, and it is enhanced with aromatic herbs, spices, and other creative touches, mussel soups are as delicious as any soup from the sea.

Generally speaking, 1 pound of mussels will release about ½ cup of liquor when steamed in water. However, this is just an approximation. Because mussels can differ in size and the amount of liquid they hold, you might get a little more or less. Regardless, you might need to add a little clam broth (or another seafood stock) to your mussel broth so that you have enough broth to make a soup.

Oh, how I'd love it if the seafood industry sold bottles of mussel broth like it does clam broth to make a purely mussel soup! Unfortunately, that does not exist yet. (Note: I'd be your first customer if you want to start a mussel broth company.)

When using mussels in soups, you have three choices after steaming them. The first is to leave the mussels in their shells. The benefit of this is that you won't have to spend additional time de-shelling them. If

you go with this option, make sure to serve the soup in wide-mouthed bowls so that the mussels sink into the broth as much as possible. Otherwise, they will be piling on top of each other and falling over the edges of the bowl. Not a big deal, but this will resemble more of a bowl of steamed mussels than a bowl of soup.

The second option is to de-shell all the mussels and then add them back into the soup later. Because there are 20 to 25 mussels in a pound, and you might be using up to 4 pounds for a four-person serving, this will involve some extra time. The upside is that you won't have to pick through shells in the soup, which can be a little bit awkward. Scooping and immediately slurping a plump mussel in a fragrant briny broth is certainly the best way to consume them in soup form. And no wide-mouthed bowls are needed. The third option is half-and-half: De-shell some of them and leave the rest in their shells.

It's totally up to you. Personally, if I'm making these soups for myself, I never de-shell them. I don't mind picking out whole mussels and following it up with a slurp of soup. It all tastes the same. But if I'm making a mussel soup for friends or family, I might de-shell them to provide my guests with an easier, cleaner presentation.

Mussel Dijonnaise Soup

SERVES 3 OR 4

There is a reason why steamed mussels with Dijon mustard and cream is a popular appetizer. They just work magic together, kind of like a great rock band. Making it into a soup by adding broth, herbs, and wine, takes it to a Led Zeppelin (or insert your favorite rock band here) sort of experience. When I was testing this recipe, it was one of the rare ones where I knew immediately that no changes were needed. My recipe testing notes read, "Nailed it! This is a 10 out of 10. An absolute *no doubter*." That said, the ratio of Dijon mustard to cream to broth is subjective. My taste buds say 2 tablespoons Dijon, 1½ cups cream, and 3 cups broth is about as perfect as "Stairway to Heaven." But that's just me. Start on the lower end of my suggested ingredient amounts, and slowly add more to taste.

Ingredients

2 to 4 cups Mussel Broth, page 88

4 to 5 pounds Atlantic blue mussels

2 cups water

2 tablespoons unsalted butter

3 to 4 shallots, diced into ½-inch pieces

2 to 3 garlic cloves, diced

½ cup dry white wine

5 to 6 fresh thyme sprigs, leaves removed and stems discarded

2 to 4 tablespoons Dijon mustard

1 to 1½ cups heavy cream

1 cup fresh parsley, loosely packed, chopped

Salt

Optional seasonings, to taste

Salt and freshly ground black pepper

Fresh parsley, chopped

Fresh lemon juice

Instructions

1. To make the mussel broth: Use the mussels and make the broth according to the instructions on page 88 (if you get less than 4 cups from steaming the mussels, add clam broth or another seafood stock to measure 4 cups)

2. Remove the mussel meats from their shells and set aside. Alternatively, you can leave them in their shells or de-shell some and leave the rest in their shells.

3. Heat the butter over medium heat in a large, wide-mouthed stockpot. Add the shallots and sauté for 5 minutes or until softened.

4. Add the garlic and sauté 1 more minute.

5. Add the white wine and thyme and simmer a few minutes or until the wine is slightly reduced.

6. Add 2 tablespoons of the mustard, 1 cup of the cream, and 2 cups of the broth. Stir together and simmer gently for 1 minute. Taste and add more mustard, cream, and broth to desired taste and consistency.

7. Add the mussels and parsley and simmer for 1 minute.

8. Add salt to taste.

9. Ladle into individual bowls and add optional seasonings to taste.

Atlantic Blue Mussel Mediterranean Soup

SERVES 3 OR 4

Imagine a classic Mediterranean mussel dish with a buttery white wine sauce served over pasta, except without pasta and more brothy deliciousness. Now imagine it with fresh Atlantic blue mussels, sun-dried tomatoes, artichoke hearts, and capers and finished off with a squeeze of lemon, Parmesan cheese, and liberal amounts of basil. That's this soup in a nutshell. And when I say liberal amounts of basil I really mean *liberal*. Seriously, don't be afraid to load it on. On the opposite end of the spectrum, be more conservative with the capers. Albeit delicious, they're intensely flavored little nuggets and even a little too much can overpower the soup.

Ingredients

1 quart Mussel Broth (page 88)

4 to 5 pounds Atlantic blue mussels

2 cups water

2 tablespoons olive oil

1 medium red onion, diced into ½-inch pieces

2 to 3 garlic cloves, diced

1 cup artichoke hearts, cut in half

1 cup sun-dried tomatoes, halved or quartered

4 or 5 fresh thyme sprigs, leaves removed and stems discarded

1 bay leaf

1 teaspoon dried oregano

2 to 3 teaspoons capers

1 cup dry white wine

2 cups freshly chopped basil, plus more to taste

Salt

Grated Parmesan cheese, to taste

Optional seasonings, to taste

Salt and freshly ground black pepper

Fresh basil, chopped

Grated Parmesan cheese

Fresh lemon juice

Instructions

1. To make the mussel broth: Use the mussels and make the broth according to the instructions on page 88 (if you get less than 4 cups from steaming the mussels, add clam broth or another seafood stock to measure 4 cups).

2. Remove the mussel meats from their shells and set aside. Alternatively, you can leave them in their shells or de-shell some and leave the rest in their shells.

3. Heat the olive oil over medium heat in a large stock-pot. Add the red onion and sauté 3 to 5 minutes or until softened.

4. Add the garlic, artichoke hearts, sun-dried tomatoes, thyme, bay leaf, and oregano and sauté another 3 to 5 minutes, stirring frequently.

5. Add the capers and white wine and simmer a few more minutes until the wine is slightly reduced.

6. Add the broth and simmer for about 10 minutes.

7. Add the mussels and simmer for 1 minute.

8. Add the basil and stir in.

9. Add salt to taste.

10. Top with grated Parmesan cheese to taste. Alternatively, leave it out and let each person add it to their individual bowls.

11. Ladle the soup into the bowls and add optional seasonings to taste.

Aromatic Mussel Soup

SERVES 3 OR 4

This is a fairly standard variation on many brothy mussel soup recipes that you'll find sprinkled in old cookbooks. Aromatic vegetables, especially fennel, and aromatic herbs, especially saffron, make for a light yet fragrant and revitalizing soup.

~~~~~~

Ingredients

1 quart Mussel Broth (page 88)

4 to 5 pounds Atlantic blue mussels

2 cups water

2 tablespoons olive oil

½ medium yellow onion, diced into ½-inch pieces

½ fennel bulb, core removed, diced into ½-inch pieces

2 to 3 garlic cloves, diced

½ cup dry white wine

2 Roma or plum tomatoes, diced into ½-inch pieces

Zest of 1 lemon

Pinch of saffron threads, crushed (about 20)

1 bay leaf

5 or 6 fresh thyme sprigs, leaves removed and stems discarded

1 cup loosely packed parsley, chopped

Salt

2 cups precooked white rice (optional)

Optional seasonings, to taste

Salt and freshly ground black pepper

Fresh parsley, chopped

Fennel fronds, chopped

Fresh lemon juice

(continued)

Instructions

1. To make the mussel broth: Use the mussels and make the broth according to the instructions on page 88 (if you get less than 4 cups from steaming the mussels, add clam broth or another seafood stock to measure 4 cups).

2. Remove the mussel meats from their shells and set aside. Alternatively, you can leave them in their shells or de-shell some and leave the rest in their shells.

3. Heat the olive oil over medium heat in a large stockpot and sauté the onion and fennel for 5 minutes or until softened. Add the garlic in the last minute.

4. Add the wine, raise the heat, and simmer for a few minutes or until it's slightly reduced.

5. Add the tomatoes, lemon zest, saffron, bay leaf, thyme, and mussel broth and simmer for 10 minutes.

6. Add the parsley and simmer for 1 minute.

7. Add the mussels and simmer for 1 minute.

8. Add salt to taste.

9. Add some of the optional precooked white rice into individual bowls. Ladle the soup into the bowls and add optional seasonings to taste.

TWO MUSSEL AND BEER SOUPS

It's hard to go wrong with an appetizer of steamed mussels enhanced with a touch of beer. Beer creates some background bitter notes that complement the sweet, briny flavor of mussels and their broth. However, it's easy to go wrong when you combine them into a soup. The bitter taste of beer can easily overpower the mussels. You want the beer flavor to come through, but not too much or not too little. Adding things like cream and citrus can help mellow things out and make the soup more palatable. The ratios of beer, stock, and cream in the two recipes that follow create a nice balance, though feel free to adjust those ratios to your taste buds when adding the cream.

The type of beer is also important. Crisp and light- to medium-bodied maltier beers such as lagers and ambers work better than heavier, darker, and hoppier beers like IPAs and stouts. These two recipes are fairly distinct from each other with different combinations of citrus, herbs, and spices. Let your intuition tell you which one you think you'd like better, and make that recipe. Then, make the other one and see if you were right! You'll see the different ways that beer, mussels, and other ingredients can play off each other. You might even be inspired to create your own mussel-beer soup using similar but different ingredients. The possibilities are endless.

Malty Mussel Soup

SERVES 3 OR 4

In this first recipe, the richer of the two, I've employed a medium-bodied amber beer. It's not so malty that it overpowers the other flavors, but it certainly enhances the delicate mussels and their broth, providing a layered flavor element that works beautifully with herbs, spices, and seasonings.

Ingredients

1 cup Mussel Broth (page 88), plus more to taste

4 to 5 pounds Atlantic blue mussels

2 cups water

2 tablespoons butter

1 fennel bulb, diced into ½-inch pieces

4 to 5 fresh thyme sprigs, leaves removed and stems discarded, or 1 teaspoon dried thyme

1 bay leaf

5 or 6 allspice berries or ½ teaspoon ground allspice

2 to 3 garlic cloves, diced

One 12-ounce bottle amber beer

1½ to 2 cups heavy cream

1 cup fresh dill, loosely packed, plus more to taste

2 tablespoons lemon juice, plus more to taste

Salt

Optional seasonings, to taste

Salt and freshly ground black pepper

Fresh dill, chopped

Fennel fronds, chopped

Fresh lemon juice

Instructions

1. To make the mussel broth: Use the mussels and make the broth according to the directions on page 88.

2. Remove the mussel meats from their shells and set aside. Alternatively, you can leave them in their shells or de-shell some and leave the rest in their shells.

3. Melt the butter over medium heat in a large, wide-mouthed stockpot. Add the fennel, thyme, bay leaf, and allspice. Sauté for 5 minutes or until fennel is softened, stirring frequently.

4. Add the garlic and sauté for 1 more minute.

5. Add the beer and 1 cup mussel broth and bring to a simmer for about 10 minutes.

6. Add 1½ cups cream and dill. Add 2 tablespoons lemon juice slowly and stir well to prevent cream from curdling. Taste. If desired, add more cream, broth, and lemon juice to taste.

7. Add the mussels and simmer for 1 minute. Add more dill, if desired.

8. Add salt to taste.

9. Ladle into individual bowls and add optional seasonings to taste.

PBR Mussel Soup

SERVES 3 OR 4

Here, my beer of choice is Pabst Blue Ribbon (PBR), a cheap brand-name lager that incites as much heated debate among beer enthusiasts as chowder among chowder-heads. Some love it, some hate it, but its light, crisp, fairly neutral flavor works perfectly in this recipe. Use another lager if you prefer.

Ingredients

1 cup Mussel Broth (page 88), plus more to taste

4 to 5 pounds Atlantic blue mussels

2 cups water

2 tablespoons butter

2 to 3 medium shallots, diced into ½-inch pieces

One 1-inch piece ginger, diced

1 bay leaf

4 or 5 thyme sprigs, leaves removed and stems discarded, or 1 teaspoon dried thyme

4 or 5 juniper berries or ½ teaspoon ground juniper

2 to 3 garlic cloves, diced

2 Roma or plum tomatoes, diced into ½-inch pieces

One 12-ounce bottle Pabst Blue Ribbon (PBR) or any lager beer

1½ to 2 cups heavy cream

1 cup cilantro, loosely packed, plus more to taste

¼ cup to ½ cup lime juice, from 1 to 2 limes, plus more to taste

Salt

Optional seasonings, to taste

Salt and freshly ground black pepper

Fresh lime juice

Fresh cilantro, chopped

Instructions

1. To make the mussel broth: Use the mussels and make the broth according to the instructions on page 88.

2. Remove the mussel meats from their shells and set aside. Alternatively, you can leave them in their shells or de-shell some and leave the rest in their shells.

3. Melt the butter over medium heat in a large, wide-mouthed stockpot. Add the shallots, ginger, bay leaf, thyme, and juniper. Sauté for 5 minutes or until the shallots are softened, stirring frequently.

4. Add the garlic and tomatoes and sauté another few minutes.

5. Add the beer and 1 cup mussel broth and bring to a simmer for about 10 minutes.

6. Add 1½ cups cream and cilantro. Add ¼ cup lime juice slowly and stir well to prevent cream from curdling. Taste. If desired, add more cream, broth, and lime juice to taste.

7. Add the mussels and simmer for 1 minute. Add more cilantro, if desired.

8. Add salt to taste.

9. Ladle into individual bowls and add optional seasonings to taste.

OYSTER SOUPS

It's hard to imagine it today, but from the second half of the 19th century up until about World War II, oysters were so prolific on the East Coast that one could get them for less than a penny apiece. Originally published in 1941, *Consider the Oyster,* a book written by the great American food writer M. F. K. Fisher, documents this time and includes recipes for several types of oyster soups, including oyster stew. Following World War II our native oyster beds experienced a precipitous decline due to overharvesting and pollution. By the 1970s oyster production in the United States had fallen to a mere 1 percent of its peak years in the early 20th century.

The good news is that in recent years there's been a resurgence thanks to better water quality, improved conservation of native oyster habitat, and a growing oyster farming industry that uses sustainable practices. The overwhelming majority of these oysters are sold to restaurants where they're consumed raw and on the half shell. Now, I'm not even going to pretend that oysters on the half shell are not the best way to consume oysters. For a brief second, that intense shot of oyster flavor, enhanced with a little squeeze of lemon (or better yet, lime!), submerges you into a subhuman realm of salty serenity. For oyster connoisseurs, it is pure bliss. But historically, they were prepared and consumed in many other ways. So, in honor of M. F. K. Fisher and all the great

cooks and seafood connoisseurs of the past, the time is now right to *reconsider* the oyster as a soup or stew. Let me give you three very specific reasons why.

First, oyster soups are delicious! Though oysters don't release nearly as much liquid from their shells as other shellfish, the liquor contained within is intensely flavorful. It delivers a powerful punch of concentrated oyster flavor that, when added to water or fish stock, infuses it with a beautiful oyster flavor. Oyster liquor is kind of like an oyster-flavored bouillon cube, only without any artificial flavorings and nasty chemicals.

Second, in soup form, oysters are more economical than raw and on the half shell. Oysters are not cheap anymore, and that's actually a good thing. Most native oyster beds have either disappeared completely or are slowly recovering. Most of what we consume is coming from well-managed aquaculture farms with a limited supply. Thus, the high cost. But you only need three or four oysters to make an intensely flavored bowl of oyster soup. A dozen oysters will make two servings of soup and possibly even three or four servings for more modest-sized portions.

And third, you get to relish the flavor of oysters much longer compared to eating them on the half shell. Each spoonful bursts with an oyster brininess that you can savor to the last drop in your bowl.

Traditionally, most oyster soups and stews are cream based, the best example being oyster stew. Oyster liquor in combination with a creamy base is as natural and delicious a fit as it is with clams. And though oyster soups without cream are actually quite rare, oyster liquor is as adaptable to a brothy base as it is to a creamy one. You'll find two purely broth-based oyster soup recipes here, as well as two cream-based ones. Twelve oysters is the minimum needed for each recipe, though you can add as many as you want. Cost can be prohibitive today, but if you can find them on the cheap, two dozen oysters per recipe would be an ideal amount.

It's important to note that finding that perfect ratio of oyster liquor to stock and/or broth can sometimes be challenging. Adding the liquor from a dozen oysters to a quart of stock and/or broth is obviously less potent than adding the liquor from two dozen oysters. Furthermore, not all oysters have the same flavor or salinity. Generally speaking, colder months are the best time to harvest and eat oysters—they're not reproducing during that time of year, and thus they retain the elements that give them a brighter, brinier flavor. Sometimes a clam broth base instead of fish stock or water (or a combination of clam broth and fish stock) helps boost the briny flavor of an oyster soup. I say it over and over throughout these pages, but recipe ingredients should never be static! Play around with ratios and ingredient amounts and always tweak things to your liking.

Finally, be careful when salting these recipes. Oysters, and oyster liquor especially, are naturally salty so very little, if any, additional salt is ever necessary.

Traditional Oyster Stew

SERVES 2

In the days when oysters were plentiful and cheap, oyster stew was a staple dish up and down the East Coast of the United States. Prior to World War II, cookbooks were replete with oyster recipes. It is thought that the popularity of oyster stew gained steam when mid-19th-century Irish immigrants, following their Catholic customs to avoid eating meat during certain religious holidays, adapted a traditional stew recipe that called for ling, a fish not found in New England waters. Oysters have a chewy texture and briny flavor that is similar to ling, so the adaptation was a natural one and oyster stew was here to stay. The dish became customary to consume on Christmas Eve in many Irish-American communities, and it caught on around the country as a tasty, simple oyster dish.

The key to a good oyster stew is simplicity. The shining star is the oyster liquor that flavors the milk or cream with an intense briny flavor that needs little adornments. Typically, a little cayenne, paprika, or celery salt might be added, but they are not necessary. Finally, there is one addition that I highly recommend, and that is a little dollop of butter. Yes, butter. Old-school New Englanders know this well (and they don't fear butter). It may sound odd to add butter to an already rich, milky stew, but it adds an extra depth of creamy richness that can be oh so very satisfying.

Ingredients

1 dozen Eastern oysters

2 tablespoons butter

1 small yellow onion or 2 to 3 shallots, about a half cup, diced into ½-inch pieces

2 cups whole milk, half-and-half, or heavy cream

Optional seasonings, to taste

Freshly ground black pepper

Dollop of butter

Pinch of paprika, cayenne, or celery salt

Instructions

1. Shuck the oysters and reserve the liquor.

2. Heat the butter over medium heat in a small to medium saucepan. Add the onions and sauté for about 5 minutes or until softened.

3. Add the oysters and sauté until the edges start to curl, a few more minutes.

4. Add the reserved oyster liquor and milk and bring to a very gentle simmer for a few more minutes.

5. Remove from the heat and serve immediately.

6. Ladle into individual bowls and add optional seasonings to taste.

Oysters Rockefeller Soup

SERVES 3 OR 4

Oysters Rockefeller is a classic, richly flavored baked oyster appetizer that typically contains spinach, cheese, and an anise-flavored liqueur. Converting this into a soup is as simple as adding some fish stock or clam broth and adjusting the ingredients to maintain all the quintessential flavors. Turns out an anise-flavored liqueur (like Pernod), oyster liquor, and fish stock (or clam broth) make for a pretty superlative broth. Not to brag, but I was pretty impressed with how well this turned out. Seven of my friends agreed. While testing these recipes I hosted an oyster soup tasting party and made all the recipes in this chapter. Hands down, this was the consensus favorite.

I was also confident I was the first person to ever make an oysters Rockefeller soup. I mean who would think to do that?! Turns out, quite a few people, including Emeril Lagasse, whose recipe ranks #1 on Google. However, Emeril's recipe, and all the other recipes in my Google search, contained cream. The liberal amounts of butter in my recipe, which is needed to cook down the spinach, adds a creaminess that my intuition says is a much better choice. Honestly, I can't imagine this recipe getting any better.

~~~~~~

Ingredients

12 to 24 Eastern oysters

8 tablespoons (1 stick) butter

2 to 3 medium shallots, diced into ½-inch pieces

2 to 3 garlic cloves, diced

¼ cup Pernod or other anise-flavored liqueur

1 quart Basic Fish Stock (page 73), Hard-Shell Clam Broth (page 86) or bottled, or a combination of both

½ cup fresh parsley, chopped, loosely packed

1 bag loose leaf spinach, about 8 ounces, loosely packed

Optional seasonings, to taste

Freshly grated Parmesan cheese (*highly* recommended)

Fresh lemon juice (*highly* recommended)

Salt and freshly ground black pepper

Hot sauce of your choice

Worcestershire sauce

Instructions

1. Shuck the oysters and reserve the liquor. Set both aside.

2. Melt the butter over medium heat in a medium stock-pot. Add the shallots and sauté for 5 minutes or until softened. Add the garlic in the last minute and stir frequently.

3. Add the Pernod and simmer for 1 more minute.

4. Add the stock, oyster liquor, and parsley. Raise the heat to a gentle boil and simmer for about 5 more minutes.

5. Add the spinach, stir in, and simmer for 1 to 2 minutes until wilted.

6. Add the oysters and simmer until the edges curl, 2 to 3 minutes.

7. Ladle into individual serving bowls and add optional seasonings to taste.

Oysters Mariniere Soup

SERVES 3 OR 4

Mariniere is a simple white wine sauce with onions or shallots that's typically enriched with butter or cream. It's often made with steamed mussels, but it suits oysters (and other shellfish) equally well. Add a little more broth and/or stock than what's typically used and voilà, we have another dish that adapts easily into a soup. This is also one of the few recipes in this book that can be enhanced (rather than muddled) when adding a roux of butter and flour. This somewhat depends on the type of wine you use (some white wines are bolder in flavor than others) and the degree of brininess in both the oyster liquor and stock and/or broth. Should all three of those make for a broth that is a little too sharply flavored for your taste buds, a roux can both soften it and, of course, give it a nice creaminess. The good news is you don't have to wait to the end to figure this out. Simply taste the broth after adding the broth and/or stock and oyster liquor and decide for yourself if you'd like to add a roux or not. Cooking should always be like this! It's truly an art form that requires constantly tasting and adjusting until you've hit that sweet moment when you know you've created your own little culinary masterpiece.

Ingredients

12 to 24 Eastern oysters

3 tablespoons butter

3 medium shallots, diced into ½-inch pieces

3 to 4 garlic cloves, diced

1 tablespoon dried thyme

1 tablespoon dried oregano

1 cup dry white wine

3 cups Hard-Shell Clam Broth (page 86) or bottled, Basic Fish Stock (page 73), or a combination of both

1 bay leaf

1 cup fresh parsley, chopped, loosely packed

1 tablespoon fresh lemon juice, plus more to taste

For optional roux (see instructions)

3 tablespoons butter

3 tablespoons flour

Optional seasonings, to taste

Freshly ground black pepper

Fresh lemon juice

Fresh parsley, chopped

Hot sauce of your choice

Old Bay or similar seafood seasoning blend

Instructions

1. Shuck the oysters and reserve the liquor. Set both aside.

2. Heat 3 tablespoons butter over medium heat in a medium stockpot. Add the shallots and sauté for 5 minutes or until softened.

3. Add the garlic, thyme, and oregano and sauté for a few more minutes, stirring frequently.

4. Add the white wine and simmer for a few minutes until slightly reduced.

5. Add the broth, oyster liquor, bay leaf, and parsley. Raise the heat to a gentle boil and simmer for about 5 more minutes.

6. Taste. If the flavors are a tad on the bold side, make a roux (this is a totally optional step!): Melt the butter in a small pan over medium heat and add the flour, whisking together for several minutes, until thickened and smooth. Drizzle this into the soup, stirring constantly, to thicken slightly.

7. Add lemon juice and taste. Add more, if desired.

8. Add the oysters and simmer until the edges curl, 2 to 3 minutes.

9. Ladle into individual bowls and add optional seasonings to taste.

Oysters Bienville Soup

SERVES 3 OR 4

Oysters Bienville is a classic baked oyster appetizer that features mushrooms, Parmesan cheese, sherry, and a rich buttery roux. Similar to Oysters Rockefeller Soup (page 194), the soup form of this classic dish is a matter of adding stock and/or broth and oyster liquor, and adjusting the other ingredients. Adding a little cream in lieu of a roux adds the perfect touch that gives this soup a velvety texture and taste. Season individual bowls with Parmesan cheese for a final touch.

Ingredients

12 to 24 Eastern oysters

4 tablespoons butter

8 ounces mushrooms, roughly chopped into ½-inch pieces

6 scallions, diced into ½-inch pieces

3 to 4 garlic cloves, diced

Generous pinch of paprika (about ¼ teaspoon)

¼ cup dry sherry or ½ cup dry white wine

1 quart Basic Fish Stock (page 73), Hard-Shell Clam Broth (page 86) or bottled, or a combination of both

1 cup cream, plus more to taste

Optional seasonings, to taste

Salt and freshly ground black pepper

Grated Parmesan cheese

Fresh lemon juice

Fresh parsley, chopped

Hot sauce of your choice

Old Bay or a similar seafood seasoning blend

Instructions

1. Shuck the oysters and reserve the liquor. Set both aside.

2. Heat the butter over medium heat in a medium stockpot. Add the mushrooms and sauté for 5 minutes or until softened. Add the scallions, garlic, and paprika and sauté for a few more minutes, stirring frequently.

3. Add the sherry and simmer 1 more minute.

4. Add the stock and oyster liquor. Raise the heat to a gentle boil and simmer for about 5 more minutes.

5. Add the oysters and simmer until the edges of the oysters curl, 2 to 3 more minutes. Turn off the heat and stir in the cream. Taste and add more cream, if desired.

6. Ladle into individual bowls and season to taste.

LOBSTER AND CRAB SOUPS

You'll find very few recipes for brothy New England lobster and crab soups, be it online or in cookbooks past or present. Lobster soups are mostly relegated to the creamy and richer lobster chowders and lobster bisques. But there is one little-known gem of a brothy lobster soup that still hangs on in Down East country, a Maine lobster stew.

Brothy crab soups are even rarer, which is to say they're virtually nonexistent in New England! Historically, crabs haven't been important commercial fisheries in New England, but that's slowly starting to change with the emergence of the rock crab and Jonah crab. So when I decided to include some New England crab soups, I went looking for inspiration in other more crab-centric regions. I found what I was looking for in Maryland and the Chesapeake Bay. There are two popular styles of Maryland brothy blue crab soups—a creamy version that's enhanced with sherry and Old Bay seasoning and a tomato-based version with lots of vegetables. Both of my recipes are inspired by those two, albeit with local New England crabs.

Maine Lobster Stew

SERVES 3 OR 4

The little-known cousin to lobster bisque and lobster chowder, a Maine lobster stew is a much simpler preparation but equally delicious. Similar to other New England–style shellfish stews, a Maine lobster stew is a brothy soup of lobster meat, lobster stock, cream, sherry, and very little else. But there are two secrets that can take it from a delicious soup to an otherworldly one. The first is to age it. If you can, be patient; resist eating the finished stew right away (easier said than done) and put it in the fridge overnight. The flavors will become more rounded and full, just like with chowders. To taste this for yourself, simply try a small portion of the stew as soon as it's done. Try to burn that taste in your memory. Maybe even rate it on a scale of 1 to 10. Then try it the next day, after it has aged, and compare.

The second secret is even lesser known. And that is to add some tomalley (the green paste inside a cooked lobster) and some coral when simmering the onions in butter. The coral is the roe, or the eggs, of a female lobster. It's a somewhat hard, dark red substance that sits inside of a fully cooked lobster. Both the tomalley and coral are considered delicacies by hardcore lobster enthusiasts, and these ingredients add a concentrated dose of lobster flavor. Admittedly, this will not be for everyone. Both can be off-putting in appearance, especially the green tomalley, but these optional ingredients are highly recommended.

Ingredients

1 cup Basic or Robust Lobster Stock (pages 78 and 79)

Two 1¼- to 1½-pound lobsters (see instructions)

3 tablespoons butter

½ small to medium yellow onion, diced into ½-inch pieces

2 to 3 tablespoons lobster tomalley and coral (optional)

¼ cup dry sherry

2 to 3 cups heavy cream or half-and-half or rich milk

Salt

Optional seasonings, to taste

Salt and freshly ground black pepper

Dollop of butter

Fresh chives, chopped

Pinch of paprika

(continued)

Instructions

1. To make the lobster stock: Use the lobsters to make the lobster stock according to the instructions on pages 78 or 79. Steam the whole lobsters, remove the meat from the shells (you'll get 2 to 3 cups total). If possible, do this 1 day ahead. Alternatively, make a lobster stock from leftover carcasses (or use a lobster stock you previously made) and purchase fresh lobster meat.

2. Melt the butter over medium heat in a medium stockpot. Add the onions and the optional tomalley and coral. Sauté about 5 minutes, or until the onions are softened.

3. Add the sherry and the 1 cup of lobster stock and simmer for 5 minutes.

4. Cut the lobster meat into small chunks. Add the meat to the pot and simmer for a few more minutes.

5. Add 2 cups of heavy cream slowly, being careful not to let it boil. Stir well and taste. For a creamier flavor, add up to 1 more cup of heavy cream (for 3 cups total) to desired taste.

6. Add salt to taste.

7. Ladle into individual bowls and add optional seasonings to taste.

New England Jonah Crab Stew

SERVES 3 OR 4

This recipe, which is inspired by creamy Maryland crab soups, is in the tradition of New England shellfish stews. In other words, it is more broth based than it is cream and roux based. Like so many recipes in this book, the unsung hero ingredient is the homemade stock—it creates fresh, sea-tinged background flavors that will keep any seafood lover silently slurping in delight.

Ingredients

2 cups Basic Crab Stock (page 82)

4 pounds Jonah crab claws

3 tablespoons butter

½ medium yellow onion, diced into ½-inch pieces

1 to 2 cups heavy cream or half-and-half

1 tablespoon fresh lemon juice

¼ cup dry sherry

2 teaspoons Old Bay or similar seafood seasoning blend

½ cup loosely packed fresh parsley leaves

Salt

Optional seasonings, to taste

Fresh parsley leaves, chopped

Fresh lemon juice

Splash of sherry

Old Bay or similar seafood seasoning blend

Salt and freshly ground black pepper

Instructions

1. To make the crab stock: Use the Jonah crab claws to make the stock following the instructions on page 82. If possible, do this 1 day ahead. You should get at least a quart of crab stock and 2 cups of crabmeat. Set the crabmeat and stock aside.

2. Melt the butter over medium heat in a medium stockpot. Add the onions and sauté 5 minutes or until softened. Add the 2 cups of crab stock and 2 cups crabmeat. Heat to just below boiling and simmer for about 5 minutes.

3. Add 1 cup heavy cream and the remaining ingredients, except the salt. Simmer gently for a few minutes, stir well, and taste. Add up to 1 more cup of heavy cream to desired taste. Add salt to taste.

4. Ladle into individual bowls and add optional seasonings to taste.

New England Summer Crab Soup

SERVES 3 OR 4

This recipe was inspired by the tomato and vegetable–based Maryland crab soups, but I greatly simplified the amount of vegetables. For whatever reason, the Maryland version includes *loads of vegetables*, which simply doesn't appeal to me. I want a pronounced crab flavor not a vegetable soup with a little crabmeat (no offense to my mid-Atlantic seafoodies). It reminded me a little of the many Manhattan clam chowders that get drowned out by too many vegetables and not enough clam flavor. So I used fresh New England summer corn in a soup base of tomatoes and crab stock with generous amounts of Jonah crabmeat (feel free to substitute rock crab, or local New England blue crab). I thought the result was absolutely outstanding. Though you could also make this in winter with frozen corn, there's nothing quite like the taste of sweet corn picked fresh from the small farms that blanket the rolling green hills and valleys of New England in summer.

Ingredients

3 cups Basic Crab Stock (page 82)

4 pounds Jonah crab claws or 2 pounds New England crab carcasses

3 tablespoons olive oil, more if needed

1 medium onion, diced into ½-inch pieces

2 cups fresh New England sweet corn, sliced off the cob (from about 2 medium ears)

3 to 4 garlic cloves, diced

1 tablespoon Old Bay or similar seafood seasoning blend

One 14½-ounce can diced tomatoes

1 cup loosely packed fresh basil or parsley, chopped

Salt and freshly ground black pepper

Optional seasonings, to taste

Old Bay or similar seafood seasoning

Salt and freshly ground black pepper

Fresh basil or parsley, chopped

Hot sauce of your choice

Instructions

1. To make the crab stock: Use the Jonah crab claws or other New England crabs to make the stock following the instructions on page 82. If possible, do this 1 day ahead. You should get at least a quart of crab stock and 2 cups of crabmeat. Set the stock and crabmeat aside.

2. Heat the olive oil over medium heat in a medium stockpot. Add the onion and corn and sauté 5 to 7 minutes until the onions are softened. Add the garlic and seafood seasoning in the last minute and stir frequently to prevent burning. Add more olive oil if necessary.

3. Add 3 cups of the crab stock and the diced tomatoes. Raise the heat and simmer about another 5 minutes or until the corn is tender.

4. Add the 2 cups crabmeat, stir well, and simmer another few minutes.

5. Add the basil and stir in gently. Add salt and pepper to taste.

6. Ladle into individual bowls and add optional seasonings to taste.

SCALLOP AND SQUID SOUPS

Squid and scallops are the only seafoods mentioned in this book that you can't use to create a stock or broth. There are no carcasses to simmer in water like with fish and lobster, nor are there liquors to collect from shells like with clams and oysters. Scallops and squid also have fairly mild flavors, which is probably why they're more often used in stews and medleys than in stand-alone broth-based soups. But that doesn't mean they can't make supremely delicious soups on their own. With a base of clam broth and some assertive seasonings and flavors, especially those in the Portuguese style, the five soups in this section are as flavorful as any others.

Portuguese Kale Soup with Scallops

SERVES 4

Sometimes called Portuguese penicillin, Portuguese kale soup is the national soup of Portugal. Staple ingredients for it include linguica or chourico, onions, potatoes, kale, vibrant Portuguese spices, and chicken stock. But there are zillions of variations and as many opinions of what's a true "authentic" version as there are with New England chowders. In my experience, every type of Portuguese kale soup has felt as equally nourishing and delicious as the next. It's one of those soups that naturally integrates different ingredients equally well, including scallops, as demonstrated in this seafood-inspired adaptation.

Ingredients

2 tablespoons olive oil, more if needed

½ medium yellow onion, diced into ½-inch pieces

1 to 2 links linguica or chourico sausage, about 1 cup total, sliced into ¼-inch rounds

3 to 4 garlic cloves, diced

½ teaspoon paprika

¼ teaspoon red pepper flakes, plus more to taste

1 quart Hard-Shell Clam Broth (page 86) or bottled, or 2 cups clam broth diluted with 2 cups Basic Fish Stock (page 73), or water

3 to 4 medium potatoes, roughly chopped into small cubes

1 pound bay scallops, whole, or sea scallops, halved or quartered

1 bunch kale, removed from stems, roughly chopped

Salt

Optional seasonings, to taste

Freshly ground black pepper

Hot sauce of your choice

Fresh parsley or cilantro, chopped

Apple cider vinegar

(continued)

Instructions

1. Heat the olive oil in a medium stockpot over medium heat. Add the onions and sausage and brown the sausage on both sides, about 3 minutes per side.

2. Add the garlic, paprika, and red pepper flakes and sauté another few minutes, stirring frequently. Add additional olive oil, if necessary.

3. Add the broth and bring to a boil. Add the potatoes, reduce the heat, cover, and simmer for 10 to 15 minutes, or until the potatoes are cooked through.

4. Remove the cover, add the scallops, and simmer a few minutes until the scallops are cooked through.

5. Add the kale and simmer until gently wilted, a few minutes more.

6. Add salt to taste.

7. Ladle into bowls and add optional seasonings to taste.

New England-Style Hot and Sour Soup with Scallops

SERVES 4

The only soups that rival my love of New England seafood soups are Southeast Asian soups. My inspiration for this recipe is tom yum goong, a traditional Thai hot and sour shrimp soup seasoned with lemongrass, galangal, fish sauce, lots of lime juice, and hot Thai chiles. I substituted significantly less-spicy jalapeños for the light-your-mouth-on-fire Thai chiles, salty clam broth for fish sauce, and ginger for galangal (also called Thai ginger). The result is a unique New England–style of hot and sour soup—zesty but less fiery, salty but more briny, and most important, instead of farmed shrimp from Asia, sustainably harvested local New England scallops.

Ingredients

1 carrot, peeled

1 jalapeño, deseeded

One 2-inch piece ginger, peeled

2 tablespoons olive oil

1 small to medium yellow onion, diced into ½-inch pieces

2 to 3 garlic cloves, diced

1 quart Hard-Shell Clam Broth (page 86) or bottled, or 2 cups clam broth diluted with 2 cups Basic Fish Stock (page 73) or water

Zest of 1 lime

¼ to ½ cup lime juice, from 1 to 2 limes

1 pound bay scallops, whole, or sea scallops, quartered or halved

1 cup cilantro, loosely packed, chopped

Salt

Optional seasonings, to taste

Salt and freshly ground black pepper

Fresh lime juice

Fresh cilantro, chopped

Instructions

1. Julienne the carrot, jalapeño, and ginger and set aside.

2. Heat the olive oil in a small to medium stockpot over medium heat. Add the onions, carrots, jalapeño, and ginger and sauté 7 to 10 minutes. Add the garlic in the last few minutes.

3. Add the broth and lime zest, bring to a gentle boil, and simmer for about 10 minutes with the cover on.

4. Add ¼ cup lime juice, stir well, and taste. Add up to ¼ cup additional lime juice to desired taste.

5. Add the scallops and simmer about 5 minutes or until tender and cooked through.

6. Add the cilantro and stir in.

7. Add salt to taste.

8. Ladle into individual bowls and add optional seasonings to taste.

Portuguese Squid Soup

SERVES 4 TO 6

This is a fairly straightforward Portuguese-style soup brimming with the flavors of the land and sea. The key is to simmer some linguica or chourico with the olive oil and veggies in the first step. Doing this releases both smoky and spicy flavors into the briny clam broth and tart tomato base. Make sure to adjust the seasonings at the end to your taste. Some extra hot sauce and a few splashes of vinegar can really open up the senses!

Ingredients

3 tablespoons olive oil

1 medium yellow onion, diced into ½-inch pieces

1 fennel bulb, core removed, diced into ½-inch pieces

2 links chourico or linguica sausage, about 2 cups total, sliced into ¼-inch rounds

3 to 4 garlic cloves, diced

1 cup dry white wine

3 cups Hard-Shell Clam Broth (page 86) or bottled, or 2 cups clam broth diluted with 1 cup Basic Fish Stock (page 73) or water

One 14½-ounce can diced tomatoes

Generous pinch of red pepper flakes

3 or 4 fresh thyme sprigs, leaves removed and stems discarded

1 bay leaf

Pinch of saffron threads, crushed (about 20; optional)

1 tablespoon apple cider vinegar

1 pound squid, rings and tentacles

Salt

Optional seasonings, to taste

Salt and freshly ground black pepper

Fresh parsley or cilantro, chopped

Splash of apple cider vinegar

Hot sauce of your choice

Red pepper flakes

Instructions

1. Heat the olive oil over medium heat in a medium stock-pot. Add the onion, fennel, and sausage and simmer for 5 to 7 minutes, stirring often, until the veggies are softened and the sausage is slightly browned. Add the garlic in the last minute.

2. Add the wine and simmer for a few minutes or until slightly reduced.

3. Add the broth, tomatoes, red pepper flakes, herbs, apple cider vinegar, and squid. Bring to a simmer. Cover and continue simmering over low heat for 15 to 20 minutes, or until the squid are tender.

4. Add salt to taste.

5. Ladle into individual bowls and add optional seasonings to taste.

Caldo Verde with Squid

SERVES 4 OR 5

This recipe is based on the classic Portuguese caldo verde soup, also known as a green soup. Traditional versions typically include a base of chicken stock with onion, garlic and potatoes that are blended into a creamy consistency. Linguica or chourico, and a hefty dose of greens, typically kale, cabbage, or collard greens are then added. My seafood rendition includes squid and substitutes clam broth for the chicken stock. It also keeps the potatoes to a minimum, and thus the consistency on the thinner side, so that the flavor of the clam broth shines through. Though some may argue these changes veer too far from the essence of a true caldo verde, all I can say is that the salty clam broth, smoky sausage, earthy greens, and tender pieces of squid is a joyous celebration on my tongue. Finally, I can't overstate how a splash of vinegar and a little drizzle of smoked paprika mixed with olive oil makes this soup taste that much more delicious.

Ingredients

3 tablespoons olive oil

2 links chourico or linguica sausage, sliced into ¼-inch rings

1 yellow onion, diced into ½-inch pieces

3 to 4 garlic cloves, diced

4 cups Hard-Shell Clam Broth (page 86) or bottled, or 2 cups clam broth diluted with 2 cups Basic Fish Stock (page 73) or water

1 pound Yukon gold potatoes, quartered

1 large bunch collard greens, removed from stem

1 pound squid, rings and tentacles

1 tablespoon apple cider vinegar

Salt

½ teaspoon smoked paprika mixed with a few tablespoons olive oil (optional)

Optional seasonings, to taste

Drizzle of smoked paprika and olive oil

Splash of apple cider vinegar

Freshly ground black pepper

(continued)

Instructions

1. Heat the olive oil over medium heat in a medium stockpot. Add the sausage and sauté until browned, a few minutes per side. Remove and set aside.

2. Add the onion and simmer for 5 minutes or until softened. Add the garlic in the last minute. Add the broth and potatoes and bring to a simmer. Cover and simmer gently for 12 to 15 minutes, or until the potatoes are cooked through.

3. Prepare the collard greens. Take 2 to 3 leaves at a time, stack them together, roll them up tightly and slice into very thin strips. Set aside.

4. When the potatoes are cooked through, transfer the soup in batches to a high-speed blender, preferably a Vitamix, and blend until smooth. Return the soup to the stockpot. Alternately, blend using a handheld immersion blender. Be very careful not to splatter hot soup!

5. Next, add the squid. Cover and simmer gently for about 20 minutes or until the squid is tender.

6. Add the collard greens to the soup. How much you add is up to you. You can really load up the soup with the greens or, if you prefer, add a more moderate amount. Either way, simmer for a few minutes until wilted.

7. Add the apple cider vinegar.

8. Taste. It should be salty enough due to the clam broth, but if not, add a little more salt to taste.

9. Add the reserved sausage and stir in. Alternatively, keep the sausage separate and let each person add to their individual serving.

10. Mix the smoked paprika and olive together and drizzle into the soup. This is optional but highly recommended. Alternatively, let each person drizzle in the mixture to their individual serving.

11. Ladle into individual bowls and add optional seasonings to taste.

Traditional Scallop Stew

SERVES 2

Here's another variation of a classic New England milky shellfish "stew"—unpretentious, unadorned, uncomplicated, unimposing, and yet so unbelievably delicious. The congruous union of rich milk, shellfish liquors, and shellfish never fails to satisfy. In the case of a scallop stew, I recommend adding a little dry white wine, which really enhances and accents the milk and clam broth. You can leave smaller scallops whole and halve or quarter larger scallops. Finally, be sure to heed the wise words of old-timer Cap'n Phil Schwind, who in his scallop stew recipe from his book *Clam Shack Cookery*, says, "Serve in hot bowls in which have been placed chunks of butter as big as walnuts."[19] You just gotta love traditional recipes.

Ingredients

2 tablespoons butter

1 small yellow onion or 2 to 3 shallots, about ½ cup, diced into ½-inch pieces

¼ cup dry white wine

½ pound bay scallops, whole, or sea scallops, halved or quartered

½ cup Hard-Shell Clam Broth (page 86) or bottled

2 cups whole milk, half-and-half, or heavy cream

Optional seasonings, to taste

Salt and freshly ground black pepper

Chunks of butter (as big as walnuts)

Fresh chives, chopped

Pinch of paprika, cayenne, or celery salt

Instructions

1. Melt the butter over medium heat in a small to medium saucepan. Add the onion and sauté for a few minutes or until softened.

2. Add the wine and simmer for a few minutes, until slightly reduced.

3. Add the scallops and sauté for 1 minute per side.

4. Add the clam broth and milk, and bring to a very gentle simmer for a few more minutes or until the scallops are cooked through.

5. Remove from the heat and serve immediately.

6. Ladle into individual bowls and add optional seasonings to taste.

Chapter 8

Bisques

Let's face it, bisque comes with a stigma. Though delicious, it has a reputation for being highfalutin; a dish that's often served in fancy restaurants in fine china bowls on white linen tablecloths by waiters wearing white gloves and tuxedos. Not my type of place. And while you can certainly get a good bisque at less pretentious places too, most people would say it's way too time intensive to make at home. Have you ever seen Julia Child's recipe for lobster bisque? Be prepared to spend the entire day in the kitchen. So why even bother, right? Let the professionals make it for you and just enjoy it on occasion. But that's the stigma, not the truth.

While I can't deny that making a bisque is a bit more detailed than, say, making chowder, it doesn't have to be so complicated that you have to spend endless hours making it. I'm sure Julia Child's recipe is out of this world, but it's not the only way to do it. With a little planning ahead and a few time-saving tips and shortcuts, anyone can make a good bisque at home.

What Is Bisque?

Bisque is a creamy, highly seasoned, pureed soup that, in its best form, is made from crustaceans such as lobsters, shrimp, crabs, and crayfish. Some think the word *bisque* comes from *Biscay*, as in the Bay of Biscay, a shellfish-rich region on the western coast of France where bisque originates. Others think it comes from the French term *bis cuites*, or "twice cooked," because to make bisque you cook the shells of crustaceans twice—first by sautéing or roasting them to deepen their flavor and then by simmering them in water, wine, and other aromatic ingredients. And that is really the essence of bisque. It's all about that beautiful, rich, luscious stock. The shells of crustaceans contain a lot of briny tissues, fats, and juices that make wonderfully flavorful stocks. Lobster is by far the most popular bisque, not just because it's so delicious but because it's the easiest of the crustaceans to make into a stock. You need only a few of those spiny beasts compared to, say, dozens of crab or shrimp.

But rules were made to be broken. You don't *have* to use lobsters or even just crustaceans. You can make great tasting bisques from other types of seafood and their respective stocks and broths too. Because once you have your stock, it doesn't take much time to make a bisque. You can then pair your stock with different types of seafood such as clams, oysters, mussels, scallops, salmon, and even whitefish for some really fun and unique twists. There is more to bisque than just lobster bisque!

Five Tips to Make Simple but Delicious Bisques

1. Make Lobster Stock Every Chance You Get

Yes, you can use other types of stocks and broths, but lobster stock really does make the best foundation for a bisque. Of course, this is not the 19th century when lobsters were thought of as poor man's food and were so plentiful that you could go out and gather them at low tide. Few Americans consume lobster on a regular basis anymore. But you might have more access to free lobster shells than you realize. See Lobster Stock (page 75) for tips. Free lobster shells are like free money! Making them into stock, which you can freeze for later use, is like investing that money in the bank. When you have lobster stock on hand, the process of making any bisque is so much simpler.

2. Use Clam Broth in Place of Lobster Stock

There's a good chance you won't have lobster stock on hand. As you know by now, I don't recommend the store-bought boxed seafood broths and stocks. But bottled clam broth can be a suitable and much quicker alternative than making lobster stock. With the exception of lobster bisque (because there's no reason not to make lobster stock from whole lobsters), you can substitute clam broth for any of the recipes in this chapter that call for lobster stock. If you feel the clam broth is too briny, simply dilute it with some water or fish stock.

3. Try Other Types of Seafood

Lobster bisque is the most iconic bisque, but historically other types of seafood were made into bisques too. Clams, mussels, scallops, crabs, and even fish can make some really interesting and delicious bisques as well. And they can be a lot easier on the wallet.

4. Use White Rice as a Thickener

There are different methods to making bisque, but the main difference comes down to the consistency. Some prefer bisques that are ultrarich, some do not. In the case of the former, a roux of flour and butter is typically used to create a smooth and creamy consistency, but, similar to making a chowder, a little too much can make it too rich and heavy. It can also obscure the flavor of the stock that you worked so hard to make.

This is why I prefer to use white rice as a thickener. It gives bisques a lighter, more delicate, slightly grainier quality compared to flour-based thickeners. White rice also has a very neutral flavor that does not interfere with the other flavors and allows that beautiful stock, the true essence of bisque, to shine through. White rice is also consistent in its consistency. A quarter cup of white rice per quart of stock creates, in my opinion, a really nice consistency. I also include some vegetables in my recipes, such as carrots and celery, which are first sautéed in butter and then cooked with the stock and rice. The cooked vegetable fiber provides some additional thickening. To thicken a bisque with rice you simply simmer the rice in the stock until it's tender and then blend everything together. Lastly, white rice is gluten-free, which allows anyone with a gluten allergy or sensitivity to enjoy bisque.

5. Use a Powerful Blender like a Vitamix

A good-quality, high-speed blender creates the perfect silky smooth consistency for a bisque. A Vitamix is the best choice, though other less pricey powerful blenders can do the job too. You could also use an immersion blender. It's certainly easier to use, as you don't have to transfer hot bisque in batches to a blender. Just be aware that it doesn't always blend things as smoothly as a powerful countertop blender.

Lobster Bisque

SERVES 4 TO 6

Think of a cover song you like more than the original version of that song. For me, that would be "Hallelujah" by Jeff Buckley (original by Leonard Cohen) or "All Along the Watchtower" by Jimi Hendrix (original by Bob Dylan). Those interpretations are so iconic that most people think they're the original versions. Well, that's kind of how I look at lobster bisque: It takes lobster and makes it taste even more like lobster than lobster itself. It's almost hard to believe that that's even possible, considering lobster is the most delicious thing on earth, but that, in a nutshell, is what a good lobster bisque is all about.

And the secret, at least to the unassuming consumer, is the rich lobster stock, which, when properly made, concentrates and enhances the flavor from both the shells and the lobstery juices inside the shells. This is why a lobster bisque requires a Robust Lobster Stock (page 79). The meat, previously separated from the shells, can then either be blended back into the bisque or added in whole chunks at the end. I prefer to blend in the meat for a further concentration of flavor. It's that double dose of lobster stock plus lobster meat that gives lobster bisque such a heavenly lobster flavor. Sherry and cream add a sweet richness that makes every lobstery slurp that much more divine.

Ingredients

4 cups Robust Lobster Stock (page 79)

Two 1¼- to 1½-pound lobsters

4 tablespoons unsalted butter

1 medium yellow onion, diced

1 carrot, diced

1 bay leaf

2 garlic cloves, diced

½ cup dry white wine

¼ cup uncooked white rice

2 tablespoons tomato paste

1 to 2 cups heavy cream

2 to 4 tablespoons sherry, plus more to taste

Salt

Optional seasonings, to taste

Salt and freshly ground black pepper

Fresh parsley, chopped

Pinch or two of paprika

Pinch of cayenne

Splash of sherry

(continued)

Instructions

1. To make the lobster stock: Use the lobsters to make a robust lobster stock according to the instructions on page 79. Steam the lobsters and reserve the meat (you'll get 2 to 3 cups total). If possible, do this 1 day ahead.

2. Melt the butter over medium heat in a medium stockpot and add the onion, carrot, and bay leaf and sauté for about 10 minutes until the vegetables are softened. Add the garlic in the last minute.

3. Add the wine, raise the heat, and simmer for several minutes or until it's slightly reduced.

4. Add the 4 cups lobster stock, white rice, and tomato paste. Bring to a boil, cover and reduce heat to a steady boil. Simmer for 10 to 15 minutes, or until the rice is cooked through. Remove the bay leaf.

5. Remove the stockpot from the stovetop and add 1 cup of the lobster meat, or more if desired. Transfer the bisque in batches to a high-speed blender, preferably a Vitamix, and blend into a silky smooth consistency. Return the bisque to the stockpot. Alternately, blend using a handheld immersion blender. Be very careful not to splatter hot soup!

6. Add 1 cup of the cream and 2 tablespoons of the sherry, simmer gently for 2 minutes and taste. Add up to 1 more cup of cream and additional sherry to desired taste. Add salt to taste.

7. Ladle into individual bowls and add optional seasonings to taste.

New England Jonah Crab Bisque

SERVES 4 TO 6

Though similar to a lobster bisque, a crab bisque has its own nuances in flavor. It's slightly sweeter, a tad brinier, and a little lighter in texture. Perhaps one day Jonah crab bisques will rival lobster bisques on New England menus. Though that day is still far off, a homemade version made with a homemade crab stock can be just as delicious as any lobster bisque.

Ingredients

1 quart Basic Crab Stock (page 82)

4 pounds Jonah crab claws or 2 pounds New England crab carcasses

4 tablespoons unsalted butter

1 medium yellow onion, diced

1 carrot, diced

1 small fennel bulb, core removed, diced

1 bay leaf

2 garlic cloves, diced

½ cup dry white wine

2 tablespoons tomato paste

¼ cup uncooked white rice

1 to 2 cups heavy cream or half-and-half

2 to 4 tablespoons sherry, plus more to taste

2 to 4 teaspoons fresh lemon juice, plus more to taste

½ cup loosely packed fresh tarragon leaves, plus more to taste

Sea salt

Optional seasonings, to taste

Salt and freshly ground black pepper pepper

Fresh tarragon leaves

Fresh fennel fronds, chopped

Pinch of cayenne or paprika

Old Bay or similar seafood seasoning blend

Fresh lemon juice

Splash of sherry

(continued)

Instructions

1. To make the crab stock: Use the crab claws or crab carcasses and make the crab stock following the instructions on page 82. If possible, do this 1 day ahead. You should get at least a quart of crab stock and 2 cups of crabmeat (if using crab claws). If using crab carcasses from a previous meal in which the meat has been consumed, you'll probably need to purchase canned crab meat (see Note). Set the stock and crabmeat aside.

2. Melt the butter over medium heat in a medium stockpot and add the onion, carrot, fennel bulb, and bay leaf and sauté for 7 to 10 minutes until the vegetables are softened. Add the garlic in the last minute.

3. Add the wine, raise the heat, and simmer for several minutes or until it's slightly reduced. Add the 1 quart crab stock, tomato paste, and white rice. Bring to a boil, cover, and reduce the heat to a steady boil. Simmer for 10 to 15 minutes, or until the rice is cooked through. Remove the bay leaf.

4. Remove the stockpot from the stovetop and add 1 cup of the crabmeat, or more if desired. Transfer the bisque in batches to a high-speed blender, preferably a Vitamix, and blend into a silky smooth consistency. Return the bisque to the stockpot. Alternately, blend using a handheld immersion blender. Be very careful not to splatter hot soup!

5. Add 1 cup of the cream, 2 tablespoons of the sherry, 2 teaspoons of the fresh lemon juice, and the tarragon. Simmer gently for 2 minutes and taste. Add up to 1 more cup of cream and additional sherry, lemon juice, and tarragon to desired taste.

6. Ladle into individual bowls and add optional seasonings to taste.

TWO CLAM BISQUES

Two types of people enjoy clams. People who like them and people who *love* them. The opinion of people who *love* clams can be summarized in four words: the brinier the better. They crave raw clams on the half shell, steamers dipped in clam broth, and the clammiest clam dishes you can possibly make.

People who like clams don't necessarily love the ultrabriny stuff. Their preferences veer more toward dishes that tone down the saltier side of clams, things like clam chowder, stuffed clams, clam cakes, and so forth.

Regardless of which category you fall into, there's a simple secret to making not just a good clam bisque but an extraordinary clam bisque. Hardly anyone knows this anymore because, let's face it, hardly anyone makes clam bisque anymore. Not even chefs. When's the last time you saw a clam bisque on a menu? I've never seen it, and I'd bet you haven't either.

Another quote from Howard Mitcham, in *Provincetown Seafood Cookbook,* who in his clam bisque recipe description, surreptitiously reveals a clue to the secret: "Now it's almost sacrilegious to ask you to do this, but this soup has to be clear and light colored, so-o-o split the bellies of the clams and rinse out the contents. (I'll never ask you to insult a clam like this again)."[20]

At the very least, Mitcham humorously acknowledges that removing the clam bellies will sacrifice flavor. But I disagree that it has to be a clear soup. After all, I'm not asking you to make this recipe for fussy paying customers. Furthermore, it takes a lot of work to split all those clams and remove the bellies! Why discard them? Most of all, the flavor of a clam bisque made with whole clams is vastly superior to one with the bellies removed. And that is the secret. If Mitcham were alive today, I'd bet a million clam bellies he'd agree.

Traditional New England Clam Bisque

SERVES 4 TO 6

If you're a hardcore clam enthusiast like myself, this classic iteration of clam bisque will satisfy your cravings and then some. Its ultra-briny flavor offers exactly what we adore: a soup that champions clams at their best and boldest!

Ingredients

For the clam broth and clam meats

3 cups Hard-Shell Clam Broth (page 86)

3 dozen littleneck clams or 2 dozen cherrystone clams

2 cups water

For the bisque

2 tablespoons unsalted butter

1 large yellow onion, diced

2 to 3 scallions, diced

¼ cup uncooked white rice

1 cup reserved whole clam meats (from the above clams, see instructions)

½ to 1 cup heavy cream

Optional seasonings, to taste

Freshly ground black pepper

Fresh parsley, chopped

Fresh chives, chopped

Pinch of paprika

Instructions

1. To make the clam broth: Clean the clams of any grit by rinsing in cold, running water and scrubbing clean.

2. Add the 2 cups of water to a large stock pot and bring it to a rolling boil. Add the 3 dozen littleneck clams or 2 dozen cherrystone clams and make the broth according to the instructions on page 86 (ignore the small discrepancies in the amounts of water and clams). You should get about 2½ to 3 cups broth total. Add ½ cup water to measure 3 cups broth total, if needed.

(continued)

3. Let the clams cool for a few minutes and then remove the clam meats from their shells. Alternatively, do this when the rice is simmering. Set the broth and clam meats aside.

4. Melt the butter over medium heat in a medium stockpot and add the onions and scallions and sauté about 5 minutes until softened.

5. Add the clam broth and white rice. Bring to a boil, cover, and reduce the heat to a steady boil. Simmer for 10 to 15 minutes or until the rice is cooked through.

6. Take ¾ cup of the reserved clam meats and add them to the stockpot. Transfer the bisque in batches to a high-speed blender, preferably a Vitamix, and blend into a silky smooth consistency. Return the bisque to the stockpot. Alternately, blend using a handheld immersion blender. Be very careful not to splatter hot soup!

7. Add ½ cup of the cream and taste. Add additional ½ cup of the cream to desired taste.

8. Ladle bisque into individual bowls and add a small handful of the remaining ¼ cup whole clam meats to each bowl. Add optional seasonings to taste.

Tomato-Clam Bisque

SERVES 4 TO 6

If you like the flavor of clams but don't necessarily crave their unadorned pure flavor, this second recipe is the one for you. The tomatoes add a little acidity and sweetness, ultimately creating a dish that softens the strong salty quality of clams but certainly still allows them to shine.

Ingredients

For the clam broth and clam meats

2 cups Hard–Shell Clam Broth (page 86)

3 dozen littleneck clams or 2 dozen cherrystone clams

2 cups water

For the bisque

2 tablespoons unsalted butter

1 large yellow onion, diced

2 to 3 scallions, diced

One 14-ounce can tomatoes

1 tablespoon tomato paste

¼ cup uncooked white rice

½ to 1 cup heavy cream

Optional seasonings, to taste

Freshly ground black pepper

Fresh basil leaves, chopped

Fresh parsley, chopped

Fresh chives, chopped

Red pepper flakes

Pinch of paprika

Instructions

1. To make the clam broth: Clean the clams of any grit by rinsing in cold running water and scrubbing clean.

2. Add the 2 cups of water to a large stockpot and bring it to a rolling boil. Add the 3 dozen littleneck clams or 1½ dozen cherrystone clams and make the clam broth according to the instructions on page 86 (ignore the small discrepancies in the amounts of water and clams). You should get about 2½ to 3 cups broth total.

(continued)

3. Let the clams cool for a few minutes and then remove the clam meats from their shells. Alternatively, do this when the rice is simmering. Set the broth and clam meats aside.

4. Melt the butter over medium heat in a medium stockpot and add the onions and scallions and sauté about 5 minutes until softened.

5. Add the clam broth, tomatoes, and tomato paste and bring to a boil. Add the white rice, cover, and reduce the heat to a steady boil. Simmer for 10 to 15 minutes, or until the rice is cooked through.

6. Take ¾ cup of the reserved clam meats and add them to the stockpot. Transfer the bisque in batches to a high-speed blender, preferably a Vitamix, and blend into a silky smooth consistency. Return the bisque to the stockpot. Alternately, blend using a handheld immersion blender. Be very careful not to splatter hot soup!

7. Add ½ cup of the cream and taste. Add additional ½ cup of the cream to desired taste.

8. Ladle bisque into individual bowls and add a small handful of the remaining ¼ cup whole clam meats to each bowl. Add optional seasonings to taste.

Mussel and Fennel Bisque

SERVES 4 TO 6

The first time I made this recipe I made it the way almost every chef makes a mussel bisque: steam the mussels, strain the broth, and reserve the mussel meats. The bisque is then made in the usual manner, but the mussel meats are added whole at the end.

To be honest, I didn't like it. It just didn't have enough mussel flavor, especially the broth. It tasted more like a mussel soup than a mussel bisque. Remember, bisques are all about a super flavorful broth. And I think mussel broth, as wonderful as it is, is just a little too tame for bisque. So I remade it but with two adjustments. First, I boosted the broth with a little clam broth. And second, instead of leaving the mussel meats whole, I pureed the majority of them into the bisque to give it a more mussel-rich flavor. It worked like a charm.

Every spoonful was thoroughly enhanced with that distinct but subtle sea character of mussels. Yes, the bisque did turn a darker color, which some chefs might find unsuitable for serving. But as a home cook, I'm not overly concerned with presentation. Nourishment and flavor are my primary concerns, and this recipe fulfills both.

~~~~~~

Ingredients

*For the mussel broth
and mussel meats*

4 cups Mussel Broth (page 88) add Hard-Shell Clam Broth (page 86) or bottled, if needed to measure 4 cups total

3 pounds New England blue mussels, rinsed and cleaned

1 cup water

1 cup dry white wine

For the bisque

4 tablespoons unsalted butter

1 fennel bulb, core removed, diced

1 medium yellow onion, diced

1 carrot, diced

1 bay leaf

2 garlic cloves, diced

¼ cup white rice

¼ cup sherry or Madeira

1 tablespoon tomato paste

1 cup reserved mussel meats

1 to 2 cups heavy cream

Fennel fronds, chopped, about ¼ cup, loosely packed

Salt

*Optional seasonings,
to taste*

Salt and freshly ground black pepper

Fennel fronds, chopped

Pinch or two of paprika

Pinch of cayenne

Pinch or two of nutmeg

Splash of sherry or Madeira

(continued)

Instructions

1. To make the mussel broth: Clean the mussels of any grit by rinsing in cold running water.

2. Add 1 cup water and 1 cup dry white wine to a large stockpot and bring it to a rolling boil. Add the 3 pounds of mussels and make the mussel broth according to the instructions on page 88 (ignore the small discrepancies in the amounts of water and mussels). You should get about 3 cups of broth total. Add enough clam broth to the mussel broth to measure 4 cups of broth total.

3. Remove the mussel meats from the shells now or do it later when the rice is simmering. Set the mussel meats aside.

4. Melt the butter over medium heat in a medium stockpot and add the fennel, onion, carrot, and bay leaf and sauté about 10 minutes until softened. Add the garlic in the last minute.

5. Add the 4 cups mussel-clam broth, white rice, sherry, and tomato paste. Bring to a boil, cover, and reduce the heat to a steady boil. Simmer for 10 to 15 minutes or until the rice is cooked through. Remove the bay leaf.

6. Take ¾ cup of the mussel meats and add them to the stockpot. Transfer the bisque in batches to a high-speed blender, preferably a Vitamix, and blend into a silky smooth consistency. Return the bisque to the stockpot. Alternately, blend using a handheld immersion blender. Be very careful not to splatter hot soup.

7. Add 1 cup of the cream and the fennel fronds and stir in. Add up to 1 more cup of cream to desired taste. Add salt to taste.

8. Ladle bisque into individual bowls and add a small handful of the remaining ¼ cup whole mussel meats to each bowl. Add optional seasonings to taste.

Scallop Bisque with Sage

SERVES 4 OR 5

Sea scallops, with their large, buttery meats are perhaps the easiest and most ideal noncrustacean shellfish to make into bisque. Because they always come shelled, all you need to do is add them to your stock, puree it all together, and then add additional herbs, cream, and seasonings. With a premade shellfish stock or broth, you can have it all ready within a half hour, easily. Sage's pine-like aroma and earthy taste beautifully harmonize with the sweet ocean flavor of sea scallops. The result is a fragrant and succulent tasting bisque.

Ingredients

4 tablespoons unsalted butter

1 medium yellow onion, diced

1 carrot, diced

1 celery stalk, diced

¼ cup dry white wine

1½ pounds sea scallops

4 cups Hard-Shell Clam Broth (page 86) or bottled, or Robust Lobster Stock (page 79)

¼ cup uncooked white rice

1 bay leaf

¼ cup fresh sage, 8 to 10 leaves, loosely packed and chopped

1 to 2 cups heavy cream

Salt

Optional seasonings, to taste

Salt and freshly ground black pepper

Sage, chopped

Pinch or two of nutmeg

Pinch or two of mace

Instructions

1. Melt the butter over medium heat in a medium stock-pot and add the onion, carrot, and celery and sauté about 10 minutes until softened.

2. Add the white wine, raise the heat, and simmer for a minute or two or until it's slightly reduced.

3. Roughly chop 1 pound of the sea scallops (reserve the other ½ pound), add to the veggies, and cook for a few more minutes.

(continued)

4. Add the broth, white rice, and bay leaf. Bring to a boil, cover, and reduce heat to a steady boil. Simmer for 10 to 15 minutes, or until the rice is cooked through. Remove the bay leaf.

5. While the rice is cooking, in a separate pan, sear the remaining ½ pound of scallops in butter or oil, a few minutes per side until browned and cooked through. Remove from the pan and set aside.

6. When the rice is cooked through, add the sage. Transfer the bisque in batches to a high-speed blender, preferably a Vitamix, and blend into a silky smooth consistency. Return the bisque to the stockpot. Alternately, blend using a handheld immersion blender. Be very careful not to splatter hot soup!

7. Add 1 cup of the cream and stir in. Add up to 1 more cup of cream to desired taste. Add salt to taste.

8. Ladle into individual bowls and add 1 or 2 of the reserved scallops to each bowl. Add optional seasonings to taste.

Oyster Bisque with Fried Shallots and Garlic

SERVES 4 TO 6

One of my favorite toppings in Southeast Asian soups is fried shallots and garlic. They add wonderful aromas, zing, and crunch to things like congees and noodle soups. It may seem unusual in a bisque, but for this particular recipe, the smoky quality of these toppings helps to slightly soften the acutely briny flavor of this dish. That said, the bisque from this recipe is still *really* briny. The reserved oyster liquor added to the clam broth makes an intensely flavored broth. Three-quarters of the oyster meats are then blended into the bisque, which ups the briny flavor even more. So be warned, this recipe is truly for oyster lovers who crave that ultra-salty tang of the sea!

Ingredients

2 dozen Eastern oysters, shucked, liquor reserved

3 to 3½ cups Hard-Shell Clam Broth (page 86) or bottled, added to oyster liquor for a total of 4 cups

3 tablespoons unsalted butter

3 medium shallots, diced

1 celery stalk, diced

½ cup uncooked white rice

¼ cup sherry or Madeira, plus more to taste

½ to 1 cup heavy cream

For the fried shallots and garlic

4 tablespoons olive oil

2 medium shallots, diced

4 cloves garlic, diced

Optional seasonings, to taste

Freshly ground black pepper

Chives, chopped

Pinch of paprika

Hot sauce of your choice

Splash of sherry or Madeira

Instructions

1. Shuck the oysters and reserve the liquor. You'll get anywhere from ½ to 1 cup oyster liquor. Add 3 to 3½ cups clam broth to measure 4 cups of broth total. Set the broth aside.

2. Melt the butter over medium heat in a medium stockpot and add the shallots and celery and sauté about 5 minutes until softened.

(continued)

3. Add the broth and bring to a boil. Add the white rice, cover, and reduce the heat to a steady boil. Simmer for 10 to 15 minutes or until the rice is cooked through.

4. While the rice is cooking, pan fry the 2 shallots and garlic. Heat the olive oil over medium heat in a small skillet. Add the shallots and sauté about 5 minutes until browned. Stir frequently to prevent burning and to brown evenly. Add the garlic and continue to stir, about another minute or two, or until the garlic also browns evenly. Transfer the shallots and garlic to a paper towel–lined plate and set aside to cool.

5. When the rice is just about done, add the sherry and 18 of the reserved oyster meats. Simmer for a few minutes or until the edges of the oysters curl.

6. Transfer the bisque in batches to a high-speed blender, preferably a Vitamix, and blend into a silky smooth consistency. Return the bisque to the stockpot. Alternately, blend using a handheld immersion blender. Be very careful not to splatter hot soup!

7. Add the 6 remaining whole oysters. Simmer a few minutes until the edges curl.

8. Add ½ cup of cream and taste. Add an additional ½ cup of cream and additional sherry to taste.

9. Ladle bisque into individual bowls and add 1 or 2 whole oysters with each serving. Add a small amount of fried shallots and garlic to each bowl.

10. Add optional seasonings to taste.

Salmon Bisque with Dill

SERVES 4 TO 6

Fish bisques are a bit of a rarity, and probably for good reason. For starters, they're not true bisques, since technically speaking, bisques are made from shellfish. Fish don't have enough of those luscious shellfish juices to create a super flavorful stock. Even a robust fish stock is not robust enough for bisque. But a good lobster stock makes a good fish bisque possible. If you don't have lobster stock on hand, clam broth is a good second choice. And salmon is the ideal fish for a fish bisque. It's pinkish red color not only creates a dish that mimics a lobster bisque in appearance, but salmon has a strong flavor that more closely resembles a true bisque than other types of fish. Tomatoes, sherry, and of course cream, add a rich sweetness that makes the dish so bisque-like that you'd never know it wasn't a true bisque.

Ingredients

4 tablespoons unsalted butter

1 medium yellow onion, diced

1 carrot, diced

1 celery stalk, diced

1 bay leaf

2 cloves garlic, diced

4 cups Robust Lobster Stock (page 79) or Hard-Shell Clam Broth (page 86) or bottled

One 14-ounce can tomatoes

1 tablespoon tomato paste

¼ cup uncooked white rice

1 pound wild Alaskan salmon

1 to 2 cups heavy cream

¼ cup sherry, plus more to taste

½ cup loosely packed dill, plus more to taste

Salt

Optional seasonings, to taste

Salt and freshly ground black pepper

Fresh dill, chopped

Fresh lemon juice

Pinch or two of nutmeg

Splash of sherry

(continued)

Instructions

1. Melt the butter over medium heat in a medium stock-pot and add the onion, carrot, celery, and bay leaf and sauté about 10 minutes until softened. Add the garlic in the last minute.

2. Add the stock, tomatoes, tomato paste, and white rice. Bring to a boil, cover, and reduce the heat to a steady boil. Simmer for 10 to 15 minutes, or until the rice is cooked through. Remove the bay leaf.

3. Add the salmon and simmer gently for several minutes or until cooked through. Transfer the bisque in batches to a high-speed blender, preferably a Vitamix, and blend into a silky smooth consistency. Return the bisque to the stockpot. Alternately, blend using a hand-held immersion blender. Be very careful not to splatter hot soup!

4. Add 1 cup of the cream and the sherry. Simmer gently for 2 minutes. Stir in the dill and taste. Add up to 1 more cup of cream and additional sherry and dill to desired taste. Add salt to taste.

5. Ladle into individual bowls and add optional seasonings to taste.

Whitefish Bisque

SERVES 4 TO 6

Outside of one recipe for a codfish bisque in *The Soup Book* by Louis De Gouy, I've never seen another bisque recipe that uses a whitefish. So I took it as a challenge. It took a few attempts, but I eventually found that a base of a robust lobster stock or clam broth and some liberal amounts of Worcestershire, sherry, and hot sauce make a surprisingly superb whitefish bisque. In this recipe I recommend starting with 2 tablespoons each of sherry and Worcestershire, but I think it needs at least double that. Don't be afraid to add as much as your taste buds crave.

Ingredients

4 tablespoons unsalted butter

1 medium yellow onion, diced

2 celery stalks, diced

2 garlic cloves, diced

2 fresh thyme sprigs, leaves removed and stems discarded

1 bay leaf

¼ cup dry white wine

4 cups Robust Lobster Stock (page 79) or Hard-Shell Clam Broth (page 86) or bottled

¼ cup uncooked white rice

1 pound whitefish of your choice (see Chapter 2 for all options)

1 to 2 cups heavy cream

2 to 4 tablespoons sherry, plus more to taste

2 to 4 tablespoons Worcestershire sauce, plus more to taste

Salt

Optional seasonings, to taste

Salt and freshly ground black pepper

Hot sauce of your choice

Fresh parsley, chopped

Pinch or two of nutmeg

Pinch or two of mace

Splash of Worcestershire sauce

(continued)

Instructions

1. Melt the butter over medium heat in a medium stock-pot and add the onion, celery, garlic, thyme and bay leaf and sauté about 5 minutes until the vegetables are softened.

2. Add the white wine, raise the heat, and simmer for a minute or two or until it's slightly reduced.

3. Add the lobster stock and white rice. Bring to a boil, cover, and reduce heat to a steady boil. Simmer for 10 to 15 minutes, or until the rice is cooked through. Remove the bay leaf.

4. Add the fish and simmer gently for a few minutes until cooked. Transfer the bisque in batches to a high-speed blender, preferably a Vitamix, and blend into a silky smooth consistency. Return the bisque to the stockpot. Alternately, blend using a handheld immersion blender. Be very careful not to splatter hot soup!

5. Add 1 cup of the cream, 2 tablespoons of the sherry, and 2 tablespoons of the Worcestershire sauce, stir in and simmer gently for 2 minutes. Taste and add up to 1 more cup of cream and additional sherry and Worcestershire sauce to desired taste. Add salt to taste.

6. Ladle into individual bowls and add optional seasonings to taste.

Chapter 9

Classic Medleys and Stews

Seafood stews and medleys are perhaps the greatest of all seafood dishes. They're like symphonies of the sea, often melding multiple types of seafood, stocks, shellfish liquors, herbs, and spices into a luscious brothy base. With so many seductive aromas and flavors mingling and merging, they can humble you, make you weak in the knees, even grateful to experience such kaleidoscopic concoctions.

Seafood stews and medleys are often multicultural, a melting pot of influences from different regions of the world, and they have undergone endless experimentations that, in time, evolved into something unique and identifiable like say, gumbo or cioppino. But attempts to define them and/or codify rules around them (what people call "authentic" recipes) are always futile. They are constantly melding and morphing into other incarnations like a continuous spectrum of light. We give the obvious differences names like "paella" or "bouillabaisse," but the closer we get, the more those differences blur and blend back into each other. There are no so-called authentic versions of any seafood stew or medley, just like there is no such thing as the color "blue," only different shades and hues of it.

Seafood stews and medleys are native to every seafaring culture on the planet, and their varieties are as vast as the ocean itself. They can be as elegant and complex as a Bach concerto or as simple and straightforward as a badass blues jam. Many recipes can encompass both extremes. Depending on your mood, your personal tastes, or even your budget, both can be equally satisfying.

Two "Rules" to Follow

That said, most seafood stews originate with fishermen or fisherwomen, who'd return with whatever they caught that day and throw it all in a stew pot. Classically trained chefs have expanded upon these rustic dishes with great ingenuity, but sometimes they overly complicate them and in so doing intimidate regular folks from making them at home. Bouillabaisse, the great seafood stew of Marseilles, is a good example. Classical French cuisine has all sorts of rules for the exact types of fish to use, the steps in which to add them, and how to serve it. Personally, my approach is more improvisational (like a badass blues jam), and besides I really don't care for rules. As far as I'm concerned there should be only two "rules" when it comes to making seafood stews at home:

1. Use Whatever Seafood You Want in Any Combination You Want

It could be one type of fish or shellfish or 10 different things. Generally speaking, the more variety, the better, especially when it comes to shellfish, because the succulent liquors contained within add wonderful depths of flavor.

2. Use Lesser-Known Species of Seafood

Seafood stews are ideal dishes for expanding your palate and knowledge of local seafood. Go to your local fishmonger and try something you've never tried before. Blackfish, black sea bass, sea robin, porgy, and dogfish are all mild New England whitefish with a tender but firm texture that are just as good, if not better, than similar conventional choices like cod and haddock.

If you can find something even more uncommon, try it! Jonah crabs, periwinkles, slipper limpets, and razor clams are rarely seen in markets but have potential if more people embraced them. If you don't live in New England, try whatever is local to you, including freshwater species. Remember, everything works in seafood stews and medleys!

SINGLE SPECIES STEWS

Most seafood stews encompass multiple types of seafood, but sometimes you'll find single species stews. To be clear, I'm not referring to the simple milk-based traditional New England shellfish stews, like oyster stew and clam stew, which are really brothy soups (and thus are included in Chapter 7). Rather, I'm referring to actual stews, which are slowly simmered, are typically thicker in consistency than soups, and come with lots of vegetables like tomatoes, potatoes, onions, and peppers. Though you'd be hard-pressed to find them on American menus, they are prevalent throughout Asia and the Mediterranean (and probably well beyond that) where you'll find endless varieties of fish, clam, mussel, shrimp, crab, squid, and even octopus stews.

The main benefit of using only one type of seafood in a stew is cost. Because as wonderful as stews and medleys that feature a wide variety of fish and shellfish are, they can also be quite pricey.

Guess what cuisine I'm going to feature as an example?

Portuguese cuisine of course! There is no better shade of cultural color to explore when it comes to seafood stews, especially as it relates to New England seafood. Portuguese cuisine with its liberal use of tomatoes, onions, peppers, herbs, and spices is a great vehicle for creating a wide variety of recipes. In the Portuguese restaurants on the south coast of Massachusetts and Rhode Island you'll find numerous seafood stews including popular choices such as mariscada, caldeirada, and paella. But you'll also find examples of stews that use only shrimp, octopus, squid, or clams. No two are the same and they're all equally delicious.

My five Portuguese recipes are just a tiny example of what's possible but, at the very least, illustrate the analogy of stews from one country being like different shades of the same color. Though united by many similar ingredients they have enough contrasts to tease your tongue with different flavor combinations. Feel free to substitute other types of shellfish in any of these five recipes; however, I've chosen the most affordable and available types of shellfish—clams, mussels, squid, and even shrimp.

Whether you choose to make all of these recipes or just one, don't forget the Two "Rules" to Follow. If you don't have a few of the ingredients for a recipe, don't worry about it. The true spirit of these recipes are with the fishermen and fisherwomen who originally created them. When you combine seafood with their stocks and broths in melting pots of veggies, herbs, and spices, seductive spellbinding things happen. Always. Like a badass blues jam.

Bouillabaisse

SERVES 8 TO 10

There are times when the beauty in this life stops you dead in your tracks. A great piece of music, a mountain vista, a Van Gogh painting. The same could be said of a good bouillabaisse. When it's made well, for a brief moment, all is right with the world.

Though you'll see more rules associated with bouillabaisse than a football game, keep in mind that bouillabaisse, like all seafood stews, has humble beginnings. Its origins are with the fishermen of Marseilles who originally used rockfish, a fish too bony to sell, in a stew. In time the stew became more refined with more and more "rules," such as the exact types of fish to include, when to add those fish in the cooking process, the inclusion of saffron, a rouille (a garlic mayonnaise), and a specific sequence of serving the broth first followed by the fish on platters. But these rules were never meant for home cooking, but rather for high-end restaurants. Whenever you see such rules, default to the true spirit of bouillabaisse and quietly move on.

You can make a simpler but no less delicious homemade version by following only three "rules." The first two barely need repeating: Use local seafood that is fresh and varied and make your own fish stock. But it's the third rule that will truly make your bouillabaisse a bouillabaisse: Make sure to include fennel, saffron, and orange zest. Those three ingredients work some serious wizardry with your homemade fish stock. My recipe includes some fennel seeds for a little extra hit of anise flavor.

One last optional "rule": If you have the time and inclination, make a red pepper rouille. Spread on some toasted bread and, when dipped in the broth, it's a truly divine accompaniment.

(continued)

Ingredients

For the optional rouille (makes about 1½ cups)

1 red bell pepper

3 to 4 garlic cloves

2 egg yolks

1 tablespoon lemon juice

Pinch of cayenne, smoked paprika, red pepper flakes, or dash hot sauce

1 cup olive oil

Salt and freshly ground black pepper

For the bouillabaisse

¼ cup olive oil

1 medium yellow onion, diced into ½-inch pieces

1 leek, white part only, sliced lengthwise and diced into ½-inch pieces

1 fennel bulb, cored and diced into ½-inch pieces

¼ teaspoon fennel seeds

4 to 6 garlic cloves, minced

4 plum tomatoes, quartered lengthwise, cored, and sliced into ½-inch pieces

1 cup dry white wine

2 quarts Basic Fish Stock (page 73) or 1 quart Hard-Shell Clam Broth (page 86) or bottled, plus 1 quart water or fish stock, more if needed

Grated zest from 1 orange

2 pinches of saffron threads, crushed (35 to 40)

4 fresh thyme sprigs

2 fresh rosemary sprigs

2 bay leaves

¼ teaspoon cayenne pepper

3 pounds littleneck clams, rinsed and scrubbed clean

1 pound blue mussels, rinsed and scrubbed clean

1 pound any lean, mild whitefish (see pages 30–36 for options)

1 pound oily, full-flavored fish (see pages 36–40 for options)

1 pound wild Gulf shrimp

½ pound scallops and/or squid (optional)

Optional seasonings, to taste

Fresh basil, chopped

Fresh parsley, chopped

Fresh tarragon, chopped

Fresh lemon juice

Salt and freshly ground black pepper

Instructions

To Make the Rouille

1. Preheat the oven broiler.

2. Remove the top of the pepper and slice into four pieces. Remove the seeds and fleshy parts.

3. Lay the pepper slices skin side up on a baking sheet and broil 10 to 15 minutes, or until the skin is charred.

4. Remove and let cool for a few minutes. Peel off the skins.

5. Add the red pepper, garlic, egg yolks, lemon juice, and cayenne to a food processor and blend well.

6. Gradually add the 1 cup olive oil in a slow and steady stream with the blade running, until the mixture thickens like mayonnaise. Add salt and pepper to taste.

To Make the Bouillabaisse

1. Heat the olive oil in a large stockpot (at least 10 quarts). Add the onion, leek, fennel bulb, and fennel seeds and sauté for about 5 minutes, or until the vegetables are softened. Add the minced garlic in the last minute.

2. Add the tomatoes and wine and simmer for several minutes until the wine is slightly reduced.

3. Add the stock, orange zest, saffron, thyme, rosemary, bay leaves, and cayenne. Cover the pot, lower the heat to medium-low and simmer for 15 to 20 minutes.

4. Add the clams and simmer 5 to 7 minutes, or until the shells open.

5. Add the mussels and simmer 3 to 5 minutes, or until the shells open.

6. Add the fish, shrimp, and optional scallops and/or squid. Add more stock and/or water, if needed. Simmer 5 to 10 minutes, or until the fish is cooked through and easily flakes apart.

7. Ladle into individual bowls and add optional seasonings to taste.

Bourride

SERVES 6 TO 8

Bourride (pronounced "boo-reed-a") may not be as famous as bouillabaisse, its world-renowned French Provençal sibling, but it is held in high esteem among those who know it well.

Bourride's defining feature is an aioli made with olive oil, garlic, lemon, and mustard that infuses the broth with flavor, slightly thickens it into a velvety texture, and turns it a gorgeous golden yellow color.

Many traditional bourride recipes call for monkfish or halibut, both excellent choices, but any firm, lean whitefish will suffice. One or two types of shellfish are also routine additions. My recipe includes mussels because the first time I made this was on Cape Cod where I scored the biggest, juiciest, most tender blue mussels (from Chatham) that I'd ever had. Add any New England shellfish your heart desires.

Ingredients

For the aioli (makes about 2 cups)

4 garlic cloves

2 egg yolks

1 tablespoon Dijon mustard

1 tablespoon fresh lemon juice

2 cups extra virgin olive oil

Salt

For the stew

¼ cup olive oil

1 large fennel bulb, cored and diced into ½-inch pieces

1 large yellow onion, diced into ½-inch pieces

2 leeks, white part only, sliced lengthwise and diced into ½-inch pieces

2 garlic cloves, minced

1 tablespoon smoked paprika

Pinch of saffron threads, crushed (about 20; optional)

1 cup dry white wine

1 cup plum tomatoes (3 to 4 tomatoes), quartered lengthwise, cored, and sliced into ½-inch pieces or 15 to 20 grape or cherry tomatoes, halved

6 cups Basic Fish Stock (page 73) or any other seafood stock and broth combo

1 cup baby, new, or fingerling potatoes, halved or quartered into bite-sized pieces

2 pounds any shellfish (combo of mussels, clams, scallops, or others)

2 pounds firmly textured whitefish such as pollock, monkfish, halibut, dogfish, black sea bass, blackfish, or others (see pages 30–36 for options)

Salt

Optional seasonings and accompaniments, to taste

Fresh parsley leaves, chopped

Fresh basil leaves, chopped

Fresh lemon juice

Salt and freshly ground black pepper

Toasted bread of your choice, topped with aioli

(continued)

Instructions

To Make the Aioli

1. Add the garlic, egg yolks, mustard, and lemon juice to a food processor and blend together.

2. Gradually add the 2 cups olive oil in a slow and steady stream with the blade running, until the mixture thickens like mayonnaise. Add salt to taste.

3. Set aside or refrigerate if making ahead.

To Make the Stew

1. Heat the olive oil in a large stockpot and add the fennel, onions, and leeks and sauté for 5 to 10 minutes until softened.

2. Add the minced garlic, paprika, and saffron and sauté 2 to 3 minutes. Then add the wine and tomatoes and simmer for several minutes or until slightly reduced. Add the stock and potatoes and simmer 10 to 15 minutes, or until the potatoes are tender. Then add the shellfish and simmer until the shells open, 3 to 5 minutes.

3. Add the fish and simmer very gently until cooked through, 5 to 10 minutes, or until the fish is cooked through and easily flakes apart. With a slotted spoon, remove all the fish and shellfish to a separate bowl or transfer them into individual serving bowls.

4. Add salt to taste.

5. Make sure the stew is barely at a simmer and add 1 cup of the aioli and whisk for 4 to 5 minutes, or until it is slightly thickened.

6. Scoop some fish and shellfish into each serving bowl and ladle the stew over. Add optional seasonings to taste and serve with toasted bread topped with aioli.

Cioppino

SERVES 8 TO 10

Originating in San Francisco in the late 19th century with Italian fisherman, cioppino has ventured far beyond its roots to become a staple on restaurant menus all across the country. As opposed to bouillabaisse, cioppino proudly boasts itself as a dish for the common man. I can hear Italian Americans all over the country, when asked how to make cioppino, answering, "However the $#!% you want!" My type of people.

It's a classic "catch of the day" sort of stew, meaning no seafood is discriminated against. Pacific Ocean fish of all shapes and sizes, often with their heads and tails attached, and Dungeness crabs, clams, shrimp, and squid, all in their shells, were staples of these original dishes.

As cioppino spread beyond San Francisco throughout the 20th century, so did the use of local seafood. For New England, that means things like quahogs, blue mussels, Jonah crab, lobster, sea or bay scallops, squid, and all the native fish we've discussed. I love adding a mix of lean and fatty fish in cioppino and include a pound of each in my recipe. But that's only a suggestion. Make like a proud Italian and loudly declare, "I'll add whatever I want!" With cioppino, that's exactly the right thing to add.

Ingredients

¼ cup olive oil

1 large or 2 medium yellow onions, diced into ½-inch pieces

4 to 6 garlic cloves, minced

6 fresh thyme sprigs

2 bay leaves

1 teaspoon red pepper flakes (optional)

2 tablespoons tomato paste

One 28-ounce can crushed tomatoes

1 cup moderate dry red wine (see Note)

1 quart Basic Fish Stock (page 73) or 2 cups Hard-Shell Clam Broth (page 86) or bottled, plus 2 cups water or fish stock, more if needed

1 tablespoon red wine vinegar

2 pounds littleneck clams, rinsed and scrubbed clean

1 pound mussels, rinsed and scrubbed clean

1 pound any lean, mild whitefish (see pages 30–36 for options)

1 pound oily, full flavored fish (see pages 36–40 for options)

1 pound wild Gulf shrimp

½ pound scallops and/or squid (optional)

Meat from ½ pound whole Jonah crab claws (optional)

Optional seasonings, to taste

Fresh parsley, chopped

Fresh basil, chopped

Salt and freshly ground black pepper

(continued)

Note

Though white wine is also a good choice, I opt for red because it pairs well with tomatoes in a stew and adds a deeper, richer flavor than white. Avoid very tannin-heavy, full-bodied red wines like cabernet, which can leave an acrid flavor. Choose more moderate dry reds like merlot or pinot noir.

Instructions

1. Heat the olive oil in a large stockpot, at least 10 quarts, add the onions, and sauté for about 5 minutes until softened.

2. Add the garlic, thyme, bay leaves, and optional red pepper flakes and sauté 1 more minute. Add the tomato paste, stir frequently, and sauté another minute.

3. Add the tomatoes, wine, stock, and red wine vinegar. Raise the heat to a gentle boil and simmer for about 5 minutes. Lower the heat to medium-low, cover, and simmer for 30 more minutes.

4. Add the clams and simmer 5 to 7 minutes or until the shells open.

5. Add the mussels and simmer 3 to 5 minutes or until the shells open.

6. Add the fish, shrimp, and optional scallops and crab-meat. Add more stock and/or water, if needed. Simmer 5 to 10 minutes, or until the fish is cooked through and easily flakes apart.

7. Ladle into individual bowls and add optional seasonings to taste.

Zarzuela

SERVES 8 TO 10

You know when you taste something from another country's cuisine that is so incredible it makes you seriously contemplate going straight to the airport and flying to that country just so you can eat it every day? That's zarzuela.

I mean it is *that* good. Let's face it, this shouldn't be a surprise considering it has the coolest name of any seafood stew in the world. Say it slowly and really emphasize that second "z." Zar-zzzzzwella! When something just sounds that romantic and exotic it is sure to taste even better.

Zarzuela hails from the Catalonia region in Spain. The dish is aptly named after a genre of Spanish musical theatre that blends many contrasting styles of music and dance. Similarly, the stew also blends contrasting ingredients. And though it bears resemblance to many other Mediterranean seafood stews, it's those contrasting elements that make it unique.

Its defining feature is an almond paste, mixed into the broth, which gives the stew a richer, heartier feel than other types of Mediterranean stews like bouillabaisse. It's also typically (but not always) enhanced with some type of cured pork like serrano ham or prosciutto.

Finally, it's also usually more shellfish-rich than other seafood stews. It's often called *zarzuela de mariscos* (*mariscos* means shellfish in Spanish) as a way to distinguish it from the theatrical genre. Fish can be added for sure, and my recipe includes it, but it's not totally necessary.

These three things—almond paste, cured pork, and shellfish-rich—create a distinctive synthesis of nutty, smokey, and briny flavors that is truly astounding and will surely stir up some passionate emotions of deep love, nourishment, and possible spontaneous travel to Spain.

Ingredients

For the almond paste

1 cup blanched almonds

2 cups loosely packed parsley leaves

3 to 4 garlic cloves

¼ cup olive oil

For the stew

Pinch of saffron threads, crushed (about 20)

1 cup dry white wine

1 tablespoon olive oil

1 large onion, diced into ½-inch pieces

1 cup cured pork, such as serrano ham, prosciutto, or chorizo sausage, diced

3 to 4 garlic cloves, minced

2 ounces brandy

2 tablespoons tomato paste

One 14-ounce can diced tomatoes

4 cups Basic Fish Stock (page 73)

2 cups Hard-Shell Clam Broth (page 86) or bottled

For the 5 to 6 pounds of 3 to 6 types of the following fresh seafood of your choice

1 pound littleneck clams, rinsed and scrubbed clean

1 pound blue mussels, rinsed and scrubbed clean

1 pound wild Gulf shrimp

1 pound squid

1 pound scallops

1 pound lobster meat, chopped into chunks

1 pound any lean, mild whitefish fillets (see pages 30–36 for options)

Optional seasonings, to taste

Fresh parsley leaves, chopped

Fresh lemon juice

Salt and freshly ground black pepper

Instructions

1. Add the saffron to the white wine and let it steep for 20 to 30 minutes.

2. Make the almond paste: Add the almonds, parsley, garlic, and olive oil to a food processor and pulse it until it forms a thick, grainy paste (don't overblend it into a smooth paste). Set it aside. For a deeper almond flavor you can roast the almonds first. Simply heat a little olive oil in a pan over medium heat, add the almonds for several minutes, stirring frequently until they are lightly browned.

3. Make the stew: Heat the 1 tablespoon olive oil in a large stockpot over medium heat. Add the onions and pork and sauté for about 5 minutes until the onions are softened. Add the minced garlic in the last minute.

4. Add the brandy and white wine with saffron and simmer for a few minutes or until slightly reduced.

5. Add the tomato paste, tomatoes, fish stock, and clam broth. Simmer another 5 to 10 minutes.

6. Add the almond paste and stir it in. Simmer a few more minutes.

7. Add the clams and mussels and simmer gently until the shells open. Stir once or twice so they cook evenly.

8. Turn off the heat. Add the remaining seafood, cover the pot, and let it cook in the heat of the broth for 5 to 10 more minutes. Stir occasionally to submerge everything in the broth.

9. Ladle into individual bowls and add optional seasonings to taste.

Zuppa di Pesce with Black Sea Bass

SERVES 4 TO 6

Zuppa di pesce, which translates in Italian as "fish soup," probably has as many variations in Italy as there are stars in the galaxy. Though it's called a soup, it's more like a stew and almost always includes a variety of shellfish.

When you make your own fish stock, your zuppa di pesce will stand out from the abundance of recipes that do not. Choosing a fish other than cod and haddock, such as black sea bass, will make it even more unique. My version keeps things pretty simple, with minimal veggies, so as to let the beautiful homemade broth really shine through.

Ingredients

2 tablespoons olive oil

3 to 4 garlic cloves, minced

One 28-ounce can San Marzano tomatoes

½ cup dry white wine (optional)

Grated zest of 1 lemon

3 or 4 fresh thyme sprigs

1 quart Basic Fish Stock (page 73)

1 pound littleneck clams, rinsed and scrubbed clean

1 pound blue mussels, rinsed and scrubbed clean

1 pound black sea bass fillets or any other lean, mild whitefish fillets (see pages 30–36 for options)

1 pound wild Gulf shrimp and/or 1 pound scallops

Optional seasonings, to taste

Fresh basil, chopped

Fresh parsley, chopped

Fresh lemon juice

Salt and freshly ground black pepper

Instructions

1. Heat the olive oil in a medium stockpot over medium heat, add the garlic and sauté for about 2 minutes, stirring frequently, being careful not to burn it.

2. Add the tomatoes and optional white wine, raise the heat to medium-high and simmer for 3 to 4 minutes.

3. Add the lemon zest, thyme, and fish stock and bring to a gentle boil. Add the clams and simmer 5 to 7 minutes, or until the shells open. Add the mussels and simmer 3 to 5 minutes, or until the shells open.

4. Add the fish and shrimp and simmer 5 to 10 minutes, or until the fish is cooked through and easily flakes apart.

5. Ladle into individual bowls and add optional seasonings to taste.

Simple Portuguese Clam Stew

SERVES 2 OR 3

Long before Portuguese immigrants descended on Massachusetts in the 1800s they were using their native clams in beautiful rich soups and stews, seasoned with a myriad of spices, and slowly simmered for hours to amalgamate all the flavors. This recipe is a brothier and quicker adaptation of the Elegant Portuguese Clam Stew (page 262), which is more traditional. When you're short on time and/or ingredients, this recipe is an excellent choice. The broth is seasoned with wine, cumin, chourico, and lime juice, and it contains more than enough flavor to satisfy and enliven the taste buds. Lemon juice is a suitable alternative to the lime juice, but I think lime juice is more rousing and provides a more natural complement to the cilantro, garlic, onion, and pepper. Don't be afraid to add hot sauce for even more kick!

Ingredients

3 tablespoons olive oil

2 links chourico sausage, diced into ¼-inch rings

1 small medium yellow onion, diced into ½-inch pieces

½ green pepper, diced into ½-inch pieces

3 to 4 garlic cloves, minced

1 teaspoon ground cumin

½ cup dry white wine

2 cups Hard-Shell Clam Broth (page 86) or bottled plus more to taste

2 dozen littleneck clams, rinsed and scrubbed clean

1 cup cilantro, loosely packed, chopped, plus more to taste

2 tablespoons fresh lime juice, plus more to taste

2 cups precooked white rice (optional)

Optional seasonings, to taste

Steamed white rice

Fresh cilantro, chopped

Fresh lime juice

Hot sauce of your choice

Red pepper flakes

Freshly ground black pepper

(continued)

Instructions

1. Heat the olive oil over medium heat in a medium stock-pot. Add the chourico, onion, and pepper and sauté 5 to 7 minutes, until the chourico is lightly browned and the vegetables are softened.

2. Add the garlic and ground cumin and sauté a few more minutes. Stir often to prevent burning.

3. Add the wine, raise the heat, and simmer for a few minutes until the wine is slightly reduced.

4. Add the clam broth and bring to a simmer. Add the whole littleneck clams, cover, and simmer for 5 to 7 minutes, or until all the shells open. Add more clam broth, if desired.

5. Add the cilantro and lime juice and stir in. Taste and add more lime juice, if desired.

6. Add some of the optional precooked white rice into individual bowls. Ladle the stew into the bowls and add optional seasonings to taste.

Elegant Portuguese Clam Stew

SERVES 3 OR 4

Compared to the Simple Portuguese Clam Stew (page 259), this recipe is more in the traditional realm, and it features lots of spices cooked via a long, slow simmer to fuse the flavors. It is one of my favorite recipes in the book, which is saying a lot because I absolutely adore them all. There are so many things I love about it, but it's the base of pure clam broth, ideally made from whole quahogs and their piquant liquor, that makes me swoon. I felt punch-drunk giddy with briny delight the first time I tried it. I've been making it for years now, constantly tweaking it and sharing it with others. Nothing but genuine love and praise is spoken about it.

It's also one of those dishes that could likely lift the spirits of any human being, no matter how dark and depressed. Because as soon as you taste it, you can immediately feel it. Your body will involuntarily take a deep, deep inhale followed by an equally deep exhale. It's just a natural reaction to something that has an instantaneous soothing effect on the body, like cuddling up with your dog by the fire on a cold winter night.

Ingredients

For the clam broth and clam meats

2 cups Hard-Shell Clam Broth (page 86) or bottled

2 dozen cherrystone or 3 dozen littlenecks clams

2 cups water

For the stew

4 tablespoons olive oil

1 link chourico sausage, sliced into ¼-inch rings

2 to 3 medium shallots, diced into ½-inch pieces

2 to 3 scallions, diced into ¼-inch pieces

½ green pepper, diced into ½-inch pieces

2 to 3 garlic cloves, minced

½ cup mushrooms, roughly diced into ½-inch pieces

4 or 5 fresh thyme sprigs or 2 teaspoons dried thyme

1 bay leaf

½ teaspoon allspice

¼ teaspoon ground black pepper

¼ teaspoon fennel seeds

½ cup dry white wine

One 14-ounce can whole peeled tomatoes

1 tablespoon wine vinegar or apple cider vinegar

1 cup loosely packed fresh parsley

Optional seasonings, to taste

Fresh parsley, chopped

Freshly ground black pepper

Hot sauce of your choice

Instructions

1. To make the clam broth: Clean the clams of any grit by rinsing in cold running water and scrubbing clean.

2. Add 2 cups of water to a large stockpot and bring it to a rolling boil. Add the 2 dozen cherrystone or 3 dozen littleneck clams and make the clam broth according to the instructions on page 86 (ignore the small discrepancies in the amounts of water and clams). You should get 2½ to 3 cups broth total.

3. Let the clams cool for a few minutes and then remove the clam meats from their shells. Set the broth and clam meats aside.

4. Heat the olive oil over medium heat in a medium stockpot. Add the chourico sausage and sauté about 5 minutes, until lightly browned. Stir often to prevent burning.

5. Add the shallots, scallions, green pepper, garlic, mushrooms, and herbs and spices and sauté another 5 to 7 minutes, stirring often.

6. Add the white wine, raise the heat slightly, and simmer for a few more minutes or until slightly reduced.

7. Add the tomatoes, vinegar, and parsley; stir and mix well with the other ingredients and simmer for a few more minutes. Crush and mash the whole tomatoes with a potato masher or some kitchen instrument to break them apart a little.

8. Add the 2 cups of clam broth and simmer with the lid off for at least 30 minutes or until the desired consistency and flavor of the stew is reached. The liquid will continue to evaporate as it simmers, and make the stew thicker and richer in flavor. Keep tasting it every so often until your taste buds tell you it's ready.

9. Add the reserved clam meats, stir in, and simmer for a few more minutes.

10. Ladle the stew into individual bowls and add optional seasonings to taste.

Portuguese Squid Stew

SERVES 8

Though a squid stew might seem a little unusual, consider this quote regarding squid by Chef Howard Mitcham in *Provincetown Seafood Cookbook:* "In the hands of a skillful cook this octopus-faced monstrosity is one of the world's greatest seafood delicacies. But poor thing, nobody knows how to cook him, except a few million Chinese, Japanese, Siamese, Vietnamese, Indonese, Micronese, Melanese, Javanese, Balinese, Nepalese, Polynese, Portuguese, Italians, and Spaniards."[21]

Yes, it would be nice if we embraced the prodigious populations of squid that swim off our shores. It would certainly be better for the health of our planet than eating farmed shrimp from halfway around the world. While our squid consumption in America has increased since Mitcham's day, most of that is in the form of calamari appetizers in restaurants. Rhode Island in particular has a growing commercial squid fishery that mostly supplies the restaurant industry. That's a good thing, but we can learn to make it at home too. A Portuguese squid stew with a rich, tangy, and briny tomato base is a *great place* to start.

Ingredients

3 tablespoons olive oil

1 large onion, diced into ½-inch pieces

1 large green pepper, diced into ½-inch pieces

6 to 7 garlic cloves, minced

2 to 2½ pounds squid, tubes and tentacles

2 teaspoons ground cumin

1 teaspoon paprika

1 teaspoon red pepper flakes

¼ teaspoon fennel seeds

½ teaspoon ground allspice

4 ounces tomato paste

Two 14-ounce cans crushed tomatoes

1 quart Hard-Shell Clam Broth (page 86) or bottled, more if needed

2 cups dry red wine

¼ cup Madeira wine or sherry

2 bay leaves

2 tablespoons Worcestershire sauce

2 tablespoons apple cider vinegar

3 cups steamed white rice

Optional seasonings, to taste

Fresh lime juice (*highly* recommended!)

Fresh parsley, chopped

Fresh cilantro, chopped

Red pepper flakes

Hot sauce of your choice

Instructions

1. Heat the olive oil over medium heat in a large heavy-bottomed stockpot. Add the onion and green pepper and sauté for about 5 minutes or until softened. Add the garlic in the last minute, stirring often to prevent burning.

2. Add the squid and sauté a few more minutes until lightly browned.

3. Add the spices and sauté until fragrant, stirring often, 1 to 2 minutes.

4. Add the tomato paste, tomatoes, clam broth, wines, bay leaves, Worcestershire sauce, and apple cider vinegar. Bring to a boil, reduce the heat, and simmer with the cover off for a minimum of 2 hours. Four to 5 hours may be necessary. Continue simmering until the desired consistency and taste is achieved. The flavors will condense as the liquid condenses. Taste as you go and adjust the flavors, adding more of anything you want. Add more clam broth, if necessary.

5. Add a scoop of steamed rice (prepare the rice about a half hour before you're ready to serve the stew) to individual wide-mouthed bowls and ladle the stew over the rice. Add optional seasonings to taste.

Portuguese Mussel Stew

SERVES 3 OR 4

Mussels alone are not the meatiest morsels for a stew. But throw in some Portuguese linguica sausage in a rich tomato base with lots of veggies and spices, and now you've got yourself a hearty *and economical* concoction. Mussels being the cheapest of all shellfish, you won't find a more affordable stew than this one.

Ingredients

3 tablespoons olive oil

2 links linguica sausage, diced into ¼-inch rings

1 medium yellow onion, diced into ½-inch pieces

1 green pepper, diced into ½-inch pieces

3 to 4 garlic cloves, minced

One 28-ounce can whole plum tomatoes

2 cups Hard-Shell Clam Broth (page 86) or bottled, or Basic Fish Stock (page 73), plus more if needed

1 cup parsley, loosely packed, chopped

¾ cup dry red wine

2 tablespoons red wine vinegar or apple cider vinegar

1 tablespoon sugar

4 or 5 fresh thyme sprigs

1 teaspoon ground cumin

1 teaspoon dried basil

½ teaspoon freshly ground black pepper

¼ teaspoon fennel seeds

Generous pinch of red pepper flakes (optional)

Salt

3 pounds blue mussels, rinsed and scrubbed cleaned

Optional seasonings, to taste

Fresh parsley, chopped

Fresh basil, chopped

Hot sauce of your choice

Salt and freshly ground black pepper

Instructions

1. Heat the olive oil over medium heat in a large stockpot and add the linguica, onions, and green pepper. Sauté for 5 to 7 minutes until the linguica is lightly browned and the vegetables are softened. Add the garlic in the last minute.

2. Add the remaining ingredients (except the salt and mussels), stir it all together, and lower the heat. Crush and mash the whole tomatoes with a potato masher or some kitchen instrument to break them apart a little.

Leave the cover off and let it barely simmer for an hour or two or until the desired consistency and flavor of the stew is reached. The liquid will continue to evaporate as it simmers, and make the stew thicker and richer in flavor. Keep tasting it every so often until your taste buds tell you it's ready. Add more clam broth, if necessary.

3. Add salt to taste.

4. Raise the heat to a gentle simmer, add the mussels, put the cover on, and steam for 3 to 5 minutes, or until the shells open.

5. Ladle into individual serving bowls and add optional seasonings to taste.

Portuguese Shrimp Mozambique

SERVES 2 OR 3

This is the only recipe that features shrimp, a seafood I've mostly avoided for the reasons I stated in Chapter 1. But it's such an iconic dish in the Portuguese cuisine of southern New England that I feel the need to include it. Just make sure to use wild-caught US Gulf Coast shrimp.

This dish gets its name from the East African country of Mozambique, which was once colonized by Portugal. Besides the shrimp, the defining characteristic of this dish is a fragrant and zesty broth made from onions, garlic, sazón seasoning, and hot sauce. Sazón is a popular spice mix used in Latin, Spanish, and Portuguese cuisine. It's often sold in spice packets that contain artificial flavors and colorings. But you can easily make your own. The only spice you may not easily find is ground annatto, which gives the broth a deep red color. Any mild paprika is a suitable substitute.

The real heat in this dish comes from the hot sauce, traditionally made from small, spicy Southern African chile peppers, known as piri piri (also called peri peri), which Portuguese colonists cultivated and adapted into their own cuisine. Portuguese piri piri hot sauce is hard to find outside specialty Portuguese markets, though you may be able to find it via online sellers. Any type of hot sauce you like is perfectly fine as a substitute.

The one variation I made compared to traditional recipes is the addition of clam broth. It gives the dish a boost in seafood flavor and a more stewlike character. Leave it out if you desire a more authentic experience, though it will be less of a stew and more of a thick sauce. The dish is often served over white rice, though it's totally optional. Including white rice will certainly make the meal a little more substantive.

Ingredients

For the sazón spice blend

1 teaspoon ground annatto

1 teaspoon ground coriander

1 teaspoon ground cumin

1 teaspoon ground oregano

½ teaspoon salt

½ teaspoon ground black pepper

For the stew

2 tablespoons olive oil

2 tablespoons butter

1 medium yellow onion, diced into ½-inch pieces

5 to 6 garlic cloves, minced

1 cup lager beer or 1 cup dry white wine

1 cup Hard-Shell Clam Broth (page 86) or bottled

2 tablespoons piri piri hot sauce (or hot sauce of your choice), plus more to taste

1 pound wild Gulf shrimp

(continued)

Optional seasonings,
to taste

Salt and freshly ground
black pepper

Hot sauce of your choice

Fresh parsley, chopped

Fresh lemon juice

Instructions

1. In a small bowl combine and mix the spices for the sazón blend. Set aside.

2. Heat the olive oil and butter over medium heat in a medium stockpot. Add the onion and sauté for about 5 minutes or until softened.

3. Add the garlic and sauté 1 more minute. Add the sazón seasoning mix and cook about 1 more minute, stirring frequently.

4. Add the beer and clam broth and bring to a boil. Lower the heat to medium and continue to simmer 5 to 10 minutes, until the liquid is reduced by about one-third.

5. Add the hot sauce and mix well. Taste and add more hot sauce to desired taste.

6. Add the shrimp and simmer until they turn pink and are cooked through, about 5 minutes.

7. Ladle the stew into individual bowls and add optional seasonings to taste.

Chapter 10

Boils

You've probably heard of a clambake, New England's great communal summertime feast of fresh shellfish, corn on the cob, potatoes, and onions. They are epic feasts, typically meant for joyous and festive occasions such as weddings, graduations, and community fundraisers. Clambakes can feed dozens if not hundreds of people. They are traditionally prepared by steaming everything in a large firepit that has been dug on the beach. The pit is lined and heated with stones and wood, layered with fresh seaweed (which produces lots of moisture and steam), and then covered with a tarp or canvas that traps in all the heat. It's a time-consuming all-day affair, so much so that many people now hire caterers to do it for them.

But you can mimic a clambake in your kitchen. It's called a clam boil and it takes a fraction of the time that a clambake does. Clam boils are typically also meant for groups of people, just on a much smaller scale.

The best thing about clam boils is that a byproduct of boiling clams, and sometimes other shellfish, is that you also get a wonderful seafood broth. This is one of the best-kept secrets of clam boils. Only really hardcore seafoodies even think to save the broth. In fact, the broth isn't frequently emphasized in New England clam boils. It's more about the clams themselves and the other ingredients. A little of the broth may be reserved for dipping the clams in, but the leftovers (of which there can be quite a bit) are often dumped down the drain. Needless to say, we will *not* be doing that in the recipes in this chapter.

My clam boil recipes emphasize the broth, which can both enhance the clam boil experience and leave you with plenty of leftover broth that you can freeze and use in many of the recipes in this book. That's what you call a win-win!

But when I say "emphasize the broth," all I mean is that we'll be enhancing it with some bottled clam broth. Most clam boils simply use water as a base. Interestingly, seafood boil traditions down south, such as those in Louisiana, where crayfish and shrimp boils are popular, often include heavily seasoned broths with ingredients like paprika, red pepper, and celery salt. While that may be fine and dandy for southern boils, too much seasoning will prevent us from using the leftover broth in a wide variety of New England seafood soups. So my recipes strive for a mostly straightforward clam flavor, with the exception of the Portuguese Clam Boil (page 280). To accomplish this I include a 1:1 ratio of water to clam broth. Once the clams release their liquor and all the other ingredients add their own subtle flavors, the broth transforms into some serious soul-soothing juju.

Basic Clam Boil Ingredients

Almost all New England clam boils include the following five ingredients:

1. Clams

Yes, clam boils include clams. I know, shocking! These are typically soft-shell clams and/or hard-shell clams, typically littlenecks. Sometimes larger hard-shell clams like cherrystones are used, but they can take up valuable space in your stockpot.

There are pros and cons to using both soft-shell and hard-shell clams in clam boils. The advantage of soft-shell clams is that you get more per pound since their shells are much lighter. Their meats tend to be slightly larger than littlenecks too. The disadvantage is that their thinner, more delicate shells can easily break amid the other ingredients in the pot. They also take more time to clean and can release some of their sand and grit into the clam boil. The advantage of hard-shell clams, besides having sturdier shells and being easier to clean, is that their liquor is stronger in flavor compared to soft-shell clams. The disadvantage of hard-shell clams is that you'll get less per pound, but that's okay because there will be so many other delicious things to eat! Nobody should go home hungry at a traditional New England clam boil. Bottom line: I prefer to use littlenecks in clam boils.

2. Potatoes

Small to medium waxy potatoes that hold their shape when boiling are best. Red, new, fingerling, Yukon Gold, and purple potatoes are all great. Avoid russet potatoes, which easily fall apart when boiled.

3. Onions

Onions are perhaps the most underrated part of clam boils. Similar to potatoes, you want smaller to medium onions. Yellow and red onions are both great. I particularly love the sweet, crisp flavor of red onions in clam boils. Whichever you choose, make sure the onions are fresh, very hard, and without any soft spots. The skin should adhere firmly to the flesh.

4. Corn on the Cob

Fresh local summer corn is always best, and this is one of the many reasons that clam boils are typically held in warmer months. But sometimes an indoor winter clam boil is just as good! In that case, you may skip the corn on the cob—though it is possible to purchase frozen corn on the cob. It will have been lightly blanched before freezing, and it will require only about half the boiling time as fresh uncooked corn of the cob.

5. Sausage

One of my favorite parts of clam boils! The crispy crunch of a juicy sausage, followed by a salty clam and a slurp of clam juice is a trifecta of flavor that has to be experienced. There are no words to explain it. You can use almost any type of sausage you want but smoked and precooked ones are best. Kielbasa, andouille, chourico, and linguica are all suitable. Even hot dogs are common in New England clam boils, especially on the Fourth of July.

Other Clam Boil Ingredients

You'll often see clam boils enhanced by mussels and/or lobsters. Feel free to add them, in any amount you want (or that will fit into your stockpot). Garlic is another frequent addition. Add a few cloves for smaller serving sizes. For larger amounts, simply slice an entire unpeeled garlic bulb in half, crosswise, and add it with the potatoes. And though uncommon for New England clam boils, you could get creative and add any other vegetables you want, such as turnips, carrots, cauliflower, green beans, and peppers.

Clam Boil Serving Sizes

It can be difficult to gauge how much to cook in a group setting. Different people have different appetites. I've heard that in Cajun country, locals will consume 4 to 5 pounds of food at a crawfish boil. Old-time stories of communal New England shellfish feasts tell similar tales of prodigious consumption. Personally, I could easily down four dozen clams and mussels (about 2 pounds) and a good pound or two of everything else. Seafood feasts can readily bring out some hefty appetites in people! It's always best to cook too much instead of too little. Save everything and have it for leftovers.

That said, our modern-day whacky nutrition climate presents challenges. People are on trendy diets, count calories, are terrified of salt and fat, and take god-knows-what medications. This means your group will probably have its share of more moderate eaters (not to mention those who don't like any seafood). That's good news if you're a seafood fanatic like myself. More for us!

My recipe serving sizes are for 8 to 10 people. Again, that's very much an estimate. An average serving per person, broken down into individual amounts, can be esimated as follows. You may have to adjust these amounts up or down.

- **Soft-shell clams –** 12 to 15 (about 1 pound)
- **Littleneck clams –** 7 to 10 (about 1 pound)
- **Potatoes –** 2 to 3 small or 1 to 2 medium
- **Corn on the cob –** 1
- **Onions –** 2 to 3 small or 1 to 2 medium
- **Sausage –** ½ to 1 link

Equipment Needed

The larger the group, the bigger the stockpot you'll need. Old-school, traditional outdoor seafood boils that serve large numbers of people utilize huge stockpots (some can be upward of 100 quarts) that are heated on portable outdoor gas stoves. My serving size of 8 to 10 people requires a fairly large stockpot. At a minimum, you'll need a 20-quart pot.

You might also consider a steamer rack insert that fits inside your pot. Simply lifting it out when everything is done is a super easy way to remove all the ingredients. Without a steamer rack you'll need a good-sized slotted spoon to scoop and transfer everything out of the pot. You could also use a sturdy strainer with a long attached handle.

How to Cook a Clam Boil

For something as simple as boiling things in water, you'd be amazed at the different methods of cooking a clam boil. It can be a little tricky to cook everything perfectly, especially with larger servings. The more people, the bigger the pot, the more challenging it will be. But all in all, most things turn out good, so don't stress it. The real joy is the shared feast with friends and family.

The size of your ingredients, how you chop and slice them, and the order in which you add everything to the pot determines how it all cooks. The idea is to cook everything as evenly as possible.

Here's my general step-by-step method:

Step 1. Bring your water and/or stock and clam broth to a boil.

Step 2. Reduce the heat slightly, add the potatoes, cover the pot, and boil for 7 to 8 minutes.

Step 3. Add the corn for 5 minutes.

Step 4. Add the onions and sausage for 5 minutes.

Step 5. Add the clams for another 5 minutes or until all the shells open.

For the potatoes, slice the smaller ones in half and quarter the medium ones. This will not only make them cook quicker, but they'll better absorb the flavor of the broth.

For the corn, slice them in half or thirds.

For the sausage, slice them in half or thirds.

For smaller onions, about the size of golf balls, you can add them whole; but for larger ones, slice them in half. I add the onions with the sausage, which is a little later in the process than most clam boil recipes. Personally, I love a *lightly boiled* onion. A light boil removes its sharp taste but retains a nice crunchy texture. Most boils add the onions with the potatoes. This almost always turns them overly soft and without much flavor. I don't understand how anyone likes a mushy, overcooked onion. I've noticed at clam boil parties that the onions tend to be the most ignored item. For this reason, I suggest adding them with the sausage.

Finally, know that depending on the size of your stockpot, it's quite possible that by the time you add the shellfish, many may not fully submerge in the water. That's fine. They'll steam right on top of everything else.

How to Serve a Clam Boil

There's no rules here, but just know that serving it is typically messy and that's part of the fun! For clam boils served inside, transfer all the ingredients into several large serving bowls. For boils served outside, typically tables are lined with newspaper and everything is dumped on top. I'm not a big fan of newspaper ink potentially leaching into my food, but do whatever you see fit. You can purchase eco-friendly jumbo brown paper rolls that can act as a table lining. Put out a few trays or empty large bowls for people to dispose of their clam shells and corn cobs.

No clam boil is complete without small dipping bowls of broth and melted butter. Make sure to serve lots of sliced lemon wedges so that each person can season their bowls to their heart's content.

Finally, fresh bread is a fairly common clam boil side dish. Trust me when I say that onc loaf will be devoured quickly, especially when it can be dipped in broth and butter. I've learned the hard way that some of your guests may eat more bread than anything else. Include at least two loaves to keep your gluten-guzzling guests happy.

Traditional New England Clam Boil

SERVES 8 TO 10

Anthony Bourdain once said, "Good food is very often, even most often, simple food." If he were alive today, I'd like to think this would be his favorite meal in this book. Because it just doesn't get any simpler than this recipe. It's no frills. No fuss. Down to earth. Rustic and hearty. Humble and unpretentious. Messy and meant to be eaten with your hands. And yet, it's just so damn delicious it could make you cry; the type of meal you have in your backyard with friends and family, an ice cold beer in hand, good music, kids and dogs running around, the sun shining, and not a care in the world. Sometimes the best food is just *so simple and so good* it's almost hard to believe.

Ingredients

3 quarts water

3 quarts bottled clam broth

8 to 10 small to medium potatoes (2 to 3 pounds), quartered or halved

2 to 3 garlic heads, unpeeled, cut in half crosswise

6 to 8 corn on the cob, cut in half or thirds

6 to 8 smoked sausage links of your choice, cut into thirds (andouille, kielbasa, hot dogs, or other)

8 to 10 small to medium onions, cut in half lengthwise or quartered

8 to 10 pounds clams (any combo of littlenecks and/or steamers), rinsed and scrubbed clean

4 pounds mussels, rinsed and scrubbed cleaned

Seasonings and accompaniments, to taste

Generous gobs of melted butter, served in small dipping bowls

Clam broth, served in small dipping bowls

2 to 3 whole lemons, cut into wedges

Bread of your choice (optional)

(continued)

Instructions

1. Bring the water and clam broth to a boil in a very large stockpot (at least 20 quarts).

2. Add the potatoes, reduce the heat slightly, cover, and boil for 7 to 8 minutes.

3. Add the garlic and corn and boil for another 5 minutes.

4. Add the sausage and onions and boil for another 5 minutes.

5. Add the clams and boil for another 5 to 7 minutes, or until the shells open.

6. Add the mussels and boil for another 3 to 5 minutes, or until the shells open. The boil is now done and ready to be served.

7. Scoop or ladle the ingredients into several large serving bowls or transfer everything to a large table lined with disposable paper.

8. Serve with the seasonings and accompaniments.

New England Blue Mussel Boil

SERVES 4 TO 6

Though relatively rare today, mussel boils were at one time a close cousin of clam boils. At least that's what old New England cookbooks tell me. The recipes I've come across also suggest that mussel boils were simpler than clam boils and some even included chicken as a cheap protein source.

Ingredients

1 quart water or Basic Fish Stock (page 73)

1 quart bottled clam broth

6 to 8 small to medium potatoes, cut in half or quartered

4 to 6 corn on the cob, halved or cut in thirds

4 to 6 sausage links of your choice (andouille, chourico, kielbasa, or other)

6 to 8 small to medium onions, cut in half lengthwise or quartered

4 to 6 pounds blue mussels, rinsed and scrubbed cleaned

Seasonings and accompaniments, to taste

Generous gobs of melted butter, served in small dipping bowls

Mussel and/or seafood broth, served in small dipping bowls

2 to 3 whole lemons, cut into wedges

Bread of your choice (optional)

Instructions

1. Bring the water and broth to a boil in a medium to large stockpot (at least 12 quarts).

2. Add the potatoes, reduce the heat slightly, cover, and boil for 7 to 8 minutes.

3. Add the corn and boil for another 5 minutes.

4. Add the sausage and onions and boil for another 5 minutes.

5. Add the mussels and boil for another 3 to 5 minutes, or until the shells open.

6. Scoop or ladle the ingredients into several large serving bowls or transfer everything to a large table lined with disposable paper.

7. Serve with the seasonings and accompaniments.

Portuguese Clam Boil

SERVES 6 TO 8

As great as a good old-fashioned New England clam boil is, sometimes it's fun to get a little more creative with the broth. This Portuguese clam boil is all about making a spicier, highly seasoned broth in the tradition of southern United States boils. In some ways I think Portuguese clam boils, with their spicy peppers and zesty seasonings, are closer in spirit to the shrimp and crawfish boils of Cajun country than New England boils.

This broth will have some heat! Tone it down or ramp it up with more or less of the paprika and red pepper flakes. Use chourico in lieu of linguica for more kick and vice versa. Adjust the flavors any way you want. You could even add some hot sauce, if needed.

I find making a highly seasoned broth a bit easier with less liquid as a base. For that reason, this recipe isn't quite as voluminous as the Traditional New England Clam Boil (page 276), thus the slightly smaller serving size. You won't get as much leftover broth, but oh how delicious it will be. Save what you can and drink it as a tonic in the following days. You may even be able to use it as a base in some of the other Portuguese recipes in this book.

Ingredients

For the broth

¼ cup olive oil, more if needed

1 large yellow onion, roughly diced into ½-inch pieces

6 to 8 garlic cloves, diced

1 tablespoon paprika

2 teaspoons red pepper flakes

1 teaspoon fennel seeds

¼ cup tomato paste

1 cup dry white wine

2 tablespoons apple cider vinegar

1 quart water or Basic Fish Stock (page 73)

1 quart bottled clam broth

1 lemon, sliced into 4 or 5 rings

For the rest of the boil

6 to 8 small to medium potatoes, quartered or halved

2 garlic heads, unpeeled, cut in half crosswise

4 to 6 corn on the cob, cut in half or thirds

4 to 6 links chourico or linguica sausage, cut into thirds

6 to 8 small to medium onions, cut in half lengthwise or quartered

3 to 4 red peppers, deseeded and sliced into large strips

8 pounds clams (any combo of littlenecks and/ or steamers), rinsed and scrubbed clean

Seasonings and accompaniments, to taste

Generous gobs of melted butter, served in small dipping bowls

Clam broth, served in small dipping bowls

2 to 3 whole lemons or limes, cut into wedges

Bread of your choice (optional)

Instructions

1. Heat the olive oil in a large stockpot over medium heat. Add the diced onions and sauté for 5 minutes or until softened. Add the diced garlic, paprika, pepper flakes, and fennel seeds and sauté 1 more minute, stirring frequently. Add a little more olive oil, if necessary.

2. Add the tomato paste, stirring frequently for 1 more minute.

3. Add the wine and apple cider vinegar and simmer for a few minutes.

4. Add the water, clam broth, and lemon slices and bring to a boil.

5. Add the potatoes, reduce the heat slightly, cover, and boil for 7 to 8 minutes.

6. Add garlic heads and corn and boil for another 5 minutes.

7. Add the sausage, onions, and red peppers and boil for another 5 minutes.

8. Add the clams and boil for another 5 to 7 minutes, or until the shells open.

9. Scoop or ladle the ingredients into several large serving bowls or transfer everything to a large table lined with disposable paper.

10. Serve with the seasonings and accompaniments.

New England Fish Boil

SERVES 8 TO 10

Fish boils are not something you'll traditionally find in New England. After all, why boil fish, a seemingly bland way to prepare it, when you have access to the world's most delicious clams and shellfish, which when boiled or steamed, release their inner juices to flavor the liquid into a most wondrous broth?

Well, you might do it if you don't live near the ocean. This is exactly why fish boils are a popular traditional dish in the Great Lakes region, especially in parts of Wisconsin. It is thought that Scandinavian immigrants brought the practice to the area, where it spread and became a popular feast for large community gatherings, much like the clam boils of New England. In fact, the ingredients are quite similar—potatoes, onions, and corn are staples in upper midwestern fish boils. I was inspired to try one with New England fish, and I was quite surprised at the results.

First, fish boils aren't nearly as dull as you might think. This is where gobs of melted butter and lemon wedges come in. Generously slather any plain ol' fish fillets with those two flavors and the fish transform into something instantly delicious. Salt, pepper, and any type of all-purpose seafood seasoning (such as Old Bay) make it that much better.

Second, a fish boil is beyond simple. It follows the exact same process as a clam boil. You'll simply add fish fillets where you'd add clams. Now the one big difference is that boiling fish fillets won't give you a very flavorful broth. So, if you have a bunch of fish stock lying around, by all means use it as your cooking liquid. If you get your fish whole, make a stock and use that. Or just use some clam broth in combination with water.

This recipe is a straightforward nod to the fish boils of the Great Lakes. No clams, mussels, lobster, sausage, or anything else other than fish and vegetables. The only difference is the use of native New England fish. Cod and haddock are a good place to start, though don't be afraid to try any local in season New England fish. Side dish options include green salad, cole slaw, pasta salad, beet salad, green bean salad, tomato salad, and bread. Particularly, cole slaw and bread frequently accompany a fish boil to make it a rounded, hearty, and satisfying meal.

Ingredients

2 quarts water or Basic Fish Stock (page 73)

2 quarts bottled clam broth

8 to 10 small to medium potatoes (2 to 3 pounds), quartered or halved

2 to 3 garlic heads, unpeeled, cut in half crosswise

6 to 8 corn on the cob, cut in half or thirds

8 to 10 small to medium onions, cut in half lengthwise or quartered

4 to 5 pounds any lean, mild whitefish or oily, full-flavored fish fillets (see Chapter 2 for all options), cut in half or into smaller pieces

Seasonings, to taste

Generous gobs of melted butter

2 to 3 whole lemons, cut into wedges

Salt and freshly ground black pepper

Old Bay or similar seafood seasoning blend

Instructions

1. Bring the water and clam broth to a boil in a large stockpot (at least 12 quarts).

2. Add the potatoes, reduce the heat slightly, cover, and boil for 7 to 8 minutes.

3. Add the garlic and corn and boil for another 5 minutes.

4. Add the onions and boil for another 5 minutes.

5. Turn down the heat to a gentle simmer and add the fish fillets. Simmer anywhere from 3 to 10 minutes depending on their thickness, or until they flake easily with a fork.

6. Gently remove the fillets to a serving platter.

7. Using a slotted spoon, ladle the rest of the ingredients into large serving bowls.

8. Serve with the seasonings and sides. The melted butter and lemon wedges will be essential for the fillets.

A Seasonal New England Fish and Clam Boil—Four Ways

SERVES 8 TO 10

The Traditional New England Fish Boil (page 276) was so surprisingly good that I was inspired to then create a hybrid fish and clam boil. After all, why not? Clams and fish go well together and are featured in countless New England recipes, especially seafood stews, so why not a fish and clam boil? I'm sure that, traditionally, any Midwesterner would have chosen to include briny shellfish in a fish boil had they had access to the ocean. You get the added benefit of creating a delicious broth! More important, fish fillets are a great way to expand our use of alternative fish species in New England. We need to be more open to using them and find simple methods for preparing them. A fish and clam boil is about as easy as it gets.

But let's do it with an eye toward seasonality and sustainability. In that spirit, I've created a very basic New England fish and clam boil recipe that you can tweak to any holiday or festive occasion. Want to make a boil for Memorial Day? Choose a fish that's in season for spring. For New Year's Day? Choose one for winter. For a birthday party in October? Choose one for fall. And so on. Summer and the Fourth of July are the most popular times for boils, but there's no reason we can't have them at other times of the year too.

Ingredients

3 quarts water

3 quarts bottled clam broth

8 to 10 small to medium potatoes (2 to 3 pounds), quartered or halved

2 to 3 garlic heads, unpeeled, cut in half crosswise

6 to 8 corn on the cob, cut in half or thirds

6 to 8 sausage links of your choice (andouille, kielbasa, bratwurst, hot dogs—great for the Fourth of July—or others), cut into thirds

8 to 10 small to medium onions, cut in half lengthwise or quartered

8 to 10 pounds clams (any combo of littlenecks and/or steamers), rinsed and scrubbed cleaned

4 pounds in-season New England fish fillets, cut in half or into smaller pieces. Consider the following:

For summer or autumn:

Black Sea Bss

Striped Bass

Bluefish

Fluke (Summer Flounder)

Porgy (Scup)

Tautog (Blackfish)

Dogfish

Atlantic Mackerel

North Atlantic Swordfish

For winter or spring:

Hake

Atlantic Pollock

Monkfish

Acadian redfish

Skate

Flounder (Yellowtail, Dab, Grey Sole; winter only)

Porgy (scup; spring only)

Bluefish (spring only)

Tautog (Blackfish; spring only)

Seasonings and accompaniments, to taste

Generous gobs of melted butter, served in small dipping bowls

Clam broth, served in small dipping bowls

2 to 3 whole lemons, cut into wedges

Bread of your choice (optional)

Salt and freshly ground black pepper (for the fish fillets)

Old Bay or similar seafood seasoning blend (for the fish fillets)

Instructions

1. Bring the water and clam broth to a boil in a very large stockpot (at least 20 quarts).

2. Add the potatoes, reduce the heat slightly, cover, and boil for 7 to 8 minutes.

3. Add the garlic and corn and boil for another 5 minutes.

4. Add the sausage and onions and boil for another 5 minutes.

5. Add the clams and boil for another 5 to 7 minutes, or until the shells open.

6. Turn down the heat to a gentle simmer and add the fish fillets. Gently boil anywhere from 3 to 10 minutes depending on their thickness, or until they flake easily with a fork. Alternatively, if your stockpot is overfilled, poach the fillets in a separate pot of boiling water.

7. Gently remove the fillets to a serving platter.

8. Using a slotted spoon, ladle the rest of the ingredients into large serving bowls or transfer everything to a table lined with disposable paper. Serve with the seasonings and sides of broth. The butter and lemon will be essential for the fillets.

Optional Seasonal Side Dishes

Boils can be enhanced with different types of simple side dishes. Here are five suggestions of side dishes to fit each season.

Summer-themed side dishes

Any green salad of your choice

Sliced watermelon or cantaloupe

Fresh tomato and cucumber slices with basil and olive oil

Cole slaw

Dill pickles

Autumn-themed side dishes

Any green salad of your choice

Apple sauce

Sliced tomatoes with olive oil and basil

Any combo of roasted carrots, beets, butternut squash, Brussels sprouts

Cole slaw

Winter-themed side dishes

Any green salad of your choice

Cornbread

Baked beans

Sauerkraut

Any combo of roasted carrots, squash, broccoli, cauliflower, fennel

Spring-themed side dishes

Any green salad of your choice

Fresh strawberries

Roasted asparagus

Roasted green beans

Roasted baby bok choy

Thanks

To Max Sinsheimer, my agent, for advocating for me, believing in this project, and guiding me every step of the way.

To the team at The Countryman Press, for bringing this book to life. Special thanks to editor extraordinaire, Isabel McCarthy, for your always thorough and prompt communication.

To Lynne Graves, photographer extraordinaire, and Ann Lewis, stylist extraordinaire, for bringing my recipes to life in photos. Additional thanks to Ann, for the use of your home for the photo shoot.

To Kathy Ver Ecke, for your outstanding online course, The Path to Getting Published. It helped me polish my book proposal and understand how to query agents, which in time, led me to Max Sinsheimer and The Countryman Press.

To Sally Ekus, for helping me draft my first book proposal and providing support and encouragement throughout.

To all those who came to my recipe tasting parties in Easthampton, Massachusetts. So much fun! More importantly, the insights and feedback were invaluable.

To Janice Beetle and Lise Wessman, for letting me make a mess of your kitchens, and for all the seafood smells that may have lingered longer than you'd liked.

To my family, for your unconditional love and support.

Notes

1. Seaver, Barton. *American Seafood: Heritage, Culture and Cookery From Sea to Shining Sea*. 45. New York City: Sterling Epicure, 2017.
2. NOAA Fisheries. "Understanding Fisheries Management in the United States." July 1, 2021. www.fisheries.noaa.gov/insight/understanding-fisheries-management-united-states.
3. Oceana. "What is Seafood Fraud." July 1, 2021. https://oceana.org/what-seafood-fraud.
4. Masury, Kate. "Eat Like a Fish." Eating With the Ecosystem. July 1, 2021. www.eatingwiththeecosystem.org/eat-like-a-fish.
5. Rhode Island Fishermen's Alliance. "New England Sustainable Seafood List." 2010. www.rifishermensalliance.com/RIFA_Seafood_Guide.pdf.
6. Mitcham, Howard. *Provincetown Seafood Cookbook*. 29–31. New York City: Seven Stories Press, 2018.
7. Daniel, Kaayla. "Why Broth is Beautiful: Essential Roles for Proline, Glycine and Gelatin." *The Weston A. Price Foundation*. June 18, 2003. www.westonaprice.org/health-topics/why-broth-is-beautiful-essential-roles-for-proline-glycine-and-gelatin.
8. Adams, Eric, and Halper, N.M. *Vittles for the Captain: Cape Cod Sea-Food Recipes*. Cleveland, OH: Modern Pilgrim Press, 1951.
9. De Guoy, Louis P. *The Soup Book: Over 700 Recipes*. 209. Garden City, NY: Dover Publications, 2018.
10. Hooker, Richard J. *The Book of Chowder*. 13. Cambridge, MA: Harvard Common Press, 1978.
11. White, Jasper. *50 Chowders: 50 Chowders*. 15. New York City: Scribner Books, 2000.
12. Schwind, Cap'n Phil. *Clam Shack Cookery*. 23. Columbus, OH: McGraw-Hill Trade, 1967.
13. De Guoy, Louis P. *The Soup Book: Over 700 Recipes*. 210. Garden City, NY: Dover Publications, 2018.
14. Frederick, J. George. *Long Island Seafood Cookbook*. 29. Garden City, NY: Dover Publications, 2011.
15. Frederick, J. George. *Long Island Seafood Cookbook*. 27. Garden City, NY: Dover Publications, 2011.
16. Mitcham, Howard. *Provincetown Seafood Cookbook*. 21. New York City: Seven Stories Press, 2018.
17. Mitcham, Howard. *Provincetown Seafood Cookbook*. 153. New York City: Seven Stories Press, 2018.
18. Peterson, James. *Fish & Shellfish: The Cook's Indispensable Companion*. 139. New York City: William Morrow Cookbooks, 1996.
19. Schwind, Cap'n Phil. *Clam Shack Cookery*. 17. Columbus, OH: McGraw-Hill Trade, 1967.
20. Mitcham, Howard. *Provincetown Seafood Cookbook*. 52–53. New York City: Seven Stories Press, 2018.
21. Mitcham, Howard. *Provincetown Seafood Cookbook*. 133. New York City: Seven Stories Press, 2018.

Index

A

Acadian redfish (ocean perch), 36
acreage, seafood, 17, 18
Adams, Harriet, 94
"All Along the Watchtower" (Hendrix), 221
ameijoas na cataplana, 115
American Seafood (Seaver), 17
antibiotics, 23, 39, 44
Aromatic Mussel Soup, 182–84
Atlantic blue mussels, 47, 178, 180, 182, 186, 188
Atlantic Blue Mussel Mediterranean Soup, 180–81
Atlantic cod, 22, 31
Atlantic mackerel, 38, 162, 284
Atlantic northern shrimp, 53–54
Atlantic pollock, 32, 156, 285
Atlantic rock crab (Peekytoe crab), 52–53
Atlantic sea scallops, 48
Atlantic wild fish, 37
Azores, 57–59

B

bacon, 94, 98
Bar Harbor Foods, 90
Basic Crab Stock, 81, 82, 140–41, 203–5, 224–26
Basic Fish Stock, 73; Bouillabaisse, 246–49; Bourride, 251–52; Caldo Verde with Squid, 215–16; chicken broth, 90; Cioppino, 253–55; New England Blue Mussel Boil, 279; New England Fish Boil, 282–83; New England-Style Hot and Sour Soup with Scallops, 210–11; Oyster Spinach Chowder, 144–45; Oysters Bienville Soup, 198; Oysters Mariniere Soup, 196–97; Oysters Rockefeller Soup, 194–95; Portuguese Clam Boil, 280–81; Portuguese Kale Soup with Scallops, 207–9; Portuguese Mussel Stew, 266–67; Portuguese Squid Soup, 212–14; Zarzuela, 256–57; Zuppa di Pesce with Black Sea Bass, 258
Basic Lobster Stock, 78–80, 134–36, 200–202
bay scallops, 48–49, 142, 207, 210, 217, 253
"beards," 47
beer, 185–89, 258
bisques, 12, 218–42
black sea bass, 34, 68, 120, 154, 244, 251, 258
blood clams, 55
blue crab, 52–53, 55, 199, 204
bluefish, 27, 37, 68–69, 128, 130, 162, 164, 284
Bluefish Chowder with Cherry Tomatoes, Basil, and Tarragon, 128-2
boils, 271–86
Book of Chowder, The (Hooker), 96
Boston Cooking-School Cookbook (Farmer), 101
bottled clam broth, 83, 90; boils, 272; lobster stock, 219; New England Blue Mussel Boil, 279; New England Fish Boil, 283; Portuguese Clam Boil, 280; Portuguese Clam Chowder, 115; A Seasonal New England Fish and Clam Boil—Four Ways, 284; Traditional New England Clam Boil, 286
Bouillabaisse, 34, 35, 244, 246–49
Bourdain, Anthony, 276
Bourride, 251–52
broths, 11–12, 65–71; bottled clam broth, 90; broths, terminology, 66; chicken broth, 90; clam boils, 58, 271, 280; clam broth, 83–87; mussel broth, 88; seagreens broth, 91
brothy soups, 148–242
bycatch, 26–27, 31, 33, 35, 52

C

Caldo Verde with Squid, 215–16
California mussels, 55
Cape Cod Commercial Fishermen's Alliance, 35
Caribbean spiny lobster, 55
chicken broth, 90

Child, Julia, 41, 218
chourico, 60, 273; Caldo Verde with Squid, 215; Elegant Portuguese Clam Stew, 262; Portuguese Clam Boil, 280; Portuguese Clam Chowder, 115; Portuguese Fish Chowder, 126; Portuguese Kale Soup with Scallops, 207; Portuguese Squid Soup, 212; Portuguese Two Fish Soup, 156; Simple Portuguese Clam Stew, 259
chowders, 11, 94–147; and sustainability, 97; Atlantic cod, 31; Atlantic mackerel, 38; bluefish, 37; Bluefish Chowder with Cherry Tomatoes, Basil, and Tarragon, 128; clam chowders 105–19; Classic Creamy New England Clam Chowder, 94; Classic New England Whitefish Chowder, 120; Connecticut Clam Chowder, 117; cooling of, 102; Crab, Bacon, and Cheddar Corn Chowder, 140; Curried Butternut Squash Squid Chowder, 146; fish chowders, 120–33; freezing, 103; haddock, 31–32; Hake and Skate Chowder, 132; halibut, 33; history of, 95–97, 149; ingredients, 98–103; leftovers, 103; Lobster Corn Chowder, 134; Manhattan Clam Chowder, 112; Milky Maine Steamer Clam Chowder, 110; Mussel Chowder with Fennel, 137; oily fish stocks and, 69; Oyster Spinach Chowder, 144; Portuguese Clam Chowder, 58, 115; Portuguese Fish Chowder, 126; quahogs (hard-shell clams), 45; Rhode Island Clam Chowder, 107; Scallop and Wild Mushroom Chowder with Chives, 142; shellfish chowders, 134–45; silver hake (whiting), 32; Smoked Haddock Chowder with a Poached Egg, 130; tautog (blackfish), 34–35; tips, 102–3; Wild Salmon Chowder, 123
Cioppino, 24, 78, 253–55
clam bisques, 227–32
clam boils, 58, 271–76, 280, 284
clam broths, 83–87, 90, 105, 191, 219
clams, 55, 244. See also clam bisques, clam boils, clam broths, and clam soups
Clam Shack Cookery (Schwind), 99, 217
clam soups, 165–75

Classic Creamy New England Clam Chowder, 105–6
classic medleys and stews, 243–270
Classic New England Whitefish Chowder, 120–22, 126
coastline, 17–18, 23, 24, 44, 117
cockle clams, 31–32, 55, 68, 127
collagen, 67
community supported agriculture (CSA), 19
community supported fishery (CSF), 19
conch, queen, 55
Connecticut Clam Chowder, 102, 117
Consider the Oyster (Fisher), 190
corn, 123, 132, 134, 140, 204, 271–85
Crab, Bacon, and Cheddar Corn Chowder, 140–41
crabs: Atlantic rock crab, 52–53; Basic Crab Stock, 82; bisques, 218; blue crab, 52–53, 55, 199, 204; broth, 83–84; Cioppino, 253; crab stock, 81; Crab, Bacon, and Cheddar Corn Chowder, 140; Dungeness, 55, 253; green crab, 52–53, 81; Jonah crab, 26, 52–53, 81, 82, 140, 199, 203, 204, 253; king crab, 55; New England Jonah Crab Bisque, 224; New England Jonah Crab Stew, 203; New England Summer Crab Soup, 204; Peekytoe crab, 52–53; red crab, 55; rock crab, 55, 199, 204; snow crab, 55; soups, 53, 81, 199, 203–5; steaming of, 81; stock, 53, 81–82; stone crab, 55
crawfish, 55, 273, 280
cream, 95, 99–103
cultural (mis)perceptions, 27
Curried Butternut Squash Squid Chowder, 146–47

D
dairy, 99–101
Delmonico's, 96
diversity, 25–27
dogfish, 35, 120, 127, 151, 244, 251, 284
Dungeness crab, 55, 253

E
eastern oysters, 49, 193–98, 237
Eating with the Ecosystem, 22, 25

Eat Like a Fish, 25, 27
Elegant Portuguese Clam Stew, 262–63
Endangered Species Act (1973), 18

F
farmed Atlantic salmon, 39–40
farmed shellfish, 44
Farmer, Fannie, 101
fennel, 71, 137; Aromatic Mussel Soup, 182;
    Basic Lobster Stock, 78; Bouillabaisse,
    246; Bourride, 251; Elegant Portuguese
    Clam Stew, 262; Lemony Haddock (or
    Black Sea Bass) Soup, 154; Lobster Corn
    Chowder, 134; Malty Mussel Soup, 186;
    Mussel and Fennel Bisque, 233; Mussel
    Chowder with Fennel, 137; New England
    Jonah Crab Bisque, 224; Oyster Spinach
    Chowder, 144; Portuguese Clam Boil, 280;
    Portuguese Clam Chowder, 115; Portu-
    guese Fish Chowder, 126; Portuguese Mus-
    sel Stew, 266; Portuguese Squid Soup, 212;
    Robust Lobster Stock, 79; side dish, 286
50 Chowders (White), 96
Fish and Shellfish (Peterson), 165
Fisher, M.F.K., 190
fisheries, , 17–26, 29–31, 39–40, 52–54, 199
fishmonger, 20
fish stock, 34, 66–74
FishWatch, 30
flatfish, 32–33
flounders, 32–33
Frederick, George, 11, 103, 176

G
gelatin, 67
geoduck clams, 55
globalization, 18
Gouy, Louis De, The Soup Book, 11, 94, 96,
    101, 241
Grace-Davies, Amanda, 132
green crab, 52–53, 81
Greencrab.org, 53
Green Crab R&D Project, 53

H
haddock, 25, 31–32, 120, 130, 154
Hake and Skate Chowder, 132–33

half-and-half, 100
halibut, 33, 96, 127, 159, 251
"hallelujah" (Buckley), 221
Hard-Shell Clam Broth, 86
hardtack, 103
Hooker, Richard, 96
hyper-regional food, 176

J
Jonah crab, 52–53, 81–82, 140, 203–4, 224,
    244, 253

K
king crab, 55
kombu, 91

L
Lemony Haddock (or Black Sea Bass) Soup,
    154–55
linguica, 60, 215, 273, 280, 115, 207, 266,
    212
Lobster Bisque, 75, 79, 218, 221–23
Lobster Corn Chowder, 75, 78, 134–36
lobster: American, 51–52; Basic Lobster
    Stock, 78; bisque, 218–23; Caribbean
    spiny, 55; Julia Child, 218; Cioppino,
    253; clam boils, 273; food for poor, 52;
    how to steam and prepare, 80; Lobster
    Bisque, 221; Lobster Corn Chowder, 75,
    78, 134–36; Maine, 51–52; Maine Lobster
    Stew, 200; markets, 25; New England
    Fish Boil, 282; Robust Lobster Stock, 79,
    235, 241; Salmon Bisque with Dill, 239;
    Scallop and Wild Mushroom Chowder
    with Chives, 142; Scallop Bisque with
    Sage, 235; soups, 52, 199–202; stock,
    65–66, 75–79, 235, 239, 241; Whitefish
    Bisque, 241; Zarzuela, 257
Local Catch Network, 20
Long Island Seafood Cookbook (Frederick), 11,
    102, 103, 176
longfin squid, 50–51

M
Mac's on the Pier, 172
Magnuson-Stevens Act, 18
Magnuson-Stevens Fishery Conservation and

Management Reauthorization Act (2006), 18

Maine lobster (American lobster), 51–52; Maine Lobster Stew, 79, 200

Malty Mussel Soup, 186–87

mangrove forests, 23

Manhattan Clam Chowder, 58, 101, 112–13, 115

Manila clams, 55

Marine Mammal Protection Act (1972), 18

Marine Stewardship Council (MSC), 21

"mashmallows of the sea," 48

Mercenaria mercenaria, 45

milk, 95, 99, 101

Milky Maine Steamer Clam Chowder, 110–11

mirepoix, 71

Mitcham, Howard, 58, 149, 156, 227, 264

monkfish, 26, 34, 41, 68, 127, 151–53, 251, 284

Monkfish (or Dogfish) Soup with Ginger, Lemongrass, and Lime, 151–53

mushrooms, 142, 198, 262

Mussel and Fennel Bisque, 233–34

Mussel Broth, 88–89; Aromatic Mussel Soup, 182–84; Atlantic Blue Mussel Mediterranean Soup, 180–81; Malty Mussel Soup, 186–87; Mussel and Fennel Bisque, 233–34; Mussel Chowder with Fennel, 137–39; Mussel Dijonnaise Soup, 178–79; PBR Mussel Soup, 188–89

Mussel Chowder with Fennel, 137–39

mussels: Atlantic Blue, 47; bisque, 219, 233; blue, 26, 248, 251, 253, 257; Bouillabaisse, 246; Bourride, 251; broths, 66; California, 55; chowder, 96; Cioppino, 253; clam boil, 273; farmed, 44; Mussel and Fennel Bisque, 233; Mussel Chowder with Fennel, 137; New England Blue Mussel Boil, 279; Portuguese Mussel Stew, 266; Traditional New England Clam Boil, 276; Zarzuela, 256; Zuppa di Pesce with Black Sea Bass, 258. *See also* Mussel Broth *and* mussel soups

Mussel Dijonnaise Soup, 178–79

mussel soups, 176–89; Aromatic Mussel Soup, 182; Atlantic Blue Mussel Mediterranean Soup, 180; beer, 185–89; Malty Mussel Soup, 186; Mussel Dijonnaise Soup, 178; PBR Mussel Soup, 188

N

National Oceanic and Atmospheric Administration (NOAA), 18, 30

Native Americans, 37

New England Blue Mussel Boil, 279

New England Fish Boil, 282–83

New England fish substitutes, 41

New England Jonah Crab Bisque, 224–26

New England Jonah Crab Stew, 203

New England Summer Crab Soup, 204–5

New England-Style Hot and Sour Soup with Scallops, 210–11

NOAA, 18, 30

North Atlantic swordfish, 38, 284

O

Oceana, 21–22

oily full-flavored fish, 36–40

onions, 57, 71, 98, 272

online buying, 21–22

other New England fish, 41

Our Wicked Fish, 132

Oyster Bisque with Fried Shallots and Garlic, 237–38

oysters: bisques, 11, 219, 237; chowders, 96, 144; Eastern, 49, 148; farmed shellfish, 44; Louis De Gouy, 96; lime, 151; Oyster Bisque with Fried Shallots and Garlic, 237; oyster liquor, 43; Oysters Bienville Soup, 198; Oysters Mariniere Soup, 196; Oyster Spinach Chowder, 144; Oysters Rockefeller Soup, 194; Pacific, 55; prices, 26; Barton Seaver, 151; shucking of, 50; *The Soup Book*, 96; soups, 190–98; stew, 148; Traditional Oyster Stew, 193; *Two If By Sea*, 151

Oysters Bienville Soup, 198

Oysters Mariniere Soup, 196–97

oyster soups, 190–98

Oyster Spinach Chowder, 144–45

Oysters Rockefeller Soup, 194–95

oyster crackers, 103

P

Pacific fish and shellfish, 41, 55

Pacific halibut, 33

Pacific oysters, 55

Pacific salmon, 39–40
Pacific squid, 55
PBR Mussel Soup, 188–89
Peekytoe crab, 52–53
periwinkles, 55
Pesto Noodle Soup with Striped Bass (or Halibut), 159–61
Peterson, James, 165
"picked toe," 53
polyunsaturated fats, 36, 68
poquauhock, 45
Portuguese Clam Boil, 58, 272, 280–81
Portuguese Clam Chowder, 58, 115–16
Portuguese cuisine, 57–60, 156, 245, 268, 270
Portuguese Fish Chowder, 126–27
Portuguese Kale Soup with Scallops, 207–9
Portuguese Mussel Stew, 266–67
Portuguese Shrimp Mozambique, 268–70
Portuguese Squid Soup, 212–13
Portuguese Squid Stew, 264–65
Portuguese Two Fish Soup, 156–58
potatoes, 98, 103, 272
Provincetown Seafood Cookbook (Mitcham), 58, 149, 156, 227, 264

Q
quahogs (hard-shell clams), 45–46, 83, 86, 105, 253, 262
queen conch, 55

R
razor clams, 55, 244
Real Milk, 99
red crab, 55
red gurnard, 35
Red's Best, 22
Rhode Island Clam Chowder, 107–9
Rhode Island Fishermen's Alliance, 29
Robust Fish Stock, 74; Bluefish Chowder with Cherry Tomatoes, Basil, and Tarragon, 128–29; Classic New England Whitefish Chowder, 120–22; Hake and Skate Chowder, 132; Lemony Haddock (or Black Sea Bass) Soup, 154–55; Monkfish (or Dogfish) Soup with Ginger, Lemongrass, and Lime, 151–53; Oyster Spinach Chowder, 144–45; Pesto Noodle Soup with Striped Bass (or Halibut), 159–61; Portuguese Fish Chowder, 126–27; Portuguese Two Fish Soup, 156–58; Rhode Island Clam Chowder, 107; Smoked Haddock Chowder with a Poached Egg, 130–31; Tomato Swordfish (or Mackerel) Soup with Fresh Italian Herbs, 162–63; Wild Salmon (or Bluefish) and Dill Soup, 164–65; Wild Salmon Chowder, 123–25
Robust Lobster Stock, 79; Lobster Bisque, 221–23; Maine Lobster Stew, 200–202; Salmon Bisque with Dill, 239–40; Scallop Bisque with Sage, 235–36; Whitefish Bisque, 241–42
rock crab, 52–53, 55, 199, 204

S
Salmon Bisque with Dill, 239–40
salt pork, chowders, 94, 95, 98, 105–46
sausage: A Seasonal New England Fish and Clam Boil—Four Ways, 284; Caldo Verde with Squid, 215; clam boil, 273–84; Elegant Portuguese Clam Stew, 262; New England Blue Mussel Boil, 279; Portuguese Clam Boil, 280; Portuguese Clam Chowder, 115; Portuguese cuisine, 58, 60; Portuguese Fish Chowder, 126; Portuguese Kale Soup with Scallops, 207; Portuguese Mussel Stew, 266; Portuguese Squid Soup, 212; Portuguese Two Fish Soup, 156; Simple Portuguese Clam Stew, 259; Traditional New England Clam Boil, 276; Zarzuela, 256
Scallop and Wild Mushroom Chowder with Chives, 142–43
Scallop Bisque with Sage, 235–36
scallops: Atlantic sea scallops, 48; bay scallops, 48; bisques, 219, 235; Bouillabaisse, 248; Bourride, 251; calico scallops, 49; chowders, 137; Cioppino, 253; clam broth, 90; "dayboat," 48; "diver," 48; dry vs. wet, 48; farmed shellfish, 44; fish markets, 25; New England-Style Hot and Sour Soup with Scallops, 210; Portuguese Kale Soup with Scallops, 207; Scallop and Wild Mushroom

Chowder with Chives, 142–43; Scallop Bisque with Sage, 235–36; soup, 206; Traditional Scallop Stew, 217; Zarzuela, 256; Zuppa di Pesce with Black Sea Bass, 258

Schwind, Cap'n Phil, 99, 217

scup (porgy), 36, 41, 284

sea robin, 27, 35, 244

Sea to Table, 22

seafood consumption, 17, 57

seafood fraud, 21–22

seagreens broth, 91

Seasonal New England Fish and Clam Boil—Four Ways, A, 284–85

Seaver, Barton, 17, 151

Shellfish Chowders, 134–47

shellfish, farmed, 44

shellfish, New England and substitutes, 54

"ship's biscuit," 103

shrimp: American consumption of, 18; Atlantic northern, 53–54; Atlantic Salmon and, 40; bisque, 218; boils, 272; Bouillabaisse, 246; buying whole, 54; Cioppino, 253; foreign, 22–25; overfishing of, 20; Portuguese cuisine, 58; Portuguese Shrimp Mozambique, 268; stews, 245; wild-caught gulf, 53–54; Zarzuela, 257; Zuppa di Pesce with Black Sea Bass, 258

silver hake (whiting), 32

Simple Portuguese Clam Stew, 259–61

skate, 27, 33, 132, 284

slipper limpets, 55, 244

Smoked Haddock Chowder with a Poached Egg, 130–31

snails, 54

snow crab, 55

Soft-Shell Clam Broth, 46, 84, 87, 110, 172–75

Soup Book, The (Gouy), 11, 94, 96, 101, 241

soups, 11–13; Aromatic Mussel Soup, 182; Atlantic Blue Mussel Mediterranean Soup, 180; Atlantic blue mussels, 47; bottled clam broth, 90; brothy soups, 148–217; Caldo Verde with Squid, 215; choosing fish for, 30–41; chowder, 102; clam soups, 165–75; Clams Newburg Soup, 170; crab, 53; crab soups, 199–205; crab stock, 81; curdling, 100; eggs, 130; fish soups, 149–64; fish stock, 73–74; gelatin, 67; Lemony Haddock (or Black Sea Bass) Soup, 154; lobster, 52; lobster soups, 199–202; lobster stock, 78–79; Maine Lobster Stew, 200; Malty Mussel Soup, 186; Monkfish (or Dogfish) Soup with Ginger, Lemongrass, and Lime, 151; mussel and beer soups, 185–89; mussel soups, 176–89; Mussel Dijonnaise Soup, 178; New England Jonah Crab Stew, 203; New England Summer Crab Soup, 204; New England-Style Hot and Sour Soup with Scallops, 210; oily fish, 69; onions, 98; Oyster Rockefeller Soup, 194; oyster soups, 190–98; Oysters Bienville Soup, 198; Oysters Mariniere Soup, 196; PBR Mussel Soup, 188; Pesto Noodle Soup with Striped Bass (or Halibut), 159; Portuguese cuisine, 58–60, 115; Portuguese Kale Soup with Scallops, 207; Portuguese Squid Soup, 212; Portuguese stews, and Manhattan clam chowder, 115; Portuguese Two Fish Soup, 156; quahogs (hard-shell clams), 45–46; scallop soups, 206–11, 217; shopping locally, 19; shrimp, 54; soft-shell clams (steamers), 46; soft-shell clam soups, 172–75; Spinach-Tarragon Clam Soup, 167; squid soups, 206, 212; squid, 51; Steamer Clam Soup in a Ginger-Garlic-Tarragon-Lime Broth, 174; Steamer Clam Soup in a Tomato-Basil-Lemon Broth, 173; Tomato Swordfish (or Mackerel) Soup with Fresh Italian Herbs, 162; Traditional Clam Stew, 166; Traditional Oyster Stew, 193; Traditional Scallop Stew, 217; Wild Salmon (or Bluefish) and Dill Soup, 164. See also bisques

Spinach-Tarragon Clam Soup, 167–69

squid, 26–27, 50–51; Bouillabaisse, 248; Caldo Verde with Squid, 215; Cioppino, 253; clam broth, 90; Curried Butternut Squash Squid Chowder, 146; longifin, 50–51; Pacific, 55; Portuguese cuisine, 58, 212, 215; Portuguese Squid Stew, 264; Portuguese Verde with Squid, 212; soup, 206, 212; stews, 245; Zarzuela, 257

Steamer Clam Soup in a Ginger-Garlic-Tarragon-Lime Broth, 174
Steamer Clam Soup in a Tomato-Basil-Lemon Broth, 173
stews, 148, 243–270; bottled clam broth, 90; Bouillabaisse, 246; Bourride, 251; Cioppino, 253; clam stew, 165; *Consider the Oyster*, 190; crab stock, 81; Elegant Portuguese Clam Stew, 262; fish for, 31–38; fish stock, 65, 73; M. F. K. Fisher, 190; J. George Frederick, 11; Maine Lobster Stew, 199; New England Jonah Crab Stew, 203; oyster, 190–91; Portuguese cuisine, 58–60; Portuguese Fish Chowder, 126; Portuguese Mussel Stew, 266; Portuguese Shrimp Mozambique, 268; Portuguese Squid Stew, 264; Portuguese stews, and Manhattan clam chowder, 115; quahogs (hard-shell clams), 46; Robust Lobster Stock, 79; scallops, 48, 206, 217; shrimp, 54; Simple Portuguese Clam Stew, 259; single species, 245–70; squid, 51, 206; *The Long Island Seafood Cookbook*, 11; Traditional Clam Stew, 166; Traditional Oyster Stew, 191; Traditional Scallop Stew, 217; two "rules," 243–44; Zarzuela, 256; Zuppa di Pesce with Black Sea Bass, 258
stocks, 65–71, 90
stone crab, 55
striped bass, 37–38, 128, 159, 162, 284
sustainability status, 29–30
Sustainable Fisheries Act (1996), 18

T
tautog (blackfish), 34, 284
Tomato Swordfish (or Mackerel) Soup with Fresh Italian Herbs, 162–63
Tomato-Clam Bisque, 227, 231–32
Traditional Clam Stew, 166
Traditional New England Clam Bisque, 228–30
Traditional New England Clam Boil, 276–78
Traditional Oyster Stew, 193
Traditional Scallop Stew, 217
"trash fish," 26–27
tuna, 18, 20, 25, 39
Two If By Sea (Seaver), 151

V
Vital Choice, 22
Vittles for the Captain: A Cape Cod Cookbook (Adams), 94

W
whelks, 55
White, Jasper, 96
whitefish, 30–36, 241–42
Whitefish Bisque, 33, 241–42
Whole Dairy Story, 99, 165
wild-caught gulf shrimp, 53–54
Wild Salmon (or Bluefish) and Dill Soup, 164–65
Wild Salmon Chowder, 123–25

Z
Zarzuela, 256–57
zuppa di pesce, 102, 258